BIKE&BREW AMERICA™

Rocky Mountain Region

**Todd
Bryant
Mercer**

VELO *press*®

VeloPress

and

Brewers Publications

Boulder, Colorado   USA

For
Amanda

Bike & Brew America: Rocky Mountain Region
© 2001 Todd Bryant Mercer

Printed in the United States of America

Distributed in the United States and Canada by
Publishers Group West

International Standard Book Number: 1-884737-91-9

Library of Congress Cataloging-in-Publication Data
Mercer, Todd Bryant.
   Bike & brew America: Rocky Mountain Region/Todd Bryant Mercer.
     p. cm.
   Includes index.
   ISBN 1-884737-91-9
   1. All terrain cycling—Rocky Mountains Region—Guidebooks. 2. Bars (Drinking establishments)—Rocky Mountains Region—Guidebooks. 3. Microbreweries—Rocky Mountains Region—Guidebooks. 4. Rocky Mountains Region—Guidebooks. I. Title:
Bike and Brew America. Rocky Mountain Region. II Title.

GV1045.5.R6 M47 2001
917.8084'34—dc21   00-054641

Cover photos: Shrine Pass (top) near Vail, Colorado; copyright 2001 Wendy Shattil/Bob Rozinski. Mountain Sun Brewery (bottom) in Boulder Colorado; copyright 2001 Galen Nathanson.
Interior photos (unless otherwise noted) by Amanda and Todd Mercer
Maps by Amanda Mercer
Cover and interior design by Ann W. Douden

Disclaimer: Neither the publishers, editors, nor author shall be held liable for the use or misuse of information contained in this book. Readers assume the risk by participating in the activities described herein. The act of operating a bicycle or any vehicle after consuming alcohol is not advocated by this book and is strongly discouraged.

VeloPress
1830 North 55th Street
Boulder, Colorado 80301-2700 USA
303/440-0601; Fax 303/444-6788; E-mail velopress@7dogs.com

Brewers Publications
736 Pearl Street
Boulder, Colorado 80302
303/447-0816; Fax 303/447-2825; E-mail bp@aob.org

CONTENTS

ACKNOWLEDGMENTS

Needless to say this book would not be here without the help and encouragement of many people—first and foremost is my wife, Amanda. Not only can she claim credit for the original idea (which I completely ignored until I could come up with it on my own at a later date), her support, editing, and honesty are the only reasons this book was ever completed. And I know Amanda joins me in expressing appreciation to our parents for supporting our dreams.

My most sincere thanks to the following people for showing support and giving me the confidence to even attempt a project of this magnitude. Michael Bey, who, desperately short of material for his club newsletter, turned to me as a last resort and tapped into more words than anyone could have suspected. Lisa Lazaroff, for her continued encouragement and faith that someone out there would actually pay for some of my ramblings. John and Kathy Sheard, for suggesting I put some of my biking stories down on paper. Miriam Snider, for giving me the time to write when I should have been doing other things. Roger Knight, for showing me what the sport of mountain biking is all about and gallantly volunteering to take part in so much of the "research" necessary for me to become "qualified" to write a book of this nature. (Not to mention helping me come up with the idea—for the second time—over a pint of beer at, you guessed it, a brewpub.)

Special thanks to all my editors along the way who have volunteered their time and talents to try and make me look good. John Masson, whose snide comments were worth more than his corrections; Michael "Iron Mike" Bey, who completely and utterly ROCKS; Anne Curzan; and, of course, my publishers Amy Sorrells at VeloPress and Toni Knapp at Brewers Publications for taking a chance on a first-time author. And thanks to all the folks at both houses who have worked so hard on this project, including Ann Douden, Mary Eberle, Toni Knapp, Amy Sorrells, Theresa van Zante, and Lennard Zinn, for making me look so good.

No thank-you would be complete without mention of all those who rode the trails and drank the ales along the way, including Amanda (of course), Roger Knight, Nick Ranson, Sean Hickman, Mark Stucky, Mark Kidder, Darrin and Jodie Griffiths, Michael Bey (yet again), and Larry Staley for getting me back on my mountain bike after a long hiatus. And thanks to Scott Sager for brewing the beer and Dale Hulsing for drinking it.

I'd also like to toast all the folks I met along the way at the bike shops, brewpubs, and everywhere else, for all the information, directions, advice, stories, rides, places to sleep, laughs, and friendly faces. In particular, Kurtis from Main Street Brewery in Cortez; Shawn and Mandy from Green River; Harley Parsons and Eric and Shannon Lafferty from Boise; Roger, Laura, Jen, Tommy, and Steve from Boulder and Fort Collins; Andrew Hoffmann and his pal Greg for that beer on top of the parking structure in Vail; and Don, for finally showing me how to find Lost Lake, also in Vail.

I also thank Denise and Doug McGarvey for getting the Bike & Brew™ web site up and running while I was out on the road. And last, but certainly not least, I thank Mark Stucky for designing the soon to be famous Bike & Brew America™ logos.

vii

PREFACE

I don't feel I stand alone when I proclaim, "I love bikes!" And, of those who stand in agreement, many also hail this next statement with equal passion, "I love beer!" For whatever reason, the two seem to go together like peanut butter and jelly; alone, each a fine delicacy, but together . . . ahhh. Words cannot describe the feeling of completeness, happiness, and nirvana—the total rapture attainable—when both are experienced in proper quantity and quality.

This bond, kinship if you will, is for me somehow fitting. My indoctrination to all things good—bikes and brews— came almost 10 years ago. I had just landed my first "real" job and had money. Lots of money. This, of course, meant two things to me: one, I could now afford to buy my first mountain bike; and two, I had more money to spend on beer.

My roommate at the time worked at a bike shop and set me up with a deal that, even to this day, seemed too good to be true. A 1990 Raleigh Tangent equipped with LX components for only $320. A steal. But more important, a mountain bike for only $320 meant even more money for beer, which brings me back to my earlier statement connecting the two.

About a month later, a buddy and I were sitting in a bar staring with much envy at a menu that listed over 300 very expensive beers from around the world. A menu so novel it even listed American beers that were not brewed by Coors, Anheuser-Busch, or Miller Brewing Company. Remember, this is back in 1990.

"I'm gonna have an Anchor Steam," my friend says, closing the menu.

"What's that?" I ask, still trying to decide between a Molson and Labatt.

"It's a beer from San Francisco—you probably wouldn't like it," he says, sounding a little smug.

What? "Why not?" I ask, feeling slightly challenged.

"Well, it's pretty bitter . . ." and so my indoctrination to what beer really is all about began as we proceeded to drink our way around the world that night.

My mountain biking was sporadic for a few years, but fortunately, I was still able to hone my beer-drinking

skills and knowledge. I also developed some brewing abilities until I was a self-proclaimed finely tuned beer connoisseur.

As brewpubs gradually proliferated across the landscape—and I quit said job—I was able to spend more time on my Raleigh and less time in the kitchen boiling wort, weighing hops, measuring specific gravity and sanitizing bottles; forever in search of the perfect pint of barley and hops. Yes, I was effectively put out of the homebrewing profession. But on the bright side, I now had access to great locally brewed beer located a stone's throw from a hard day on the trails.

More time in the saddle improved my biking skills, and I began traveling farther and farther from home in search of sweeter singletrack, bigger hills, and, yes, better beer. Fortune has smiled upon me more than a few times, and I've managed to sample some of the best riding and finest brews North America has to offer. I'm trying to ride it all, from the great Floridian swamps to the Rockies of Colorado, from the red sands of Moab to the top of Mount Tamalpais. Along the way, I'm also trying to drink it all. From nitrogen taps in Seattle to hand-pumped brews in Michigan, from cask-conditioned ales in Kansas to unfiltered hop-fests in Boulder. I've braved alcohol-starved Utah only to get blasted by a Trappist Tripel–style ale in Missouri boasting an alcohol content of 12%! Through all this, only one truism has remained constant: no matter where I travel there is always prime singletrack and quality handcrafted beer—you just need to know where to look.

And now, as a new millennium begins, it is high time to share this hard-won knowledge with you—the millions of mountain-biking, beer-loving kindred spirits out there.

Bike & Brew America: Rocky Mountain Region is the first of six regional mountain-biking, beer-drinking guides to the sweetest, most heroic, or just plain twisted, nasty, sicko singletrack rides you could ever find yourself on, followed by the best brewpubs you could ever find yourself in.

There's always fine print, so here's some to let you know where I'm going. *Bike & Brew America* outlines the best mountain-bike trails in the country that are situated within a 30-minute (or so) drive of the best brewpubs in the country. Sometimes a pub is on the way to great riding or a trail is on the way back from some place where there was great beer. Understand that you have to get to and from the trail somehow, and, unfortunately, brewpubs are usually not located right at the trailhead. Although, sometimes they are, as you will soon see. . . .

Also, because I happen to like quaint, old-fashioned stuff, buildings with some character, and downtown areas with a lot of history, that's where I envision Bike & Brew enthusiasts to be spending most of their evenings. In other words, if it became a choice between hitting the strip mall for a chain brewery or driving a little farther into town for a nineteenth-century building and cool downtown aura, I invariably drove the extra five minutes. I believe, just as the scenery makes up part of a good mountain-bike ride, your surroundings, while drinking the fruits of your daily labor, make for a better beer.

And now, without further ado, let's begin our search for the perfect Bike & Brew experience in the most glorious of locales, America's Rocky Mountains.

INTRODUCTION

Bike & Brew America is a comprehensive series of guide-books to America's best mountain-bike trails and best brewpubs. But why mountain bikes and brewpubs? What is the attraction mountain bikers feel toward microbrewed beer in general and brewpubs in particular? Beyond the obvious answer—both mountain biking and brewpub frequenting are great fun and offer endless hours in the company of good friends—what pairs these two seemingly random activities together is called *character*.

Mountain biking and brewpubs say something about a person's character. They speak of a person who enjoys freedom and following a path less traveled. They speak of individuality, someone who likes trying new and different things. One who enjoys the atmosphere, the experience, and the trip—not just the destination. Not to mention someone who likes to ride bikes and drink good beer.

And just as mountain biking and drinking real beer offer a glimpse into a person's character, so too do they open a window into a region's character. Each trail and each brewpub tell something about the area where they are located. A trail tells about the outdoors, the wilderness, the area's geography and its flora and fauna. A brewpub tells a tale of history, philosophy, local pastimes, local cuisine, and age-old beer styles. What better way to sample a town's character than by exploring its historic streets and stopping in at the local brewpub for a taste that can be found no other place in the world?

As mountain bikers know, every trail—no, every *ride*—is different. Terrain, elevation, distance, climate, companions, and weather—all add up to make each ride new and exciting. As each trail is unique, molded out of the local geography, each brewpub is also a creature of its environment. Different architecture, atmosphere, food, people, and, of course, beer give each brewpub a character all its own. This individuality is what having a pint at the local brewpub is all about.

So I ask you, what better way is there to explore an area than by biking its trails and drinking its ales? And, what better way to find out about the Rocky Mountains' trails and ales than by reading this book?

How to Use This Book

This is not a book series describing random collections of trails and brewpubs. These guidebooks present a carefully researched selection of the best trails that are located near great brewpubs. Each entry guarantees its readers a great day of biking and a great night of eating and drinking. It effectively eliminates the guessing game all traveling bikers encounter at one time or another.

No longer will mountain bikers planning a trip endure endless frustrating hours searching through stacks of old magazines trying to locate that barely remembered article detailing a great ride that may be near where they're headed. Readers will now find all rides in a particular geographic region of the United States under one cover, six books in all.

Each section begins with an introduction to the state's overall Bike & Brew (B&B) character and a locator map marking the places to be covered. The chapter then proceeds to detail each featured trail and brewpub in a fun, conversational style. A road map showing both trail and brewpub locations, as well as the local bike shop and additional trails and watering holes accompanies each trail and brewpub pairing.

Online Web Site

In order to combat the greatest problem with all guidebooks, that of its information becoming dated, Bike & Brew America maintains a web site at www.bikeandbrew.com. This site continually offers trail and brewpub updates, which will allow your copy of *Bike & Brew America: Rocky*

Mountain Region to remain up-to-date until a complete revision is required. Reader input, comments, and suggestions are welcomed for online posting and future editions. All Bike & Brew pubs, trails, and bike shops with a web site are also linked to this site for easy pretrip planning reference and are indexed by state, town, trail, and brewpub.

Descriptions of Rides and Brewpubs

In this book, I have methodically organized the descriptions to assist the reader in finding specific aspects of each ride and brewpub. Thus, for each city, town, or area for which I endorse a Bike & Brew pair, I offer brief teasers covering the attractions and scenery and then full descriptions in the following format:

TRAIL NAME: Well, its most common name anyway.

THE SCOOP: What to expect on the trail in about ten words or whatever it happens to take.

RIDE LENGTH AND TYPE: The ride's distance in miles and what kind of ride it is—out-and-back, loop, town-to-town, balloon-on-a-string, or "variable." Variable trails are part of a large trail network and are rarely ridden the same way twice.

THE BIKE: Details covering what the ride is like including terrain, elevation, trail conditions, scenic opportunities, trail highlights, and directions, when appropriate.

DIFFICULTY: A general rating of novice, intermediate, or advanced and a short explanation of why this rating was applied. Although I didn't intend to restrict the trails in this book to a particular difficulty rating, most trails I selected are intermediate and intermediate to advanced because this level just happens to be the difficulty most people consider makes for the best or most "classic" of rides.

AEROBIC DIFFICULTY (1–5): A subjective rating used to describe the physical conditioning needed to successfully complete a trail with a smile still on your face. The easiest trails are rated a 1 and the hardest, steepest, highest-elevation trails are rated a 5. Most Bike & Brew trails fall in the 2–4 range with 3 being the most common.

ROCKY MOUNTAIN AEROBIC DISCLAIMER: If you are not from the Rockies, or from somewhere else where the typical ride begins above 5000 feet, add 1 to the aerobic difficulties listed here until you become acclimated.

TECHNICAL DIFFICULTY (1–5): Another subjective rating used to describe the technical skill needed to successfully complete a trail without having to dismount and walk over or around obstacles—not to mention making a face plant, hitting a tree, or falling off a cliff. The smoothest of trails are rated a 1; the most twisted, gnarly, rocked-out, rooted, off-camber, mountaintop trails are rated a 5. Again, most Bike & Brew trails fall in the 2–4 range, and a technical difficulty of 3 is the most common.

DIFFICULTY DEFINITIONS: Although all systems of rating difficulty are subjective, the following descriptions should give you a way to measure where you stand, understanding you may fall into one category technically and another aerobically.

DIFFICULTY LEVEL 1: You definitely enjoy your beer more than your bike. Rarely have you ridden on singletrack trails. Perhaps until recently you have preferred to lead an inactive lifestyle.

DIFFICULTY LEVEL 2: You are a "social cyclist" who rides singletrack occasionally. You lead a fairly active lifestyle and are interested in seeing what adding a little more mountain biking to your routine has to offer.

DIFFICULTY LEVEL 3: You are comfortable riding singletrack, train regularly, and are looking to improve your skills. You may even race occasionally just to see where you stand among your peers.

DIFFICULTY LEVEL 4: You're a good rider. You know it, your friends know it, and your mom and dad know it. You train regularly and do well when you race.

DIFFICULTY LEVEL 5: When you race, other racers know your name. You regularly clear obstacles other accomplished cyclists only dream of. Basically, you're the mountain biker everyone else wants to be.

WARNINGS: Any trail-specific warnings beyond the standard "wear your helmet, keep your eyes open at all times, carry food and water, carry tools, know how to use those tools, maintain your bike regularly, and know how to get back to your car." Examples of what may be included are crowded trail conditions, extreme weather conditions, dangerous animals or other critters known to inhabit that particular part of the country, fragile environmental areas, and hazards such as flat-causing cactus needles, poison ivy infestations, complicated trail intersections, and pretty much anything else that may make your day uncomfortable. However, all the warnings in the world won't help if you don't heed them, take the proper precautions, and use common sense wherever you ride.

ROCKY MOUNTAIN WARNING: Sudden storms are a constant threat during summer afternoons in the Rocky Mountains. A bright and clear mountain morning can turn ugly in a matter of minutes at high altitudes. You should pack a windbreaker and try to ride in the morning and always be prepared for the eventuality of a thunder and lightning storm popping up at any time. If you should get caught in one, even before rain or hail starts falling move away from exposed terrain, leave your lightning rod— that is, your bike—and find a low valley or ditch to wait out the storm. Though fierce, they usually don't last long, and it's better to be safe and miss happy hour than be struck by lightning and miss the brewpub altogether.

OTHER TRAILS IN THE AREA: Summary of at least two other rides, of varying difficulty, located in the area.

CONTACTS: The local land managers' address and phone number. When these folks are also the ones with the all-important trail map, their location is noted on the map of the area. Otherwise, it's always a good idea to give them a call before your visit to learn about other vital information such as current trail status, camping opportunities, or more detailed directions. Also included is a general contact such as the Chamber of Commerce or Tourist Information Center just to make sure all travelers' questions will be answered. The general contact follows the local land managers' information.

MAPS: Where you can get the most current maps of the trails described. Frequently the maps are free, created by the local bike shop for out-of-town riders such as yourself. Sometimes, in popular mountain-bike destinations, an enterprising individual has created a detailed map of many local trails (or a narrative guide) that is available at a nominal cost. Unless you enjoy exploring on your own and don't care when you get home, such maps are very useful and worth a stop to pick one up.

BIKE SHOP: Source of the local knowledge for all traveling bikers and where all riders new to an area should begin their day. The shop proprietors and/or employees are the experts on the trails. Besides being where the free maps are usually located, bike shops are the place to check on trail conditions, get directions, or score any last minute purchases or repairs.

BREWPUB NAME: The official name.

BREWPUB INFORMATION: The address, phone number, and web address (if available).

ATMOSPHERE: A short description of the brewpub's setting, surroundings, feel, and character.

THE BREW: A detailed account of the brewpub's features, its history, and, of course, its beer.

PRICE OF A PINT: How much a pint of beer costs regularly and, more important, the ifs, ands, and buts of the almighty happy hour.

OTHER BREWS IN THE AREA: Just as there is always more than one good trail in an area, there is always more than one good place to get a brew. This section summarizes other brewpubs, microbreweries, or other local bars that serve good beer and attract the mountain-bike crowd.

QUOTE: An original, insightful, or humorous quote or fact overheard on the trail or at the brewpub is included in each B&B pairing.

A WORD ABOUT THE MAPS PRINTED HEREIN: The maps included in this book are artistic renditions of the states and cities, towns, and areas described. That's not to say the maps are inaccurate, just that distances may be longer, or shorter, than they appear. Not to worry, the street names are correct and directions are straightforward, so rest assured you will arrive at the primary trail, brewpub, and bike shop. With all that stated, please be aware that in some instances, the maps will point you to trails or breweries off the page. When this is the case, it is because it was not practical to fit all secondary details on the map. Please obtain detailed directions from the maps described in the map paragraph of each Bike & Brew section.

LEGEND FOR MAPS

 Pint Glass & Fat Tire ~ Bike & Brew America destination

 Single Fat Tire ~ Trail or trailhead location

 Full Pint Glass ~ Brewpub or microbrewery location

 Double Fat Tires ~ The all-important bike-shop location

 Star ~ Other important locations such as landmarks, land manager, tourist information, or beer joint that is not a brewpub or microbrewery

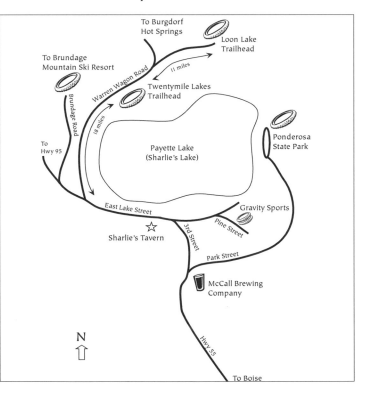

BIKING ADVICE FROM THE INTERNATIONAL MOUNTAIN BICYCLING ASSOCIATION (IMBA): Have fun out there, but please don't forget to live by the International Mountain Bicycling Association's Rules of the Trail:

1. Plan ahead.

2. Always yield trail.

3. Never scare animals.

4. Ride on open trails only.

5. Control your bicycle.

6. Leave no trace.

IMBA works to keep trails open for mountain bikers by encouraging responsible riding and supporting volunteer trail work.

⚙I·M·B·A
International Mountain Bicycling Association

BIKING AND DRINKING ADVICE FROM BIKE & BREW AMERICA: Always wear your helmet! And as in other aspects of life, this advice is more easily followed if we Bike & Brew travelers drink responsibly and NEVER drink and drive OR ride. See you on the trail, in the brewpub, and maybe even in the bookstore!

CHAPTER ONE

COLORADO

Colorado's dominating mountain ranges and its many national forests offer great midsummer, alpine-type mountain biking, and the state's numerous restored mining towns offer unique handcrafted beer and excellent food. In a nutshell, Colorado has everything the Bike & Brew traveler could ever need or want: great mountain biking and great beer.

Colorado

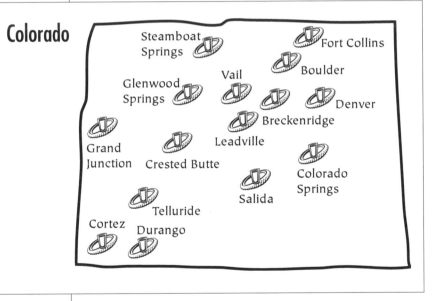

Steamboat Springs

Fort Collins

Vail

Boulder

Glenwood Springs

Denver

Breckenridge

Grand Junction

Leadville

Crested Butte

Colorado Springs

Salida

Telluride

Cortez

Durango

Rising up out of eastern Colorado's Great Plains, the Southern Rocky Mountains dominate much of the state. This monstrous band of mountains includes more than 50 peaks rising above 14,000 feet in elevation. Combining this impressive display of geography with Colorado's 12 national forests and other public lands creates the perfect stage for intermediate and advanced mountain biking.

The fact that Colorado is the highest state in the union—

averaging just about 6800 feet—does make the biking season in the mountains a little shorter and a bit more aerobically difficult than other biking destinations in the country. However, both the Front Range (the eastern slopes of the Rockies) and the Colorado Plateau and Grand Valley areas (the western slopes) are at lower elevations and enjoy a much milder climate than the central Rockies, meaning, your season of fat tire fun can be extended to almost 12 months a year.

Now, all the biking in the world wouldn't be completely satisfying without a fresh beer to go with it. And that's where Colorado again stands frothy head and cool shoulders above the other Rocky Mountain states. The gold and silver mining booms of the mid–nineteenth century spurred Colorado's early growth as prosperous mining towns sprang up throughout the mountains. The mines have long since closed, and these boomtowns have turned to another source of revenue: tourism.

As a tourist destination, Colorado is king. Spectacular scenery, abundant wildlife, a colorful history, hunting, fishing, over 20 ski resorts, and, of course, mountain biking attract visitors from all over the world. This flow of tourism has been a natural catalyst for the other important Bike & Brew ingredient: fresh beer.

Brewpubs in these historic towns are often set in beautiful old buildings restored to their former glory and offering a unique glimpse into the town's past. And, because all of these towns are already vacation destinations, they present plenty of other distractions for the complete vacation appeal. Basically, Coloradans love their microbrewed beer as much as their outdoor sports, and you'll never have to travel far for either while visiting this Rocky Mountain Bike & Brew paradise.

Boulder

Sitting at an elevation of just over 5000 feet and nestled in the foothills beneath the picturesque, giant rock slabs known as the Flatirons, Boulder is everything Bike & Brew America is all about, right down to the fact that, at last count, there were five brewpubs and three microbreweries pumping fresh beer inside the city limits of this town of less than 100,000 people. Thanks to an environmentally conscious populace there's plenty of green space loaded with biking as challenging and as scenic as anywhere in the Rockies. The Boulder area boasts of more than 200 miles of horseback, hiking, and biking trails and almost 100,000 acres of Open Space just waiting to be explored. As an added bonus, the restaurants and bars are smoke free except in designated, enclosed smoking rooms. The facts that Boulder enjoys over 300 sunny days a year (more than San Diego) and *Outside Magazine* recently rated the place the Number One Sports Town in America only support your decision to make Boulder a mandatory destination on any serious Bike & Brew tour.

Walker Ranch Open Space

THE SCOOP: Thigh-burning downhill, lung-burning uphill, and rolling, tight-switchbacked singletrack through awesome forest-fire devastation.

RIDE LENGTH AND TYPE: 7.2-mile loop that can be done in either direction and all the way from town.

THE BIKE: Just minutes up Flagstaff Mountain (by car) and just behind (west of) the Flatirons, the Walker Ranch Open Space offers mountain bikers just about everything. A mix of extended downhilling and climbing, rolling singletrack following the contours of the mountain, and technical problems that'll have all but the best cyclists on foot (or on their faces). It also features a fantastic section of switchbacks that is just barely 100% rideable if your membership at the gym is up to date.

The forest-fire season of 2000 hit Walker Ranch hard, forcing the Open Space there to be closed for a few months. Andrew Hoffman of Boulder County Open Space says it will reopen soon and "will give a unique feel to an already great ride." The area provides an excellent chance for a firsthand glimpse of the devastation resulting from forest fires but also an opportunity to see the regrowth potential of the wilds.

Now back to the trail. This trail in its entirety can be done as a loop in either direction from the trailhead. Alternatively, it can be ridden as a counterclockwise out-and-back to a required bike-portage section and/or, again from the trailhead, as a clockwise ride down the steep switchbacks of the **Columbine Gulch Trail** to the east of the trailhead. At the bottom of Columbine Gulch, you can either turn around and indulge in a quad-burning ascent of those same switchbacks or find nearby **Pika Road** that eventually climbs all the way to **Flagstaff Drive** and back to your car.

If it's your first time on the trail, it's probably best to do it as a loop. The trail is well marked and well traveled so you shouldn't get lost. The counterclockwise route starts out with a descent down an old doubletrack, the **South Boulder Creek Trail,** before crossing the creek at the bottom of the valley. Once across the creek, you'll learn what climbing is all about in the Rockies. Don't try to power up it. Ease back when the terrain allows so that you'll have plenty of gas to make it to the top. Your reward is a serene section of singletrack known as the **Crescent Meadows Trail** that seems to do all the pedaling for you. This trail ends all too soon with a couple technical spots and a hike-a-bike section that takes you once more across the creek and up another doubletrack, the **Eldorado Canyon Trail,** on the other side. Then it's around the hill and up the steep switchback of the Columbine Gulch Trail that ends right at the parking lot.

Now, after you're finished with Walker, draw straws to figure out who has to drive the rig back down to the brewery. The rest of you get to partake in the scream down Flagstaff Drive via bike all the way to the Sun.

DIFFICULTY: Intermediate to advanced. This is another example of a trail that can give advanced riders everything they've been looking for and more. However, by skipping the switchback section, it's a picture-perfect intermediate trail as well.

AEROBIC DIFFICULTY (1–5)

4

TECHNICAL DIFFICULTY (1–5)

4

WARNINGS: This is Boulder and outdoor activity is religion here. Watch for other mountain bikers and hikers on this trail and abide by IMBA's Rules of the Trail. If you plan on biking Flagstaff Drive either up, down, or both, make sure you play it safe and stay on the right side of the road. Flagstaff is an extremely winding road with dozens of blind corners for both motorists and cyclists. Also, check your brakes before any trips down the mountain; it's easy to pick up lots of speed on this steep section of mountain road. And if that's not enough warning for you, then this area is also known as a mountain lion habitat, so be on the lookout. Mountain lions are not very brave and they usually stay hidden, especially from large, biking humans, but if you happen to get lucky and spot one, don't turn your back on it. Raise your arms, jump up and down, and make lots of noise if it appears hostile.

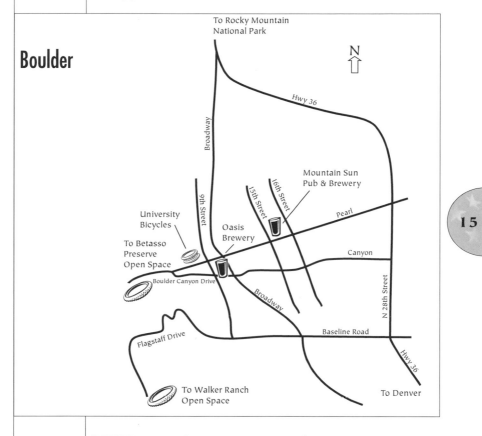

Boulder

To Rocky Mountain National Park

N

Hwy 36

Broadway

Mountain Sun Pub & Brewery

9th Street

15th Street

16th Street

Pearl

University Bicycles

Oasis Brewery

To Betasso Preserve Open Space

Canyon

Boulder Canyon Drive

Broadway

N 28th Street

Flagstaff Drive

Baseline Road

Hwy 36

To Walker Ranch Open Space

To Denver

OTHER TRAILS IN THE AREA: The Front Range is loaded with riding opportunities, and Boulder has some of the best ones. If it's your first time in the mountains and you're a little unsure of what extended climbs and altitude will do to you, then check out the Betasso Preserve Open Space 6½ miles west of town and just off Boulder Canyon Road (State Highway 119). Although the **Betasso Trail** itself is only a 3-mile loop, it's all tight singletrack, it's in the mountains, and you can reverse directions as many times as you want if you need more miles. This trail is perfect for beginners, but fun for everyone. Another way to add miles is to ride to the Betasso Trail. The first 4 miles are along the **Boulder Creek Path** before it ends, forcing you to finish the climb on **Boulder Canyon Road** before turning onto **Sugarloaf Road** and finally **Betasso Road.** This will add 6½ miles each way. Add two laps around the trail and you'll have a cool 19 miles.

A great intermediate ride that is 100% singletrack and not too far into the mountains is **Sourdough Trail (no. 835)** from County Road 116 to Brainard Lake Road. The trail is a little more than 5½ miles one way and offers the occasional outstanding view of the surrounding mountains and foothills through the thick pine forest.

Want even more heavy-duty action than the trails already described offer? Then try what the locals call the Walker Ranch Super Loop. Park at the brewery, climb the 8½ miles up **Flagstaff Drive**, do the trail, and then come back down. All by bike. An incredible day in the saddle and guess what? It begins and ends right at the Mountain Sun Pub & Brewery.

CONTACTS: Boulder County Parks and Open Space Department, 2045 Thirteenth Street, Boulder, CO 80306; (303) 441-3930. Boulder Chamber of Commerce, 2440 Pearl Street, Boulder CO 80302; (303) 442-1044.

MAPS: Like most trails managed by the Boulder County Open Space Department, the trails are mapped out for you right on the trailhead kiosk, often with small map pamphlets you can take with you. Even without a map, the trails are well marked and worn. If you're planning on spending a couple of days in the area, a great idea is to buy Latitude 40 Inc. & ZIA Map's *Boulder County Mountain Bike Map* for $9.99. It shows all the trails mentioned here plus many more.

BIKE SHOP: University Bicycles, 839 Pearl Street, Boulder, CO 80302; (303) 444-4196. On the west end of the Pearl Street Mall, it's right in the mix and mere blocks from both the Mountain Sun Pub & Brewery and the Oasis Brewery.

Mountain Sun Pub & Brewery

1535 Pearl Street
Boulder, Colorado 80302
(303) 546-0886

A view of the Mountain Sun Pub & Brewery from busy Pearl Street in downtown Boulder.

ATMOSPHERE: Tie-dyed University of Colorado students meet peace-loving Rastafarians in the "love your neighbor feel" that emanates from this Pearl Street building.

THE BREW: Ah Boulder! Some call it Planet Boulder, the People's Republic of Boulder, Baghdad by the Flatirons, or 35 square miles surrounded by reality. Call it what you will, it has everything a crunchy, free-thinking, politically correct, environmentally aware, hip endurance athlete would want and a price tag that shows it. At the center of this enlightened melting pot is the Pearl Street Mall—a pedestrian-only street where restaurants, specialty shops, and street performers all strive for your attention with the beckoning foothills as a backdrop. Located right off the eastern end of the Pearl Street Mall, the Sun's location puts it in the middle of all of the action. Not in many other places will you find advanced-degree intellectuals sitting beside angst-ridden youths just old enough to get a hand around a pint of beer.

The chalkboard beer list tastefully displays the Mountain Sun Brewery's current selection of handcrafted ales.

The Sun is one large room that ends with the bar, the kitchen, and finally the brewery. Filled with booths and tables, the place draws a crowd seven nights a week. Peaceful paintings of suns and moons cover the walls, seeming to smile down with looks of benign self-indulgence over the crowded bar. Old concert posters from bands like the Grateful Dead and The String Cheese Incident are but background decorations when placed next to the "chalkboard" beer list.

The board draws attention. Not only does it list the beers currently on tap, it does so in such an artistic way that you want to try every single beer listed. And with over a dozen house beers tapped at any given time, that's saying a lot.

Beers at the Sun are unfiltered hop-aggrandizing festivals that celebrate all that is good with beer in Colorado. You absolutely cannot go wrong with any of the beers the Sun puts out. Even the Sun's lightest ale, **Quinn's Golden Ale,** does not cry "sell out." It's still full of flavor and character. Next on the entry-level beers is the **Annapurna Amber,** named after the tenth-highest mountain in the world and meaning "goddess rich in sustenance." This beer is so full of malt that it could practically be called a brown. On to the bigger beers, and you've arrived at the **Colorado Kind Ale.** A Sun favorite and hop lovers' delight. This beer takes the meaning of hops to a new level. But things really start picking up with the **Isadore Java Porter,** originally brewed because the "brewers were weary of drinking stout for breakfast." Well this brew should fix that problem with its coffee aroma and flavor mixed perfectly with that of a fine porter. It'll make a coffee drinker out of anyone.

PRICE OF A PINT: Happy hour starts late in these parts. When the bell strikes 10:00 P.M., pints go from $3.00 down to $2.00. If you happen to be there on a Tuesday, wear your Mountain Sun T-shirt, and your pints will be only $2.00 all day. Don't have a Mountain Sun T-shirt? Buy one Tuesday and the first round is on the house. Put it on and the rest are only $2.00 all day long.

OTHER BREWS IN THE AREA: If you're not in the mood for dreadlock hair extensions and the smell of patchouli, check out the nearby **Oasis Brewery** at 1095 Canyon, (303) 449-0363. Located just south of the Pearl Street Mall, this place serves up outstanding beers in a spacious Arabian-styled building complete with an outdoor patio, good food, and fair prices.

19

Breckenridge

Located deep in the Rocky Mountains, Summit County is an easy 75-mile Interstate 70 drive west of Denver and a fat tire and beer lover's dreamland. Originally a gold rush mining town, Breckenridge was founded in 1859 by the lure of quick riches. Now, the four world class ski resorts of Arapahoe Basin, Breckenridge, Copper Mountain, and Keystone Resort all sit within 30 miles of each other, making this a winter vacation paradise. In the summer, when mountain bikes replace skis as the toy of choice, the Arapaho National Forest surrounding the area turns into a bona fide Bike & Brew playground.

And like the four points of the star that is Lake Dillon, the resort towns of Breckenridge, Dillon, Frisco, and Keystone each has a brewpub. Only here for one day? Then the Colorado Trail and Breckenridge Brewery & Pub in the historic mining town of Breckenridge constitute the requisite destinations. Two days, then add the Peaks Trail with the Backcounty Brewery in Frisco. However, with the number of trails and breweries in this valley, you could easily spend a week here and never see the same trail twice and never set foot in the same brewery twice.

The Colorado Trail

THE SCOOP: High-country alpine ride with mountain views, faultless singletrack, manageable climbs, and swooping downhills.

RIDE LENGTH AND TYPE: 23½-mile loop, 16 of which is singletrack.

THE BIKE: In Breckenridge (often shortened to Breck), Bike & Brew America once again turns the mountain biker's attention to a short segment of the Colorado Trail, a non-motor-vehicle recreational trail extending almost 500 miles from Denver to Durango. This part of the trail can be ridden as an epic 32-mile out-and-back or as a loop in either direction by incorporating Tiger Road, which parallels the trail.

The recommended route begins on Tiger Road, a nice way to warm up those legs on a brisk mountain morning and do some of the climbing on smooth dirt before you actually drop into the trail. The road also means there are plenty of bailout opportunities and options for shorter rides if the more than 23 miles is a little too much for you. Or, if you're in for the long haul, then tack on the 3½-mile paved bike trail from Breck and leave your car or truck at the brewery, an option that will total right around 30 miles. Now that's a day on the trails!

Assuming you've parked at the **Gold Hill Trailhead** along State Highway 9, ride the 5½ miles to where **Tiger Road** connects with North, South, and Middle Fork Roads. Take **Middle Fork Road** by staying to the right another 2.3 miles to where the **Colorado Trail** cuts across it. The path on the north side of Middle Fork Road is where you drop in on the Colorado Trail and things begin to get interesting.

You are immediately engulfed in quality singletrack rising and falling along the base of Wise Mountain. The trail rolls along the contours of the mountain for the first 2½ miles, staying at about 10,000 feet of elevation and occasionally emerging from the trees to give you refreshing views of the Tenmile Range.

Now don't get lulled into thinking you're not going to have to work for these views. After passing over North Fork Road and continuing the trail on the other side, you immediately begin a manageable 1000-foot climb. This climb continues for the next 2½ miles along West Ridge to your highest point of elevation, which is just over 11,000 feet.

As you climb, the forest becomes more mature, and Keystone Ski Area comes into view just across the next valley. Two trails that together constitute **West Ridge Loop** will take you down into Keystone if you really want to make this ride a doozy.

Not up for an all-day event? Then stay tuned to the Colorado Trail and prepare for an unimaginable 5 miles, almost all of which is downhill. This section of slightly off-camber singletrack is an absolute joy, with the trail swooping along the side of the mountain and just rocky and rooty enough to encourage you to keep your mind on business. It's possible to pick up quite a bit of speed along this section, but avoid the temptation to do so. Switchbacks come up quickly, and locking the brakes to make the turn will erode the trail.

After this meaty downhill, you'll be in for one last small climb before the trail finishes in grand fashion with smooth gliding singletrack and a couple of tight switchbacks before spitting you out at a four-star RV resort (only near a ski town) and right across State Highway 9 from your car. Delightful!

DIFFICULTY: Intermediate. The trail itself has very few technical obstacles, and the climbs are moderate compared to some in the Rockies. A moderately conditioned biker from the lowlands, below 5000 feet, should have no problem handling this trail, even though the elevation averages right around 10,000 feet.

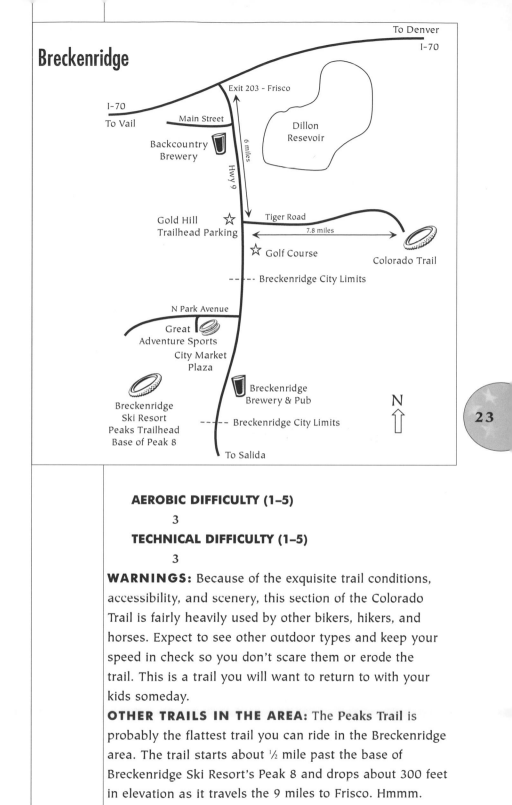

Breckenridge

To Denver
I-70

Exit 203 - Frisco

I-70
To Vail

Main Street

Dillon
Resevoir

Backcountry
Brewery

6 miles

Hwy 9

Gold Hill
Trailhead Parking ☆

Tiger Road

7.8 miles

Colorado Trail

☆ Golf Course

---- Breckenridge City Limits

N Park Avenue

Great
Adventure Sports
City Market
Plaza

Breckenridge
Brewery & Pub

N
⇧

Breckenridge
Ski Resort
Peaks Trailhead
Base of Peak 8

---- Breckenridge City Limits

To Salida

AEROBIC DIFFICULTY (1–5)

3

TECHNICAL DIFFICULTY (1–5)

3

WARNINGS: Because of the exquisite trail conditions, accessibility, and scenery, this section of the Colorado Trail is fairly heavily used by other bikers, hikers, and horses. Expect to see other outdoor types and keep your speed in check so you don't scare them or erode the trail. This is a trail you will want to return to with your kids someday.

OTHER TRAILS IN THE AREA: The Peaks Trail is probably the flattest trail you can ride in the Breckenridge area. The trail starts about ½ mile past the base of Breckenridge Ski Resort's Peak 8 and drops about 300 feet in elevation as it travels the 9 miles to Frisco. Hmmm.

Either turn around and return the way you came, use the paved bike trail that connects Frisco and Breck, or have a car waiting for you at Frisco and head immediately over to Backcounty Brewery. Although this can be considered a novice ride, the trail still has something for everybody— and, with a brewery on either end of it, you can't go wrong. By combining the **Burro Trail** with **Spruce Creek Loop,** you can create an advanced ride of about 11 miles that also leaves right from **Breckenridge Ski Resort.** And the ski resort is also a mountain-bike park with chairlifts running during the summer, providing easy access to a multitude of trails on the mountain.

CONTACTS: U.S. Forest Service, Dillon Ranger District, P.O. Box 620, 680 Blue River Parkway, Silverthorne, CO 80498; (970) 468-5400. Breckenridge Chamber of Commerce, 137 South Main, Breckenridge, CO 80424; (970) 453-5579. Summit County Chamber of Commerce, (970) 668-2051. Breckenridge Resort Chamber, (970) 453-6018.

MAPS: Summit County is extremely bike friendly. The county publishes a free *Summit County Bike Trail Guide,* which covers the trails listed here with directions and maps. These are always available at Great Adventure Sports bike shop, and Breckenridge Brewery & Pub usually has a few copies on hand as well.

BIKE SHOP: Great Adventure Sports, 400 North Park Avenue, Suite 13B, Breckenridge, CO 80424; (970) 453-0333; www.greatadventuresports.com. Located in the City Market Plaza and visible as soon as you enter Breck, the shop has all the maps and trail directions you're gonna need.

Breckenridge Brewery & Pub

600 South Main Street
Breckenridge, Colorado 80424
(970) 453-1550

ATMOSPHERE: Large, friendly, two-story ski-town brewery with patio seating on both lower and upper levels that overlook the Tenmile Range and Breckenridge Ski Resort.

THE BREW: Sitting at an elevation of 9600 feet, Breckenridge is a true high-country ski town loaded with small boutiques, curio shops, cafés, and restaurants. This is also where the successful Breckenridge beers originated when an enterprising ski bum met a wealthy lawyer on the ski lifts in 1989 and decided to open Breckenridge Brewery & Pub. Soon huge success at the brewpub dictated the opening of a microbrewery in Denver's Lower Downtown. Eleven years and many award-winning beers later, Breck is one of the largest, most well known, regional breweries in the country. Regardless, this is where you want to be after a hard day on some high-country singletrack.

Great happy hour specials and a mellow atmosphere attract the types who would rather be on skis or a bike than behind a desk. The large two-story brewing system sits right behind the bar, so while sipping a pint, all can see the brewers hard at work. In addition to a large bar area downstairs, the brewery also has a separate room for playing pool and watching ESPN on the tube. Upstairs is where most of the dining takes place alongside more fantastic views of the Tenmile Range.

The four award-winning regular Breckenridge flavors are always on tap with a couple of seasonal specials. The four

"Never trust a local who tells you the ride is a loop and mostly downhill."
—ROGER, TOMMY, AND CHIP WHILE LOST IN THE WOODS ON A LOOP RIDE THAT WAS SUPPOSED TO BE MOSTLY DOWNHILL.

25

Looking out on Breckenridge Ski Resort and the 12,998 ft. Peak 8 of the Tenmile Range from the Breckenridge Brewery and Pub's upstairs deck.

standards are the light, easy-drinker **Mountain Wheat,** the medium-bodied and more interesting **Avalanche Ale,** the strong and hoppy **Breckenridge India Pale Ale** (known locally as liquid heroin in honor of its 6% alcohol content), and the coffee-flavored **Breckenridge Oatmeal Stout.** In addition to this award-winning lineup, Breck also offers two seasonal beers—a good bet, because the brewers can express themselves when brewing these recipes—whereas the four main guns are pretty much set in stone.

PRICE OF A PINT: Considering you're knee-deep in a ski town, Breck runs some spectacular happy-hour deals. To begin, pints drop from $3.00 to $2.00, and pitchers are $6.00, Monday through Friday between 3:00 and 6:00 P.M. Then on Monday nights, things get really crazy when women drink for free and men only pay $1.00 for pints after 10:00 P.M. On Wednesdays, pool is free, and pitchers are only six bucks all day long.

OTHER BREWS IN THE AREA: Summit County is loaded with brewpubs. The Dillon Reservoir area has no less than four with Breckenridge Brewery and **Backcountry Brewery** in Frisco making up the best one-two punch in Summit County. So after you're finished with Breckenridge, be sure to stop by Backcountry Brewery on the corner of State Highway 9 and Main Street. Can't miss 'em on your way to or from Interstate 70.

Colorado Springs

Located on a plateau at the base of the Front Range about 60 miles south of Denver, Colorado Springs starts out at 6500 feet above sea level and is nestled at the foot of the famous 14,110-foot Pikes Peak. Founded as a resort in 1871, the discovery of gold in the nearby hills quickly catapulted Colorado Springs to early prominence. The historic Broadmoor Hotel is the crowning local achievement of one of the gold rush barons. From the U.S. Olympic Committee Headquarters and their state-of-the-art Olympic Training Center to the 7-11 Velodrome, Colorado Springs offers a very active, health-minded community. A cycling-friendly town, the network of bike paths throughout the city makes it worth the effort to explore by peddle power.

And, if singletrack and fresh beer are what you desire, epic riding is just minutes away from a great downtown brewery. North Cheyenne Canyon Park offers classic Front Range riding on crushed red-rock singletrack and fantastic views of the mountains and the city. Top that off with the Phantom Canyon Brewing Company and its great Colorado brews served up in a historic downtown setting, inside, outside, upstairs, or down. Come for a pint and stay for dinner—this place could be Colorado's best brewpub and is definitely where you want to be after a day on the trails in the Springs.

North Cheyenne Canyon Park

THE SCOOP: Miles of classic riding only 4 miles from downtown.

RIDE LENGTH AND TYPE: A loop from downtown to Captain Jacks to Chutes and back to town is about 18 miles and just scratches the surface of a near-limitless trail system.

THE BIKE: Pairs like this are what Bike & Brew America is all about. North Cheyenne Park lies a mere 4 miles from the heart of downtown Colorado Springs, which just happens to be the location of both the brewery and a great bike shop. Within the park are pine forests, streams, waterfalls, vistas that'll stop you in your tracks, and miles upon miles of singletrack trails, doubletrack trails, and dirt roads. The only limiting factors here are desire and time.

A great way to introduce yourself to the multiple trails crisscrossing the park is from the **High Drive Trailhead** that is located a little over 3½ miles inside the park entrance where **North Cheyenne Canyon Road** ends in a dirt parking lot. Either ride your bike (for a 7½-mile 1500-foot climb from downtown) uphill to High Drive or drive out, park the car or truck, and grab the helmet 'cause this is where the fun begins.

From the parking lot, **Gold Camp Road** maintains a nearly constant elevation, climbing gently to the left as it follows the terrain, whereas High Drive takes off in an uphill direction, picking up the climb where the paved road of North Cheyenne Canyon left off. For the true goods—and to teach you what North Cheyenne Canyon terrain is all about—hit the classic Captain Jacks Trail by heading west on the Gold Camp Road (closed to motor vehicles) for about ½ mile, keeping an eye out for a singletrack off to your right. Take this singletrack and be prepared for a decent climb as you switchback on the fairly exposed mountainside above the parking lot. The trail comes to a tee after about 1 mile of climbing. Left and west takes you to **Jones Park Trail** whereas east puts you on **Captain Jacks Trail**, the subject of this story.

Almost immediately after the intersection you begin down a 2-mile descent that will make you feel like The Captain. Just keep your ship pointed in a downward direction and way too soon you'll pop out onto **Gold Camp Road** (not to be confused with High Drive, which you will have crossed higher on the trail). Now you have some thinking to do. Left (east) down Gold Camp takes you to the fabled **Chutes**—a couple of miles of berm-filled, twisting, downhilling—and back to the Springs. Right (west) takes you back up to the High Drive parking lot where the possibilities are once again endless and longer trails can be fully explored.

DIFFICULTY: Intermediate to advanced. Novice bikers may find the combination of altitude, extended climbing, switchbacks, and loose surfaces a little intimidating. Reverse that, and intermediate to advanced bikers may find the combination of altitude, extended climbing, switchbacks, and loose surfaces a little invigorating.

Bike & Brew America prepares to ride the Captain Jacks Trail at High Drive Trailhead in North Cheyenne Canyon Park, Colorado Springs, Colorado.

AEROBIC DIFFICULTY (1–5)

3

TECHNICAL DIFFICULTY (1–5)

3

WARNINGS: A couple words of warning. Having a park this close to town is good for you—your game is just minutes away. But it's also good for other trail users, so PLEASE be aware of hikers. Captain Jacks, Chutes, and Columbine Trails all offer great downhilling opportunities but are also easily accessed by the Colorado Springs hiking population—especially the **Columbine Trail**, which you might want to stay off of altogether during prime weekend hours. Just remember to always say *Hi* and give way. This park is too good to lose.

OTHER TRAILS IN THE AREA: A real gem called

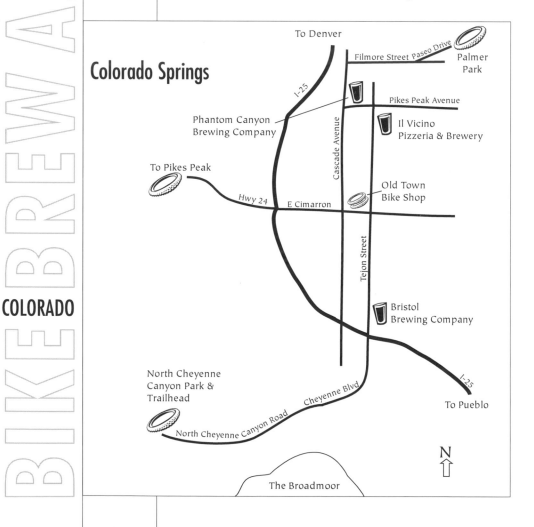

Colorado Springs

To Denver

Filmore Street Paseo Drive

Palmer Park

I-25

Pikes Peak Avenue

Phantom Canyon Brewing Company

Cascade Avenue

Il Vicino Pizzeria & Brewery

To Pikes Peak

Hwy 24   E Cimarron

Old Town Bike Shop

Tejon Street

Bristol Brewing Company

North Cheyenne Canyon Park & Trailhead

Cheyenne Blvd

I-25

To Pueblo

North Cheyenne Canyon Road

The Broadmoor

N

Palmer Park offers 600 acres of in-town singletrack with trails as easy, or difficult, as you want. Located northeast of the brewery, you can get there by using the **Pikes Peak Greenway Trail** to the **Templeton Gap Trail** or by driving north past the brewery on **Cascade Avenue** to **Fillmore Street.** Go east (right) on Fillmore Street and then left (northeast) on **Paseo Drive.** Park at the trailhead provided and then drop in and explore.

With Pikes Peak rising above you, it's hard not to imagine what it would be like to downhill from 14,000 feet. Got a little bit of cash stashed away? Give **Pikes Peak Downhill Bike Tours** a call at (888) 593-3062. This business offers downhill tours that begin at the 14,110-foot summit. Nothing like 19 miles of downhilling to make you thirsty.

CONTACTS: North Cheyenne Canyon Park Starsmore Discovery Center, 2120 South Cheyenne Canyon Boulevard, Colorado Springs, CO 80903; (719) 578-6146 or (719) 578-6147. Colorado Springs Chamber of Commerce, 2 North Cascade Avenue, Suite 110, Colorado Springs, CO 80903; (719) 635-1551.

MAPS: *The Colorado Springs Trails Network Map* outlines North Cheyenne Canyon Park as well as many other trails in the area. It's available at Old Town Bike Shop for $4.99.

BIKE SHOP: Old Town Bike Shop, 426 South Tejon Street, Colorado Springs, CO 80903; (719) 475-8589. Old Town Bike Shop just happens to be located 4 blocks from Phantom Canyon Brewing Company and about 4 miles from North Cheyenne Canyon Park. Be sure to stop in for any last-minute items, maps, or questions about the trails. The owners and employees are bikers and know the land better than anyone.

Phantom Canyon Brewing Company

2 East Pikes Peak Avenue
Colorado Springs, Colorado 80903
(719) 635-2800
www.phantomcanyon.com

ATMOSPHERE: The Phantom Canyon Brewing Company is located in the heart of downtown Colorado Springs; the brewpub occupies the early twentieth century Cheyenne Building that is on the National Historic Register. From the moment you ride up, you realize this place is gonna treat you right. Situated not more than 5 feet from the sidewalk patio tables are multiple bike racks just waiting for your exhausted bike. Lock it up and prepare yourself for some of the finest beer Colorado has to offer.

THE BREW: As you make your way through the front doors, you will pass beneath the building's namesake, Chief Two Moons of the Cheyenne Indians, whose stone face scowls down from above the entrance. The first floor serves as the main dining room, brewhouse, and bar. Large windows dominate the south and west walls, and a beautifully restored period bar occupies the east. High tin ceilings, ceiling fans, and tap handles as far as the eye can see round out the décor. If a quiet beer or indoor dining is the goal, go no further, you have arrived.

However, if you're more interested in looking at the mountains while keeping a loving eye on your bike, then the outdoor sidewalk patio is for you. Or, if you're just not quite ready to settle down, then head up to the Phantom Canyon's billiard hall on the second floor to stretch those legs. Here you'll find 11 pool tables plus TVs, music, and a livelier, if a little less refined, crowd.

Cheyenne Chief Two Moons watches over Phantom Canyon Brewing Company's front door.

But no matter where you settle, you're gonna be in for great beer and fantastic food. With six standard beers on tap and a few rotating taps, Phantom Canyon has something for everyone. For those out there who are self-proclaimed softies for hand-drawn ales, the brewers will keep you happy with their **Phantom IPA (India pale ale** for the uninitiated) and **Zebulon Peated Porter,** both always on the hand pump. Also, be sure to try the **Railyard Ale** for an all-around smooth drink, perfect after a day on the trails. There's not a bad beer in the bunch, so order freely depending on your mood or try a sampler if you can't decide and then pick the one that suits your fancy.

PRICE OF A PINT: Happy hour is from 3:00 to 6:00 P.M. every day, so plan your ride accordingly as pints go for the incredibly low price of $1.75! If you get lost and arrive late, expect to pay the standard $3.25. Have one too many Saturday night? Come back for a Sunday brunch and a $2.00 Bloody Mary to get you back in the saddle again.

OTHER BREWS IN THE AREA: Phantom Canyon is the best brewpub in town, but if you're looking for some great local beer to share with the locals, head over to **Bristol Brewing Company's Tap Room**— also situated very conveniently on the way to and from the trailhead at the Tejon Street–Cheyenne Boulevard intersection. The Bristol doesn't serve food, but it does serve and distribute some great beer. Don't leave town without at least a six-pack.

If you're visiting Colorado Springs on a Sunday be sure to check out the local **Il Vicino Pizzeria & Brewery** (part of the Il Vicino chain that originated in New Mexico) at 11 South Tejon between 3:00 and 5:30 P.M. when pints are half price and the local riders start arriving after a day on the trails.

"Killer lead back there!"
—PACE LINE OF MOUNTAIN BIKERS PAUSE AT HIGH DRIVE AFTER SPINNING UP NORTH CHEYENNE CANYON ROAD BEFORE DISAPPEARING INTO THE DIRT BEYOND.

Cortez

So you have a long week for a mountain-bike vacation, half in Moab and half in Durango. What could be more perfect, from slickrock to alpine conditions in 3 hours— barely enough time to hydrate before your next ride, right? Well, how's this for a proposition: Cortez, Colorado. It's on the way, has slickrock and alpine riding plus plenty of fresh, local beer. Basically, the only thing it doesn't have is the crowd.

Perhaps you're a bit of a history buff as well as a Bike & Brew fiend. Then Cortez is doubly the place for you. Just 10 miles west of Mesa Verde National Park, Cortez serves as the research center for the study of the prehistoric Ancestral Pueblo people, once called the Anasazi, a Navajo word meaning *Ancient Ones*, most noted for their ability to build castle-like cliff dwellings.

Some of the most magnificent dwellings are found in Mesa Verde National Park, but the entire region abounds with ruins and archaeological sites. In fact, both the Sand Canyon Trail and East Rock Trail are loaded with these ruins, and most of the time they are within sight of the trail itself.

Downtown Cortez offers the Main Street Brewery and Kokopelli Bike & Board, so do yourself a favor and take time out from the yearly journey to Moab and Durango for a little break, right here in Cortez. And remember, if you're headed to Utah, this may be the last time your beer rates above 3.2% alcohol by weight. Alternatively, if you're from Utah, this is the first watering hole since Moab.

Sand Canyon and East Rock Trail

THE SCOOP: Slickrock, mesas, cacti, singletrack, and, get this, ruins of Ancestral Puebloan cliff dwellings.

RIDE LENGTH AND TYPE: There are actually two connected trails in this area. The out-and-back Sand Canyon Trail is 6 miles and the East Rock Loop is close to 10 miles. The first 3½ miles of Sand Canyon and then back to the connector trail to complete the East Rock Trail total right around 12 perfect miles.

THE BIKE: About 15 miles west of Cortez lie Sand Canyon and East Rock Trails. Originating from the same trailhead, these two trails can be combined for almost 20 miles of slickrock and singletrack riding with the only thing getting in your way being the incredible ruins of Ancestral Puebloan cliff dwellings.

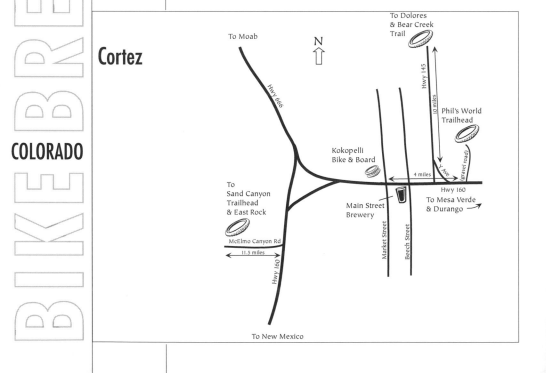

Cortez

To Moab

N

To Dolores
& Bear Creek
Trail

Hwy 666

Hwy 145

10 miles

Phil's World
Trailhead

Kokopelli
Bike & Board

Y Ave

(gravel road)

4 miles

To
Sand Canyon
Trailhead
& East Rock

Main Street
Brewery

Hwy 160
To Mesa Verde
& Durango

McElmo Canyon Rd

11.5 miles

Market Street

Beech Street

Hwy 160

To New Mexico

One of many Ancestral Puebloan cliff dwellings along Sand Canyon Trail.

Sand Canyon Trail is a fairly moderate 6-mile out-and-back trail with the most threatening part being the ruins. (It'll be hard to keep your eyes on the trail as you pass by them.) Once you're finished with Sand Canyon, take the cutoff trail to **East Rock Trail.** Here you are well advised to keep your eyes on the road as East Rock is tighter and more technical than Sand Canyon. Both trails wind through slickrock, dwarf-growth forests of Rocky Mountain juniper (cedar to the locals) and Colorado piñon. Under your tires will be dirt and, yes, a little bit of sand. It is called Sand Canyon after all.

Perfect day? Ride all 10 miles of the East Rock Trail, then pack a lunch and hike (or bike) the first 3½ miles of Sand Canyon so you can take time to truly experience the ancient ruins along the trail. And, of course, there is no better way to finish your perfect day than with a stop at the Main Street Brewery back in Cortez. There you go. A little hike, bike, and brew.

DIFFICULTY: Intermediate. East Rock contains a couple advanced sections but nothing that will defeat the determined rider.

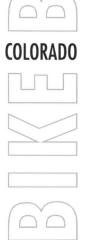
AEROBIC DIFFICULTY (1–5)

2

TECHNICAL DIFFICULTY (1–5)

3

WARNINGS: Ruins of Ancestral Puebloan cliff dwellings are everywhere—so please read the warnings and keep your bike on the main trail. If you'd like a closer look, dismount and walk to the site. There's talk of making this area a national monument. If that happens, we mountain bikers don't want to give "them" any reason to ban bikes from the area. If damaging ancient archaeological sites isn't enough to worry about, you also have cryptobiotic crust to contend with. Beware of the thin, dark, mineral crust on much of the soil out here. It's a critical part of the desert soil-building process so be careful not to step, ride, or urinate on it. Need any more incentive to stay on the trails out here? Cactus needles. Lots of 'em.

OTHER TRAILS IN THE AREA: Sand Canyon and East Rock Trails are at a fairly low elevation (5443 feet at the trailhead), which makes for some HOT riding in the summer. If it's too hot, head north through Dolores to the **Bear Creek Trail** for a great summer 20-mile intermediate out-and-back. And just a couple of miles from downtown Cortez is **Phil's World Trailhead,** an intermediate to advanced mesa ride of winding, technical trails that total about 7 miles.

CONTACTS: Bureau of Land Management, San Juan Resource Area, 701 Camino Del Rio, Durango, CO 81301; (970) 882-7296. Cortez Chamber of Commerce, 928 East Main Street, Cortez, CO 81321; (970) 565-3414.

MAPS: Free hand-drawn maps and directions to all the trails mentioned here are available at Kokopelli Bike & Board in downtown Cortez.

BIKE SHOP: Kokopelli Bike & Board, 30 West Main Street, Cortez, CO 81321; (970) 565-4408 or (800) 565-6736. Kokopelli is the place to go for all trail information in the area. It has free maps of these trails plus a few more. Pick up some maps and whatever else you need, and then hit the trails or head across the street and east one block for some brews at the Main Street Brewery.

Main Street Brewery

21 East Main Street
Cortez, Colorado 81321
(970) 564-9112
www.mesacerveza.com

ATMOSPHERE: Colorado Highway 160 becomes Main Street in downtown Cortez, and it's here you'll find the Main Street Brewery, another classic western-town building with tin ceilings and wooden floors. The main level has been divided into a casual family dining area and a tavern with a long wooden bar down the length ending with the brewhouse. And that's where classic ends and the quirky fun begins, right down to the copper urinals in the men's room. (Sorry ladies, nothing quite that exciting in the women's room.) Above the bar is a mural with so much going on it'll take you two pints just to sort out the mix of images. But lest we mountain bikers get ahead of ourselves once again: first, da beers.

THE BREW: Although Main Street does not do seasonals, when you have eight standards on tap, you don't really have to. If you were out in the desert too long, quench your thirst with the nicely hopped **Pale Export.** Winter rides deserve the excellent, easy-drinking, dark and smooth **Schnorzenboomer Doppelbock.** On a spring or fall day the **Winter Ale**—which just happens to be a combination of the Export and Doppelbock—really hits the spot and is an excellent all-around drinking beer. Designated drivers, or those who just want to taste some fantastic root beer, must try Main Street's homemade **Honey Root Beer.** It's honey-colored as root beer was meant to be and tastes out of this world.

"Avoid Heart Attacks— Drink Beer."
—MAIN STREET BREWERY LOGO, TRUE WISDOM AT LAST!

Main Street Brewery's hop-vine mural welcomes thirsty bikers off of Cortez's Main Street.

As you sample the taps, be sure to check out the afore-mentioned mural above the bar, understanding that you can't leave until you find Waldo. He's up there; you just have to know where to look. Tired of that, head down to the stone-walled basement where video games, pool, foos-ball, and TV await those so inclined. Here, and elsewhere, you will find various words of wisdom painted about the walls and ceiling, most of which can be applied to biking

COLORADO

in some fashion or another. "Letup and Lose" and "Nerve Succeeds" are two that seem particularly applicable.

PRICE OF A PINT: Main Street has no happy hour so expect to pay between $2.75 and $3.75 a pint depending on the flavor you chose. Hey, nobody's perfect!

OTHER BREWS IN THE AREA: Cortez has only the one brewery, and you can pick up some of its beers under the Mesa Cerveza label just about anywhere in the area, package or draft.

Crested Butte

Known as one of the first places to embrace mountain biking as a legitimate activity, Crested Butte has always placed sport above all else, even claiming that people have skied here longer than they've had cars, plumbing, or electricity. Though that may be pushing it a bit (or maybe not), the fact remains that Crested Butte is removed from the real world by virtue of being located 9000 feet above sea level in a dead-end valley surrounded by nothing but mountains and wilderness. A strong mining history has left this quaint mountain town with one of the largest national historic districts in Colorado, and a strong biking history makes Crested Butte the perfect place for the Mountain Bike Hall of Fame, which is located in downtown Crested Butte, a mere block away from the breweries. Mountain bikes, cruiser bikes, and just plain old junkers dominate the town as the primary means of transportation. And with hundred of miles of singletrack to explore, and more being developed all the time, mountain biking is now the favored summertime pastime. Come for a week, and you won't even get close to riding it all. The Crested Butte Brewery and Idle Spur Restaurant, as well as the Eldo Restaurant, Bar, & Brewery hold up their end of the bargain by delivering good beer and entertainment after a hot day on the trails.

401 Trail

THE SCOOP: 8 miles of the best singletrack and best views anywhere.

RIDE LENGTH AND TYPE: 30-mile town-to-town ride, which can be shortened if a car is used to drive up past the town of Gothic to one of the many parking areas.

THE BIKE: The biking excitement starts with the 401 Trail, a classic slice of Crested Butte singletrack with views of Schofield Pass and the spectacular valley leading there. The 401 is normally ridden as a town-to-town ride and is one of those beautiful trails where most of the initial climb is on dirt road. In fact, you climb all the way from 9000-foot downtown Crested Butte to 10,700-foot Schofield Pass by the time you reach the beginning of the singletrack and the 401 Trail proper. Although this is 13 miles of dirt road separating you from actual singletrack, it is a scenic, low-traffic, and trouble-free ride.

The 401 Trail's single-track summit at 11,150 ft., with the Elk Mountain Range and Maroon Bells-Snowmass Wilderness disappearing to the north.

You make your way past Mount Crested Butte Resort, through the strange little town of Gothic, and up **Gothic Road** until it turns into the narrow, 4x4 **Schofield Pass Road.** When the Schofield Pass Road starts getting steeper, you'll know you're getting close to the goods.

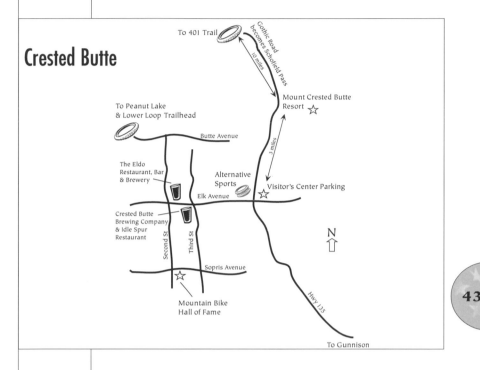

Crested Butte

To 401 Trail

Gothic Road becomes Schofield pass

10 miles

Mount Crested Butte Resort

To Peanut Lake & Lower Loop Trailhead

Butte Avenue

3 miles

The Eldo Restaurant, Bar & Brewery

Alternative Sports

Visitor's Center Parking

Elk Avenue

Crested Butte Brewing Company & Idle Spur Restaurant

Second St

Third St

N

Sopris Avenue

Hwy 135

Mountain Bike Hall of Fame

To Gunnison

The **401 Trail** singletrack starts directly on top of the pass off to the right. Keep in mind that you've only completed "most" of the climb up to this point. Now you have a 600-foot finale over the next 1½ miles through forests of huge pines and over black loamy soil and twisted roots. The incline isn't too steep, but remember this is taking place at over 10,000 feet, and the thin air gives a whole different kind of hurt. Persevere and you will break through the timberline for some striking views of the surrounding Maroon Bells–Snowmass Wilderness Areas and the peaks over 14,000 feet high forming the Elk Mountains to the north.

A switchback descent takes you across lush mountain fields filled with small wildlife and flowers that earned Crested Butte the additional title "Wildflower Capital of Colorado." A few water-filled drainages keep the ride interesting, and views of the valley keep the ride unforgettable.

Just when you think this is as good as it gets, prepare for a B&B Hotmile (that is, *perfect* in every way, shape, and form) as you effortlessly glide along the exposed side of Mount Bellview with nothing but singletrack ahead and nearly vertical meadows all around you.

Following that perfect mile, you drop into a stand of aspens for a little technical duty, but—rest assured—the trail stays prime, and the singletrack fantasy remains firmly in place. It's not far after the aspens that you get to your first bailout point. If you're not interested in another extended climb, now is your chance to break for Gothic Road and pedal back to town. If you're up for another 1½-mile, 600-foot climb along the Maroon Bells–Snowmass Wilderness Boundary, cross the access road and return to the 401 Trail where it crosses the river.

After the climb you can expect another descent, but not quite as smooth as the first. Ranchers let their cattle roam free here, and the areas around the water crossing can get pretty muddy and torn up by the cows as well as by horse riders and bike traffic.

Then, after a little over 8 miles of singletrack, it's over, and you can point your bike back toward the Butte and the Idle Spur for a "mostly" downhill ride back to town.

DIFFICULTY: Intermediate to advanced. There are plenty of roots and rocks on the trail, and things can get pretty slippery after the cows have come home.

AEROBIC DIFFICULTY (1–5)

4

TECHNICAL DIFFICULTY (1–5)

4

WARNINGS: There is some serious exposure on the B&B Hotmile so if you don't like heights, this one ain't for you. Cow paddies and horse puckies make the mud that much more juicy, and things also get slippery under the many pine-tree stands and multiple stream crossings.

OTHER TRAILS IN THE AREA: Nothing is too easy at 9000 feet, but there are a couple of rides that are kind to lowlanders who are stretching their lungs for the first time.

The best "novice" ride in the area is **Snodgrass**, a 9-mile loop close to town. Unfortunately, this trail closes in mid-August when the owner runs his cattle across it. Check with Alternative Sports for the current status. If Snodgrass is closed, the next best thing is the **Lower Loop.** Just over 1½ miles from town, it makes for a great town-to-town ride with 5 miles of well-marked singletrack. This 8-mile loop from town is perfect for working up a thirst without almost killing yourself. However, if near-death experiences are what defines mountain biking to you, the locals can't stop talking about the **Reno-Flag-Bear-Deadman Trail**— which is what you'll be unless you're up for an all-day advanced epic ride with three extended climbs and three extended descents.

CONTACTS: U.S. Forest Service, Taylor River Ranger District, 216 North Colorado, Gunnison, CO 81230; (970) 641-0471. Crested Butte Chamber of Commerce, 601 Elk Avenue, Crested Butte, CO 81224; (970) 349-6438 or Mount Crested Butte–Crested Butte Chamber of Commerce, 7 Emmons Road, Mount Crested Butte, CO 81230; (800) 545-4505.

MAPS: With the Mountain Bike Hall of Fame right down the street, you would think there would be some sort of free trail guide to the area. Not so. The best thing to do is go to Alternative Sports and study the wall map or pick up an *Aspen/Crested Butte/Gunnison Recreation Topo Map* for $10.00 to make sure you get it right. Guess Crested Butte doesn't need to work at attracting bikers—we already know about the place.

BIKE SHOP: Alternative Sports, Crested Butte, CO 81224; (970) 349-1320; www.alternativesports.com. A fun little shop without an address but right across from Crested Butte's Chamber of Commerce and Visitor's Center (a great place to park for free and explore the town by foot or bike). The folks at Alternative Sports keep a whiteboard out front with current trail conditions and a large trail map of the area hanging in the front hallway. Come on in, ask a lot of questions, and take good notes.

Crested Butte Brewing Company and Idle Spur Restaurant

226 Elk Avenue
Crested Butte, Colorado 81224
(970) 349-5026

ATMOSPHERE: Country lodge feel with roughhewn logs for support columns and beams. Log cabin interior with tables and chairs to match adds to the western ambiance of the place.

The 12,516 ft. Whetstone Mountain reflects off of Nicholson Lake just outside of Crested Butte.

THE BREW: Ah, Crested Butte, where cruisers, clunkers, and mountain bikes outnumber cars two to one. One of the few ski towns where the streets aren't completely packed with slowly moving cars and parking is a joke. Public bike racks at every street corner encourage this trend and create the perfect setting for the second half of a B&B pair to remember.

The Idle Spur in Crested Butte is home to award-winning Red Lady Ale, named after Red Lady Basin atop 12,392 ft. Mount Emmons just outside Crested Butte.

The Idle Spur is a large long building with antique ski paraphernalia on the wall and a large fieldstone fireplace to encourage après-ski activities. During the summer months, the Elk Avenue patio comes to the fore. The setting is perfect for Lycra-clad mountain bikers to take in pints of fresh brew while watching the vibrant downtown, or simply sit and gaze at beautiful Mount Crested Butte towering over the town from the northeast.

Regardless of what you're doing while having a pint, just make sure you're having one. Expect eight different beers on tap at all times with the Big Three (**Red Lady Ale, White Buffalo Peace Ale,** and **Rodeo Stout**) always present and the other taps rotating through 13 or so

"We gotta brew the light ones because of all the Texans."
—YOUNG, ANONYMOUS BARTENDER AT THE IDLE SPUR, DEFENDING THE FAMILY'S HONOR.

different recipes. The Big Three are award winners—the Red Lady Ale is the flagship and best-selling Crested Butte beer. The White Buffalo is a decent American pale, and the stout is a real sweet and smooth treat served on nitrogen.

The Spur's best beers come from the rotating five. Don't miss the **Extremely Special Brew,** Crested Butte's big and bold version of an "ESB," an excellent rendition of an English strong ale, and the **New World Pale Ale,** a very good India pale ale rendition. For the big beer lover, Crested Butte puts out **Old Groper Barleywine,** which is ready to drink after just five weeks in the tank. However, a batch can last nearly two years—just sitting there, getting bigger and better as time goes by.

And the food? Absolutely everything you would expect from a four-star steakhouse. If it's in the budget, this is the place for a cut of beef. If it's not, then have another pint and call it even as **Teocalli Tamale** is right across the street waiting for your business.

PRICE OF A PINT: In 1999 the Crested Butte Brewing Company tried a "Season's Pass" where $100 got you all the beer you could drink from May through September. It, ah, didn't work out as the promoters planned, so things are back to normal for a ski town, that is, $3.25 pints with happy hour from 3:00 to 5:00 P.M. when beers drop to $2.50. Better than nothing but, oh, that Season's Pass. . . .

OTHER BREWS IN THE AREA: Right across the street is **The Eldo Restaurant, Bar, & Brewery** which proudly proclaims itself, "A sunny place for shady people." Nothing fancy here, but a great upstairs deck with $1.50 house pints from 4:00 'til 8:00 P.M. every day of the week. The beers are solid with the **Mahogany Ridge India Pale Ale** taking honors. The Eldo gives you cheap beer and a very casual atmosphere. A local hangout: expect smoke, bar food, and a pool table in back.

Denver

As the capital and largest city, Denver is Colorado's commercial, financial, and cultural center. Known as the Mile High City, because the 15th step on the Capitol Building is exactly 5280 feet above sea level, Denver is located on the western edge of the Great Plains just before the foothills and mountains of the Front Range take over, giving the city a spectacular backdrop and unforgettable sunsets. For a major metropolitan area, Denver delivers like a champ in the Bike & Brew world. The mountains prevent much potential urban sprawl to the west—thus providing the riding—and Coloradans' love of good beer ensures that more than enough breweries are operating in her capitol city. In fact, the Lower Downtown area of town, known as LoDo, has no less than six brewpubs and microbreweries alone. With major interstate highways riddling the area, neither trails nor pubs are far from each other and make excellent stops on the way to some high-country riding in the mountains beyond.

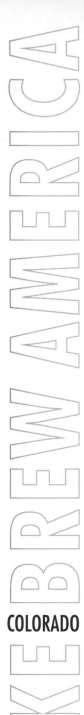
Matthews-Winters Park

THE SCOOP: Technical climbs and descents filled with rocks and sand welcome you to riding in the Rockies.

RIDE LENGTH AND TYPE: 7.6-mile singletrack loop.

THE BIKE: Practically within spitting distance of downtown Denver is the 1127-acre Matthews-Winters Park. Located right off Interstate 70 just before it turns uphill and enters the mountains, this is a popular after-work ride for the locals. Don't let the rather short 7.6-mile loop fool you. This is a ride you'll want to be ready for, or it will eat you up and spit you out.

Ridden clockwise (recommended unless you really like punishment), the trail begins with a 200-foot climb out of the parking lot up onto the **Dakota Ridge Trail** (also known as **Hogback Ridge** if you grew up here). This is the least of your problems. As you regain your senses from

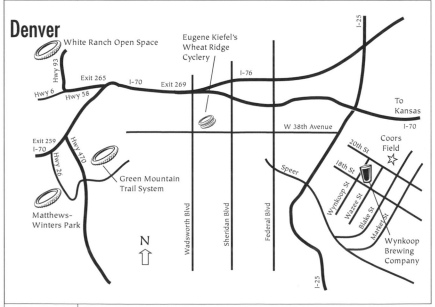

Denver

White Ranch Open Space

Eugene Kiefel's Wheat Ridge Cyclery

I-25

Hwy 93

Exit 265 I-70 Exit 269

I-76

Hwy 6 Hwy 58

To Kansas

I-70

W 38th Avenue

Coors Field

Exit 259 I-70

Hwy 470

Hwy 26

20th St

18th St

Speer

Green Mountain Trail System

Matthews-Winters Park

Wadsworth Blvd

Sheridan Blvd

Federal Blvd

Wynkoop St

Wazee St

Blake St

Market St

Wynkoop Brewing Company

I-25

N
↑

the steep climb at high altitude, you are immediately thrown into a rocky, sandy melee where you'd better be on your game or you'll end up a casualty. The sounds of Interstate 70 will be of little concern as you concentrate on short but technical descents and climbs. Spectacular views of the Front Range stretch off to the south, and the sprawl of Denver lies below—but you'll have to dismount to properly enjoy them.

Things get a little more reasonable when you come off the Dakota Ridge Trail onto **State Highway 26.** Here a quarter-mile excursion north (left) from where the trail picks up on the other side of State Highway 26 is the Dinosaur Ridge National Historic Site and an interesting interpretive display with dinosaur tracks embedded in the rock cliff rising next to the highway.

Roger Knight rides the Morrison Slide Trail in Matthews-Winters Park, with the deadly Hogback Ridge behind and the Great Plains stretching into the distance.

Once you've recovered from your Hogback episode under the pretenses of a prehistoric science lesson, climb back up State Highway 26 to where the **Red Rocks Trail** picks up where Dakota Ridge left off. Although the Red Rocks Trail is not as technical, it's still a demanding climb. You can add a couple of miles by looping in the **Morrison Slide Trail**, which takes you to the highest point of this trail network (almost 6800 feet) and provides some spectacular views of the Denver area. Then it's all downhill and back to your car on the tame and smooth **Village Walk Trail,** just what the doctor ordered after some of your earlier stunts.

Not enough for you? Either do it again or turn around and go the other direction. Do that and you're looking at what one local called the "Best climb in the state."

DIFFICULTY: Advanced, although intermediate riders will survive if they don't mind walking their bikes a bit. Do the trail in the counterclockwise direction and crank both the aerobic difficulty and technical difficulty up to a 5.

AEROBIC DIFFICULTY (1–5)

Clockwise 4

Counterclockwise 5

TECHNICAL DIFFICULTY (1–5)

Clockwise 4

Counterclockwise 5

WARNINGS: This section of the Front Range is in the most populated area of Colorado. Expect other trail users at all times and especially after work. If you can get to the trail before the evening rush, you'll be doing yourself a favor.

OTHER TRAILS IN THE AREA: A great trail system that offers miles of relatively easy dirt roads and trails is the **Green Mountain Trail System.** It sits conveniently next to, and is reachable from, Matthews-Winters Park.

With 18 miles of trails that range between intermediate and advanced, the **White Ranch Open Space,** just outside Golden, offers an excellent array of Front Range riding. With an elevation gain of almost 2000 feet, the 3.4-mile **Belcher Hill Trail Climb** gives you access to the park's many single-track alternatives. Be on the lookout for deer, bears, mountain lions, bobcats, elk, and wild turkeys as you explore this excellent alternative just north of Denver.

CONTACTS: Jefferson County Open Space, 700 Jefferson County Parkway, Suite 100, Golden, CO 80401; (303) 271-5925. Denver Chamber of Commerce, 1445 Market Street, Suite 400, Denver, CO 80202; (303) 620-8070.

MAPS: Jefferson County Open Space provides kiosks with permanent maps and printed map pamphlets at the trailhead of most trails, including Matthews-Winters Park and White Ranch Open Space.

BIKE SHOP: Eugene Kiefel's Wheat Ridge Cyclery, 7085 West Thirty-Eighth Avenue, Denver, CO 80033; (303) 424-3221 or 1-888-ridewrc; www.ridewrc.com. Voted number one cycle shop in the country, this place is home to Ron Kiefel (seven-time Tour de France racer) and unlimited knowledge about the local riding scene. Stop by and tell Eugene and company what you're looking for, and they'll send you to any one of eight or nine outstanding places to ride within 30 minutes of downtown Denver and the Wynkoop Brewing Company.

Wynkoop Brewing Company

1634 Eighteenth Street
Denver, Colorado 80202
(303) 297-2700
www.wynkoop.com

ATMOSPHERE: Large nineteenth-century warehouse turned into a spacious three-story brewpub with maple floors, pressed metal ceilings, timber columns, and large windows overlooking Denver's Lower Downtown or LoDo (pronounced LOW-DOE by those in the KNOW; low because it's the end of Denver nearest the Platte River).

THE BREW: Wynkoop, Colorado's oldest brewpub, is located smack in the heart of Denver's picturesque Historic Warehouse District, an area filled with grand old buildings dating from a time when the architecture and

Wynkoop Brewing Co. exterior from across Wynkoop St.
(COURTESY OF WYNKOOP BREWING CO.)

53

design of a building had as much to do with proclaiming a business's wealth as with serving a purpose. The area has recently experienced a renaissance and is once again thriving, only this time with trendy residential lofts, coffee houses, bookshops, restaurants, sport stadiums, and, you got it, breweries.

On the inside of Wynkoop, you will find the large main level split evenly with casual dining on one end and the expansive bar area, sporting two nitro taps and no less than six beer engines pouring cask-conditioned beers, on the other. Off one side of the bar, the old loading dock has been turned into an outdoor patio that overlooks Union Station, train tracks, and, ironically enough, Coors Field. A pool hall fills the equally large upstairs with 22 tables, darts, shuffleboard, music, and plenty of TVs. The basement contains the beer-aging cellar and Impulse Theater, which does "competitive comedy" on Thursday, Friday, and Saturday evenings.

But what about the beer, you ask? Just as impressive a selection, featuring seven regulars and a seasonal floating tap. Many of these beers are served on nitrogen or using a beer engine so their flavors run deep and authentic. You really can't go wrong with any beers in the lineup, but if you still need a nudge, the **Wixa Weiss** is an excellent unfiltered German wheat whose yeast comes all the way from Maisbock, Germany. Looking for something bigger, then the cask-conditioned **Imperial India Pale Ale** and **St. Charles Extra Special Bitter** are both sure bets. The **Quinn's Scottish Ale** seasonal is also cask conditioned, smooth, and so full-bodied you can practically smell the roasted malt climbing right out of the glass.

PRICE OF A PINT: During daily happy hour from 3:00 to 6:00 P.M., the 20-ounce English draws go from $4.00 to $2.50 and the regular pints drop from $3.50 to $2.00.

OTHER BREWS IN THE AREA: Denver has 16 breweries, and many of them are right here in the Lower Downtown area. By venturing to the other side of downtown, you can get an English experience if you "nip in for a pint" at **Pint's Pub**, 221 West Thirteenth Avenue, Denver, CO 80204; (303) 534-7543. At Pint's, you are immersed in

English atmosphere right down to the huge Union Jack hanging from the wall and over 200 single-malt scotches suspended upside down over the bar—that's right, directly over the bar. In an effort to get away from "cold and fizzy," as the Brits call American draft beers, Pints keeps two "live" beers on tap. That's the British way of saying cask conditioned and served at room temperature. Truly a beer-drinking experience that should not be missed.

Durango

The historic town of Durango was established in 1880 as a mining town. The Durango-Silverton Railroad was completed in 1881, cementing the town's future as the commercial hub of southwest Colorado. During these early days, Durango was the classic Wild West town, with commonplace shootouts in the streets, robberies, and lynchings. Today, the famous Durango-Silverton run is still active, but instead of cattle and gold it carries tourists and sightseers between the two towns. The highlight of this service is the yearly Iron Horse Bicycle Classic, a weekend of racing whose main event is a bicycle race against the train to Silverton.

Because of events like these, the incredible network of trails that has grown around the town in the surrounding San Juan National Forest, and the fact that multiple professional mountain-bike racers call Durango home including Juli Furtado, Ned Overend, and John Tomac, it's easy to see why Durango has been called the Mountain Bike Capital of the World. In this world of biking called Durango, the Colorado Trail is a true classic with buff singletrack, heart-breaking climbs, and fantastic views. It shouldn't be missed during any visit, and neither should Carver Brewing Company. Without getting too far ahead of ourselves, here's one last big fat hint: the bagels are fine and happy hour is 4:00 to 6:00 P.M. every day, so plan your town-to-town ride accordingly.

Colorado Trail, Dry Fork Loop, Hoffheins Connection Trail

THE SCOOP: Lush mountain singletrack just 4½ miles from the brewery.

RIDE LENGTH AND TYPE: A 25-mile town-to-town loop, 16 of which is on dirt.

THE BIKE: What better way to introduce yourself to alpine riding than a ride that leaves right from a historic downtown area and returns 25 miles later, having offered climbing, switchbacks, mountain singletrack, and great descents?

Your introduction to the Mountain Bike Capital of Southwest Colorado (there are just so many great places to choose from these days . . .) should begin right downtown on Main Avenue at Carver Brewing Company. Bakery by day, brewery by night—what better combination is there than that? Grab a coffee and bagel; then hop on your bike heading north on **Main Avenue.** Before you is an approximately 4½-mile road ride via **Twenty-Fifth Street** and the

Todd Mercer and his dog, Nikki, have a SKA microbrew while making some notes on the Hermosa Creek Trail in Durango, Colorado.

Junction Creek Road to the start (or finish) of the famed **Colorado Trail.** From the trailhead, you dip into well-worn singletrack as you continue to follow the Junction Creek valley in a gradual but steady climb into the wilds. The scenery here is fantastic so be sure to take it in, but be careful or you might find yourself on an unexpected side journey down into the creek.

Pleasantries are over as soon as you cross Junction Creek because you immediately begin to climb out of the valley to Gudy's Rest. Here two things will happen: (1) Foot traffic will diminish drastically, and (2) you will sit down on Gudy's and take in the amazing view of the valley below. After you have taken in your fill, or finished the other half of that bagel, press on west along the Colorado Trail. Here, the climb continues but in a much more gradual fashion. About when you begin a nice little descent, you will come to the junction with the **Dry Fork Loop.** Take it, and you will immediately be involved in a 3.2-mile section of trail that is 100% downhill, 100% singletrack, and 100% fun. In your euphoria, keep an eye peeled for the **Hoffheins Connection Trail.** Miss it and plan on a road ride back into town. Take it and experience a short climb back to Gudy's Rest where you can earn back some of those frequent-climber miles with an outstanding descent down the switchbacks under Gudy's. At this point, it is pretty much a glide retracing your path all the way back to Carver Brewing Company where you can concentrate on the brewery aspect of the establishment in a little more detail.

DIFFICULTY: Intermediate. A significant proportion of this ride is climbing at altitudes above 7000 feet, so a good set of lungs is in order along with a little finesse as you climb the switchbacks up to Gudy's.

AEROBIC DIFFICULTY (1–5)

3

TECHNICAL DIFFICULTY (1–5)

3

WARNINGS: This part of the Colorado Trail is very easy to access for bikers and hikers. Be on the lookout for both, especially on your way up to and back down from Gudy's Rest.

OTHER TRAILS IN THE AREA: Durango is a place much like Moab—no one comes for just one ride. Because this will also apply to you, make sure your second ride is the 20-mile **Hermosa Creek Trail.** This ride can either be done as a one-way shuttle from Purgatory Ski Resort or as an out-and-back from the south end as long as you want to go. The scenery on this ride epitomizes the alpine forest with ponderosa pines, aspens, mountain views, streams, and wildlife everywhere.

The first trail to become rideable each spring, and where the locals head for some close-to-town training, is the

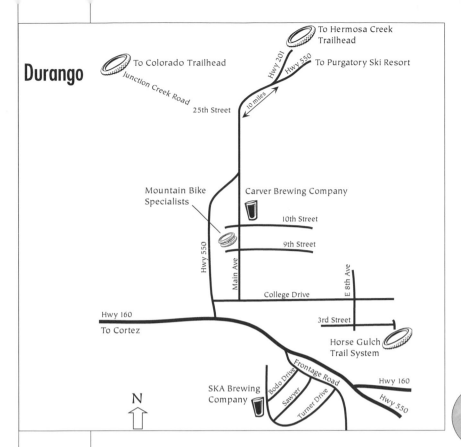

Durango

To Colorado Trailhead

Junction Creek Road

25th Street

To Hermosa Creek Trailhead

Hwy 201

Hwy 550

To Purgatory Ski Resort

10 miles

Mountain Bike Specialists

Carver Brewing Company

10th Street

9th Street

Hwy 550

Main Ave

College Drive

E 8th Ave

Hwy 160

To Cortez

3rd Street

Horse Gulch Trail System

Frontage Road

Hwy 160

SKA Brewing Company

Bodo Drive

Sawyer

Turner Drive

Hwy 550

N

Horse Gulch Trail System. Expect a moderate ride with some steep and rocky ridges. Perfect for some late afternoon miles.

CONTACTS: U.S. Forest Service, San Juan National Forest, 701 Camino Del Rio, Durango, CO 81301; (970) 247-4874. Durango Chamber of Commerce, 111 South Camino Del Rio, Durango, CO 81301; (970) 247-0312.

MAPS: The *Durango Area Recreation Map* outlines all the trails covered here plus many, many more. It costs $4.00 and is available at Mountain Bike Specialists bike shop.

BIKE SHOP: Mountain Bike Specialists, 949 Main Avenue, Durango, CO 81301; (970) 247-4066. Across the street and down one block from Carver's, this is the place to go for all your biking needs. The shop has great maps and helpful information, and did I mention it is only one block from the brewery?

Carver Brewing Company

1022 Main Avenue
Durango, Colorado 81301
(970) 259-2545

ATMOSPHERE: One of the original breweries in Colorado, Carver's started out as a bakery in 1986 before adding the brewery in 1988. So, initially when you walk in, the tiled floor and marble countertops might make you think you're in the wrong place. But press on, and you'll soon find reassurance in the form of almost a dozen tap handles welcoming you from behind the bar.

THE BREW: Carver's keeps around seven of its own beers on tap and a few from the local competition—both SKA Brewing Company and Steamworks Brewing Company have a beer flowing here. How's that for a little confidence and class?

Now that you're sure you're in the right place, hang out up front for a little conversation and The Weather Channel (once again, here is a business showing proper attention to customer interests) or head to the back patio for a little outdoor sport and live music on Thursday and Saturday evenings. Okay, now that we mountain bikers have settled in, let's talk beers.

Mid-summer and looking for a thirst quencher, check out **Miner's Gold**, a nice, flavorful ale, sweet and very smooth. If you're not a fan of the lighter beer brethren, then the **Old Oak Amber** is a local favorite. But regardless of where you start your day, it wouldn't be complete without a **Colorado Trail Nut Brown** both in symbolism and in taste.

At some places you might move to stouts as the night starts drawing to a close, but at Carver's make sure you finish with the cask-conditioned **Big Griz Barleywine**, which has been a Grand Champion at the Real Beer Festival. Not a bad pedigree. . . .

PRICE OF A PINT: Happy hours are indeed happy as they save you a buck off the $3.00 standard from 4:00 to

6:00 P.M. every day and from 9:00 to 10:00 P.M. Mondays, Tuesdays, and Wednesdays.

OTHER BREWS IN THE AREA: Steamworks Brewing Company is right around the corner from Carver's and offers some good atmosphere. But for the true Durango packaged goods, head down to the Bodo Industrial Park and home of **SKA Brewing Company.** A microbrewery since 1995, these experts brew up some tasty beers. Among their brews is the annual **Face Plant Ale** for the Iron Horse Bicycle Classic; a percentage of the proceeds from this ale goes to support Trails 2000, the local trail maintenance outfit in Durango. Philanthropy aside, SKA just opened up a funky tap room where pints are only $2.00 all day long. What more is there to say? Don't leave town without at least a six-pack. A little hard to find, head east on State Highway 160 to Bodo Drive. Take a right on Bodo; then a left on Frontage and a right on Stewart Street. SKA is located at the corners of Stewart and Turner at 545 Turner. It's worth the trip and worth taking a six-pack or two to go.

"What do you like about your job the most?"

"Drinking beer."

—DAVE THIBODEAU, CO-OWNER OF SKA BREWING COMPANY.

Fort Collins

Home to Colorado State University and just northeast of Rocky Mountain National Park, Fort Collins is a cultural and tourist destination as well as home to miles of biking trails and a number of breweries. The northernmost Colorado Front Range city, Fort Collins gets its name from its commission by Lieutenant Colonel William O. Collins as a military fort in 1864. Incorporated in 1873, the town grew up around the town square, an area that was designated as the Old Town Historic District in 1984. Again the cornerstone of Fort Collins, the Old Town Square is a popular destination for shoppers and diners and the perfect historic setting for a couple of brewpubs. The list is long but essential stops include CooperSmith's, Linden's, and the New Belgium Brewing Company. The list of trails is just as long, but Horsetooth is the place to ride if you're looking for some raw mountain climbing and miles of singletrack close to town.

Horsetooth Mountain Park

THE SCOOP: Great mountain singletrack within riding distance of downtown Fort Collins.

RIDE LENGTH AND TYPE: Variable—trail network with 25 miles of trails that can be explored for days.

THE BIKE: The fact of the matter is you don't have to travel far into the Rockies for some epic riding. Fort Collins has the Horsetooth Mountain Park in the Front Range Foothills just minutes from downtown.

You'll hear the familiar Front Range crunch of crushed red rock mixed with pine needles beneath your tires as you climb the service roads and singletrack through ponderosa pines, huge boulders, and the strange rock formations that give the park its name. Mixed in are plenty of views of Horsetooth Reservoir, Fort Collins, and the mighty plains stretching off to the east.

Because there are a multitude of well-marked trails running through this area, you can pretty much explore on your own without risk of getting lost. However, a few pointers may be in order before you set off on the trails. The Westridge Trail affords fantastic views of Rocky Mountain National Park in the distance and Horsetooth Rock (Horsetooth Mountain Park's namesake), up close, but this trail will keep you hurting on the climb, and you better be nimble on the descent. Wathen Trail connects to Westridge and is best as a descent. Although Wathen is a little less demanding than Westridge, you'll still get bumped around quite a bit by the rocks. Stout Trail is an absolute pleasure and can be followed all the way to the East Service Road. The East Service Road itself is a real grunt, but a great nontechnical way of getting to the top and access to the Westridge Trail.

A nice, 12-mile or so route is accessible by taking the doubletrack leaving from the **West Service Road** parking lot north to the **Wathen Trail**. Continue to the **Stout Trail** and take that to the **East Service Road**, then to the **Westridge Trail**, and finally back to your car. The more adventurous-minded will find that Stout Trail also leads to **Sawmill Trail**, which in turn takes you to the **Nomad Trail** and eventually to the rest of the **Valley Trails** below Horsetooth Park. The Valley Trails lead north to Lory State Park and another 20-mile network of smoother trails and roadways. A great circuit for the hardy when done from Horsetooth or town.

DIFFICULTY: Intermediate to advanced. There are some ways around the trail network that are not as demanding as others. The East Service Road is a grueling climb, and Westridge is very technical from either direction. By avoiding those two trails, you can keep the riding intermediate. Riding either (or both) of them end to end puts you into the advanced category.

Always considerate, Roger Knight yields to all trail users, including the occasional goat, on Stout Trail in Horsetooth Mountain Park.

AEROBIC DIFFICULTY (1–5)

  3–4

TECHNICAL DIFFICULTY (1–5)

  3–4

WARNINGS: Horsetooth Mountain Park charges $6.00 a carload or $2.00 a ride-in biker, so bring cabbage accordingly. Lory State Park also charges $4.00 a carload or $2.00 a biker, but you only have to pay in one park to use both for the day.

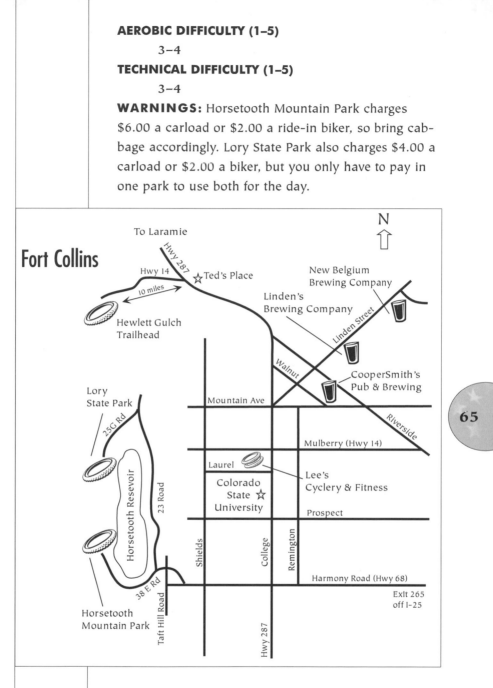

Fort Collins

To Laramie

N

Hwy 287

Hwy 14

Ted's Place

New Belgium Brewing Company

Linden's Brewing Company

Linden Street

10 miles

Hewlett Gulch Trailhead

Walnut

CooperSmith's Pub & Brewing

Lory State Park

25G Rd

Mountain Ave

Riverside

Mulberry (Hwy 14)

Horsetooth Resevoir

23 Road

Laurel

Lee's Cyclery & Fitness

Colorado State University

Prospect

Shields

College

Remington

Harmony Road (Hwy 68)

38 E. Rd

Taft Hill Road

Horsetooth Mountain Park

Hwy 287

Exlt 265 off I-25

OTHER TRAILS IN THE AREA: As already mentioned, **Lory State Park** offers a few miles of easy singletrack and more miles of dirt roads. These can be ridden as a novice ride or connected to Horsetooth Mountain Park for a more advanced ride. Another great beginner to intermediate ride is the **Hewlett Gulch Trail** in Poudre Canyon. Plan on getting wet for this one as there are 18 stream crossings—on the way out! The easiest way to do this ride is as an out-and-back by turning around at mile 4.8—just before the descent. Or you can make it a bit more technical, "balloon-on-a-string" ride by following the singletrack down that hill and around the "balloon" for an 8.4-mile total.

CONTACTS: Larimer County Parks Department, 1800 South County Road 31, Loveland, CO 80537; (970) 679-4570. Fort Collins Chamber of Commerce, 225 South Meldrum Street, Fort Collins, CO 80524; (970) 482-3746.

MAPS: There are a couple of maps available for the Fort Collins area. *Roughcuts: Best Mountain Bike Rides in Fort Collins* covers the local area and *Front Range Rider* covers more ground but costs $14.95. Both of them are available at Lee's Cyclery & Fitness.

BIKE SHOP: Lee's Cyclery & Fitness, 202 West Laurel, Fort Collins, CO 80521; (970) 482-6006 or (800) 748-BIKE. On your way to the brewery, this shop is open seven days a week, has the appropriate maps, and can pretty much take care of anything else you may need while on the road.

CooperSmith's Pub & Brewing

Number 5, Old Town Square
Fort Collins, Colorado 80524
(970) 498-0483
www.coopersmithspub.com

There's plenty of bike parking at CooperSmith's "pubside" patio, right on historic Old Town Square.

ATMOSPHERE: Two buildings separated by a brick sidewalk with brew tanks and fermentation vessels visible in both. Patios on both ends of what they call the "Pubside" are perfect for people-watching on the historic Old Town Square and Mountain Avenue. The lower and darker building next door—known as "Poolside"—is outfitted with tournament pool tables, leather couches, and more dining. It is the logical place for a little late-night fun.

THE BREW: The original CooperSmith's Pubside was once two separate buildings on one historic site, but now these buildings are connected back to back. Thus the main entrance is in the middle. The patios on either end stand where the front doors of past businesses once welcomed their patrons. Inside Pubside, which opened in 1989, you'll find a classic bar setup with ceiling fans, wood floors, and glass windows looking in on the brewhouse on one side and a long bar stretching down the other. The rest of the building is occupied by the dining room and kitchen.

Next door is the newer one-story building housing Poolside. True to the name, 12 tournament-size tables, plenty more dining area, TVs, and cushy leather couches are spread throughout the large building. A nice long bar is just waiting to serve up CooperSmith's house brews to thirsty diners and pool players.

Regardless of where you end up, you'll find the same quality brews including seven regular CooperSmith beers and a specialty or two. Of the regular brews, the **Poudre Pale Ale** is the lightest pale offered and a long-time favorite. Not far behind in popularity is the **Punjabi Pale Ale,** an excellent India pale ale served via beer engine and packing quite a punch with a high alcohol content and loads of Cascade hops. Another great CooperSmith beer is the **Albert Damm Bitter,** an extra special bitter also served via the engine, slightly warm and less carbonated than normal drafts.

Looking to **Get Frank**? Well, give one a try. The mix is two-thirds Punjabi Pale and one-third **Not Brown Ale.** A favorite with the employees, not to mention the bartender named Frank, who came up with it. Another CooperSmith novelty is the ever-popular **Sigda's Green Chili Beer.** Loaded with peppers, this one takes a little getting used to, but there is no denying its use in a Bloody Mary the morning after. . . .

PRICE OF A PINT: Happy hour daily from 4:00 to 6:00 P.M. and again from 10:00 P.M. until midnight when pints are only $2.00 down from $3.25 each.

OTHER BREWS IN THE AREA: Right around the corner from CooperSmith's, and also on the Old Town Square, is **Linden's Brewing Company.** Smaller and quieter than CooperSmith's, it's a great place for a subdued conversation. That is, at least until the live music starts up later at night. Then it's the place to go and dance to some of the best young talent Fort Collins has to offer.

Of course, no trip to Fort Collins would be complete without a stop at the Mother Ship of mountain-biking microbrew. **New Belgium Brewing Company,** the home of **Fat Tire Amber Ale,** calls Fort Collins home, and no Bike & Brew pilgrimage would be complete without a top at its tasting room. It's located just up the road at 500 Linden Street or check the company out at www.newbelgium.com.

"Yeah, this chili beer has some peppers in it, but it ain't as hot as my hiney!"
— JENNIFER PRANTL, TRIES A SIGDA'S GREEN CHILI BEER ONE WARM FALL EVENING WHILE SITTING ON COOPER-SMITH'S OLD TOWN SQUARE PATIO.

69

Glenwood Springs

Glenwood Springs is an Interstate 70 town with some character. The expressway makes Glenwood busy, and being on the main artery to Aspen doesn't help the traffic. But it's here before the mountains rise up and the journeys over the passes begin that Bike & Brew America was born. It was February of 1999, on a return from a weekend of stellar biking in Fruita, and a pint was needed before undertaking the long trip through the mountains. It was during that pint, while savoring the complete happiness of a weekend well done, that it hit. Maybe others would enjoy this novel concept of mountain biking and having a great beer afterward. Just maybe.

Located on the western edge of the deep Rockies, the historic town of Glenwood Springs hosts the "World's Largest Outdoor Hot Springs Pool," a travel destination for over one hundred years. Now a complete hotel and athletic club, the Hot Springs Lodge & Pool is open year-round to the public; its slightly mineralized waters are maintained at a hot 90 degrees in the two-block-long main pool and a 104 sizzling degrees in the smaller therapy pool. Can you think of a better way to end a day in the saddle than that? Soaking it up, you'll be surrounded by Red Mountain to the west and Lookout Mountain to the east and able to see your earlier stint on Boy Scout Trail as well as the Canyon Brewing Company where Bike & Brew America was born just across Interstate 70.

There must be something special about Glenwood Canyon if Bike & Brew America arose from its brew tanks. And, sure enough there is. The beer is outstanding, and the ride is close to epic. So come for the nostalgia, but stay for the trails and later, for the beers and hot springs. Who knows—soaked in hops, barley, and 104-degree water—you might come up with the plot for the next great American novel!

Boy Scout Trail

THE SCOOP: Climb dirt road, ride perfect singletrack, descend like a mad dog.

RIDE LENGTH AND TYPE: A 20-mile loop with shorter variations possible.

THE BIKE: It's only fitting that a particularly phat trail awaits those who make the pilgrimage to Bike & Brew America's birthplace. Boy Scout Trail—more accurately known as the **Bear Creek Loop**—encompasses 4 miles of pavement, 3 miles of graded dirt road, 3½ miles of 4x4 road, 5 miles of perfect singletrack, and a 3-mile finale of white-knuckle descending that'll make you sassy for a pint awaiting you directly below at the Glenwood Canyon Brewpub.

   This town-to-town ride begins and ends right at the brewpub, so find some parking nearby and make your way south of town 4 miles via **Grand Avenue.** Grand Avenue ends at **State Highway 82** and the Buffalo Valley Motel. Be careful, but cross the busy 82 where **Red Canyon Road (County Road 115)** makes its way up onto Lookout Mountain. The next 3 miles ascend 1000 feet to **Lookout Mountain Road (County Road 120,** which is just past the bus turnaround) where the road degrades a little, and the climbing continues up another 600 feet of elevation gain to the **Forest Hollow Trailhead.** Now you're following a true 4x4 road (**Trail 535**), and things begin to get interesting with striking views of 12,953-foot Mount Sopris and the rest of the Elk Mountains reaching south all the way to Aspen. A little more climbing over the next 1.8 miles brings you to the ill-marked cutoff from the main 4x4 road to a fast doubletrack descent. Watch carefully and take the **Forest Hollow Trail** singletrack that branches off to the left after a little less than 1 mile.

Just as you begin to wonder how this trail made it to Bike & Brew America's birthplace, you land on a B&B Hotmile. Through pine-needle–layered singletrack, cut right into the side of Lookout Mountain, you'll be gliding through an aspen and pine forest without obstacle or worry. This kind of torture goes on for the next 5 miles with hardly a change in elevation. Just you pedaling along on blissful singletrack following the contours of the mountain with occasional views of Glenwood Canyon and the interstate far down below.

After those 5 miles, you round the mountain to find Glenwood Springs and the brewery right beneath you. Just past this vision of light is the trail marker indicating that you have arrived at the last segment of your journey, **Boy Scout Trail** proper. Now things get really interesting, so check your brakes and pay attention to detail as you begin your 1400-foot descent into the valley. This is a switchback trail with plenty of opportunity to slam on your brakes to make a turn. Resist the temptation to speed down this section! See if you can control your entire descent and reduce the erosion caused by careless skidding.

All too soon, you're dropped right out on the top of **Eighth Street** for a screaming downhill all the way to the brewery. Bike & Brew forever!

DIFFICULTY: Intermediate to advanced. By doing all of the climbing on dirt and 4x4 roads, this is a very aerobically doable ride. Technically there is not much to worry about until the last 3 miles of Boy Scout where the downhill section is eroded, tight, and steep.

AEROBIC DIFFICULTY (1–5)

3

TECHNICAL DIFFICULTY (1–5)

4

WARNINGS: Make sure you have your directions down pat. The turn onto County Road 120 and the turn onto Forest Hollow Trail can be missed if you're not paying attention. Other than that, there is exposure on the 5 miles of Forest Hollow but nothing too terrifying if you keep your mind on business.

OTHER TRAILS IN THE AREA: For a more advanced but shorter version of Boy Scout Trail, try starting at the top of Eighth Street and going up the aforementioned switchbacks. This approach will entail about 1400 feet of elevation gain over about 2.3 miles. Ouch. Do the 5 perfect miles of Forest Hollow, turn around when you hit the doubletrack, and return the way you came.

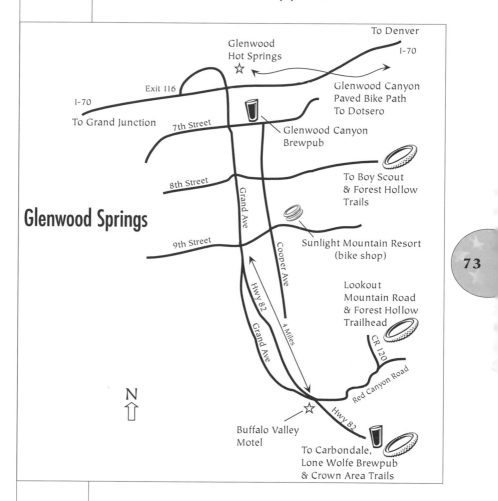

There's not much easy riding in Glenwood because of its mountain canyon location, but there's always the paved **Glenwood Canyon Bike Path** that stretches 16 miles along Interstate 70 to Dotsero. Mellow riding can also be found to the west in Rifle, where the land is more forgiving. Also, try south in Carbondale and the **Crown Area Trails.**

CONTACTS: Bureau of Land Management, 50629 Highways 6 and 24, Glenwood Springs, CO 81602; (970) 947-2800. U.S. Forest Service, White River National Forest, 900 Grand Avenue, Glenwood Springs, CO 81601; (970) 945-2521. Glenwood Springs Chamber of Commerce, 1102 Grand Avenue, Glenwood Springs, CO 81601; (970) 945-6589.

MAPS: Bike shops in Glenwood Springs, the Chamber Resort Association, the Bureau of Land Management, and the U.S. Forest Service all got together and put out the *Trails Guide to Glenwood Springs, CO,* and it is available for $1.00 at Sunlight Mountain Resort bike shop.

BIKE SHOP: Sunlight Mountain Resort, 309 Ninth Street, Glenwood Springs, CO 81601; (970) 945-9425 or (800) 445-7931. Two blocks from the brewery, pick up a map and ask your questions of the knowledgeable staff. There is free public parking across the street behind the Forest Service Office.

Glenwood Canyon Brewpub

402 Seventh Street
Glenwood Springs, Colorado 81601
(970) 945-1276

ATMOSPHERE: Historic setting in downtown Glenwood Springs. A noisy and friendly front bar has large windows looking out on the train station and mountains beyond.
THE BREW: It was while sitting in one of the front bar's booths back in 1999 that Bike & Brew America was born. The setting is perfect: close to the highway, mountains on all sides, a historic downtown building that once served as a bottling plant, and beer. Lots of fresh, handcrafted beer in a nonsmoking environment.

Although you may never make it past the front bar area, the restaurant is actually quite large. A dining area with a second, more subdued bar is located behind the entrance. Farther back is a pool room complete with tournament-sized tables, foosball, TVs, and comfy leather couches. So pick your sport, be it beer, dinner, or games, and find yourself a seat at the most holy of grounds, Bike & Brew America's birthplace.

Regardless of heritage and pedigree, we mountain bikers have come for the beer. Glenwood has the usual rundown of lighter beers such as the **Hanging Lake Honey Ale**, the **Grizzly Creek Raspberry Wheat**, and a decent **Canyon Trail Pale Ale.** But once you step up from there, the going gets good. The **Whitewater Hefeweizen** is a truly spectacular German hefe. Close your eyes, and you might just start thinking it is a **Hacker-Pschorr Weisse** in your hands. Excellent beer. Other good beers must include the locally revered **Vapor Cave IPA** (India pale ale). Spoken of

"Hey, Roger, what do you think of a book telling about great bike trails with great brewpubs nearby?"
—AND BIKE & BREW AMERICA WAS BORN.

in hushed tones with knowing looks around town, this one will have you claiming an unstoppable desire to climb Boy Scout straight up first thing in the morning.

Other gems include the **Red Mountain Extra Special Bitter.** Not only does the T-shirt for this brew have a mountain biker making tracks on Red Mountain, it's served on nitrogen and is a smooth, malty, genuine rendition of an extra special bitter. If you're a nitro-head, then the **Shoshone Stout** is also for you. Served on nitrogen, this full-bodied, smooth, malty stout is perfect with a game of pool.

PRICE OF A PINT: Happy hour is on Sundays and Thursdays from 4:00 to 6:00 P.M. when pints are only two bucks. Why Sundays and Thursdays? No one knows. A Pint of the Week rings in at $2.50. Not bad, because a regularly priced pint is $3.00, but the brewpub does pick the flavor for you. This is also a great place to pick up a growler to go. Only $8.00 filled, you get the brown glass growler jug with directions right on it on how to protect and consume the contents. Now that's neighborly.

OTHER BREWS IN THE AREA: Glenwood Canyon is the only brewery in Glenwood, but 15 minutes down the road in Carbondale is the **Lone Wolfe Brewpub.** Located at 403 Main Street and right next to the Ajax Bike Shop, you can get directions to some local riding and have a beer all within 20 feet. This is also the closest you're gonna get to fresh beer near Aspen because the long-time brewpub, The Flying Dog (later, the Howling Wolf), is no longer.

Grand Valley

If you're headed to Moab from the east there is a real good chance you're using Interstate 70 to get there. Well, just before you hit the Utah border there is another little mountain-bike morsel that may be just as singletrack friendly as your destination, maybe even more so: Grand Valley, home to the Kokopelli's Trail, 18 Road, and the Lunch Loop Trail biking area.

Grand Valley comprises the area surrounding Grand Junction, Fruita, and Loma. Located barely 5 miles from the beautiful Colorado National Monument and in the heart of many famous dinosaur digs, Grand Junction was named after the Colorado River's previous name of "Grand River" and its "junction" with the Gunnison River. Located on the temperate, dry, and not-so-elevated western slopes, the trails here stay rideable most of the year. So, while the rest of Colorado is under the powdery white stuff, the riding is just gettin' good in Grand Valley. Recently, the quantity and quality of that riding have been attracting attention away from Moab, Utah, barely 100 miles away, and the Grand area has become a mountain-bike mecca of its own. Well, maybe it's the riding and maybe it's the beer. Just 30 miles from the Utah border, Grand Junction also forms Colorado's last bastion of fresh, full-octane beer. Since the opening of the Rockslide Restaurant & Brewery, you no longer have to live in fear of the proverbial B.Y.O.B. sign right below the "Welcome to Utah" sign. Just stop in at Rockslide and fill up the old travel growler on your way through the 3.2 state.

Kokopelli's Trail

THE SCOOP: 13 miles of breathtaking singletrack offering spectacular views of the Colorado River.

RIDE LENGTH AND TYPE: Variable loops and bailouts possible with the 26-mile Grand Loop taking the cake.

THE BIKE: If you have only one day to ride in the Grand Valley area, then the place to start on this slice of singletrack heaven is the eastern end of the 145-mile Kokopelli's Trail, an incredible trail stretching from Loma, Colorado, all the way to Moab, Utah, via dirt roads, doubletrack, and singletrack. And guess what? All 13 miles of that singletrack is right here in Grand Valley overlooking the mighty Colorado River!

To take advantage of this choice singletrack, this end of Kokopelli's has been divvied up into three separate sections known as **Mary's Loop, Lion's Loop,** and **Troy-Built Loop.** Riding all three segments of trail and returning the way you came is known as the **Grand Loop,** a 26-mile singletrack out-and-back orgy for advanced riders only!

Consider chopping off one section at a time, 'cuz the singletrack gets progressively more difficult as you ride west. Mary's Loop, the easternmost trail, is the easiest, Lion's Loop is a solid intermediate ride, and Troy-Built reaches the advanced ranks. Start at Mary's and work your way west. Turn around or bail on a dirt road when you get tired.

The trails follow the cliffs and ridges hundreds of feet above the Colorado River and offer views that will astound even hardened veterans. The trails are a singletrack mix of slickrock, hard-packed sand, and clay. However, doing them as individual loops puts you on 4x4 and gravel roads for the return ride. Fortunately, local volunteers are currently creating singletrack loop returns for those of you who disdain roads when riding fat tires.

DIFFICULTY: Intermediate to advanced. By sticking to Mary's Loop, the ride is almost a beginner ride. Add on Lion's Loop and Troy-Built, and you are dealing with an intermediate and then advanced ride. However, access to gravel roads throughout the ride make for excellent bailout points, so you can drink your fill of singletrack before coasting back to the car and making your way to Grand Junction and the brewery.

AEROBIC DIFFICULTY (1–5)

2–4

TECHNICAL DIFFICULTY (1–5)

2–4

WARNINGS: Riding along hundreds of feet above the Colorado River gives some of the best views in the business. On the other hand, hundreds of feet above anything is still a nasty fall if you get too close to the edge. Be careful. Also, you're in cryptobiotic-crust territory, so stay on the trail. That black or dark brown crust you see on the ground is vital to the desert's ecology and takes years to build—so stay off it. And, although riding is darn near a year-round activity here on the desert-like western slopes of the Rockies, don't ride right after a rain. The soil contains bentonite clay that turns into a cement-like substance that sticks to tires and clogs brakes, drive trains, and cranks until your bike is an immovable object.

OTHER TRAILS IN THE AREA: The Kokopelli's Trail is only one of many riding areas in the Grand Valley area. The next destination you'll want to hit is **18 Road.** The parking lot butts right up to the Bookcliffs, a line of cliffs, ridges, and hills marking the north side of Grand Valley and stretching from the Rockies west all the way into Utah. Crisscrossed by desert trails through juniper forests, this area has everything from fun little short and sweet rides like **Prime Cut** and **Chutes and Ladders** to the very popular epic called the **Edge Loop.** Closer to Grand Junction and Rockslide Brewery, and perfect for a little town to town ride, is the **Lunch Loop Trail** which offers several loops of singletrack including the **Ribbon Trail** and

Gunny Loop. Both use **"Widow Maker Hill"** to gain access. This area is perfect for working up a thirst without enduring the drive time over to Fruita.

CONTACTS: Bureau of Land Management, 2815 H Road, Grand Junction, CO 81506; (970) 244-3000. Fruita Chamber of Commerce, 325 East Aspen Avenue, Fruita, CO 81521; (970) 858-3894.

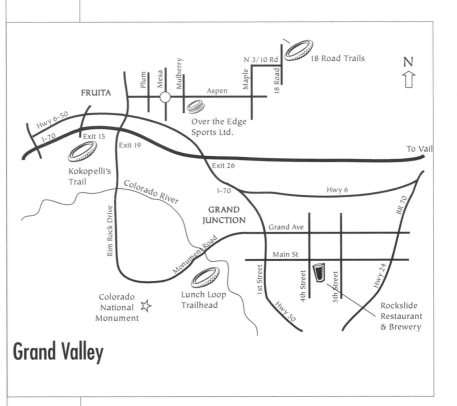

Grand Valley

MAPS: Over the Edge Sports Ltd., located in downtown Fruita, has detailed topographic maps of the area for $2.00 and the complete *Fruita Fat Tire Guide* for $10.00. The price of the map (or guidebook) brings as much detailed advice and directions as you need.

BIKE SHOP: Over the Edge Sports Ltd., 202 East Aspen Avenue, Fruita, CO 81521; (970) 858-7220; www.gj.net/~ edge. When told how lucky they are to be right in the middle of what might be the best high-desert riding in the country, Troy and Rondo just smile. In 1995, on their way to Moab to manage the Poison Spider Bike Shop, a stop in Fruita and a taste of the heralded Kokopelli's Trail was too much to resist. They never left. Fortunately for the rest of us mountain bikers, not only did they start a fantastic shop, but they've been building and promoting trails in the area ever since. So stop and give the place a try. You just might decide to stay too.

In Grand Junction, and right near the brewpub, is Geared Bicycles, 549 Main Street, Grand Junction, CO 81501; (970) 245-7939; www.gearedbikes.com. Check them out if you're only interested in Lunch Loop and don't plan on making it over to Fruita.

Rockslide Restaurant & Brewery

401 Main Street
Grand Junction, Colorado 81501
(970) 245-2111

ATMOSPHERE: Located in historic downtown Grand Junction, right on the Pedestrian Shopping Mall, this is a perfect B&B layover. The brewery takes up two old brick storefronts, one for the dining and the other to house the brewhouse, bar, and kitchen.

THE BREW: The brewhouse peeks out through large glass windows at Main Street, and the original building's worn brick wall separates the spacious dining room from the bar and kitchen. The entire restaurant is adorned in light-colored woods with a slight southwestern theme.

Rockslide recently changed brewers and with the change came recipes that are a little bolder and a little bigger. The new brewer, Justin Bauer, hails from Boulder where microbrews rule. It has not taken long for Justin to tweak a few measurements here and add a few ingredients there, making the beers fuller without alienating his regular customers.

You have to keep in mind that beer education on the western slope is not quite as advanced as on the Denver side of the Continental Divide. Still, you will be pleasantly surprised by what Rockslide has to offer after a hard day on the trails.

Of the standards, all the beers are solid with the **Cold Shivers Pale Ale** being the most fun. The **Big Bear Stout** is smooth and sits well after a February ride along Kokopelli's. Keep the rotating eighth tap in mind when visiting, as the beer from it is always Justin's personal creation and a sure bet to be good. Regardless of what you settle in with, all of Rockslide's beers are served with a CO_2 and nitro mix, which keeps them smoother and nicer than normal draft beer.

PRICE OF A PINT: Plan to finish your ride before 4:00 P.M. because that's when Rockslide's happy hour starts. From 4:00 to 6:00 P.M. and 10:00 P.M. to midnight, pints are half price at $1.50. Appetizers are also half off regular price. Now that's a happy hour (or two).

OTHER BREWS IN THE AREA: It's only a matter of time before Fruita gets a brewpub or Grand Junction gets another one. In the meantime, go to Rockslide when in the Junction and go to **The End Zone** for good beer and food when in Fruita.

"How big do you want to draw the circle?"

—THE RESPONSE FROM TROY RARCIK, CO-OWNER OF OVER THE EDGE SPORTS, WHEN ASKED BY TRAVELING BIKERS HOW MUCH RIDING THEY'VE GOT AROUND FRUITA.

Leadville

Leadville weighs in at an elevation of 10,152 feet as the highest incorporated city in the country. At that elevation, it doesn't take long to get above the tree line, and it doesn't take long before you're sucking wind like a fish out of water. Leadville's existence is a result of various mining booms that focused on gold, silver, lead, and zinc over the past century and a half. Although the last operating mine, the Black Cloud Mine, closed in 1999, remnants of Leadville's boomtown past are everywhere. Inside the city limits, this history can be traced through the elegant old Victorian mansions and prestigious brick buildings. Out on Leadville's trails, the past can still be seen in the dark mining tunnels, discolored dredging piles, and the now-still mining towers.

The world moved past Leadville as fast as the metal ores disappeared, and Leadville has only recently begun a historic revival to boost its failing economy. Not as far along as other ski and Interstate 70 towns in more accessible locations of the Rockies, Leadville is out of the way, and it shows. For now. Surrounded by the San Isabel National Forest and only about 30 miles from Colorado's highest peak, the 14,433-foot Mount Elbert, there is plenty to do for any outdoor enthusiast. The town itself has a lot of potential with a colorful history and plenty of historic buildings in various stages of renovation. And now that the crucial element of a brewpub has been added to the mix, it's only a matter of time before Leadville booms again.

St. Kevin, Turquoise Lake Loop

THE SCOOP: Old mining roads full of history—both new and old—mixed with rocky and technical singletrack.

RIDE LENGTH AND TYPE: 20-mile loop.

THE BIKE: Because of Leadville's heritage, old mining roads and trails cover the land around town, making the area perfect for mountain biking during the four or so months the trails are snow free at this high elevation. The problem is finding the trail that is just right for you. Ask three people in Leadville what the best trail to ride is, and you get three different answers. Or, ask the same person once and get three different answers. What this means is there are that many worthy rides in the area; it just depends on what you're looking for.

Leadville is probably best known in the biking world for the sick and brutal Leadville 100—a 100-mile mountain-bike race derived from the even-sicker Leadville 100 ultra-marathon running race! However, a good loop in which to introduce yourself to Leadville's mining history, race history, and natural beauty is the St. Kevin, Turquoise Lake Loop. Close to town, it can be ridden straight from the brewery for an extra 4 miles each way, or you can drive to the lake and park.

The majority of the ride incorporates 13 or so miles of the Leadville 100 bike course. This will give you a taste of what it's like to ride and climb at over 10,000 feet without actually having to race 100 miles. While climbing on the old mining roads used for the race, try to imagine what it would be like to compete against hundreds of other bikers. But, don't forget to take a look around. You will climb past old mine remnants while taking in unparalleled views of Leadville and the Mosquito Range, as well as closer views of Turquoise Lake below and the Sawatch Range directly above you.

After the mining roads and a blistering-fast, paved-road descent, you divert from the course and begin a 6½-mile section of singletrack right along the shores of Turquoise Lake. Both breathtakingly beautiful and challenging, the first 4 miles of the singletrack are very rocky and require advanced riding skills. However, things smooth out soon, and the last 2½ miles travel through camping, picnic, and boating areas. A perfect place to stop and go for a rather chilly dip before climbing back on the rig for the trip over to Boomtown Brewpub.

DIFFICULTY: Intermediate. The climbing is on old mining roads, but the elevation is up there. The singletrack at the west end of Turquoise Lake is the only technical difficulty you will encounter during this ride, and there is not so much of it that an intermediate biker cannot get off and walk for a bit.

AEROBIC DIFFICULTY (1–5)

3

TECHNICAL DIFFICULTY (1–5)

3

WARNINGS: The Greater Leadville Chamber of Commerce supplies free biking maps at the Visitor's Information Office in Leadville. However, the directions are sometimes hard to interpret, and you need to rely solely on mileage as your indicator of when to turn, or not to turn. In other words, you better have a cycle-computer and be real careful about reading directions from these maps. There are many mining roads throughout the area, and one wrong turn pretty much looks like any other right turn.

OTHER TRAILS IN THE AREA: For another historic intermediate ride through Leadville's Silver Mine district that includes a nice bit of alpine singletrack, check out **Seventh Street** to **Ball Mountain Pass Trail**. Leaving right from the brewery, this ride shows you the old silver mines east of Leadville up close and personal. Like some kind of strange apparitions out of an old *Wild, Wild West* episode, crooked towers and ramshackle buildings fill the valley just below Ball Mountain and Mount Evans. Although not the picturesque beauty most often associated with rides in the Rockies, this ride does offer a valuable link to America's past and the reason for most of the historic towns in Colorado.

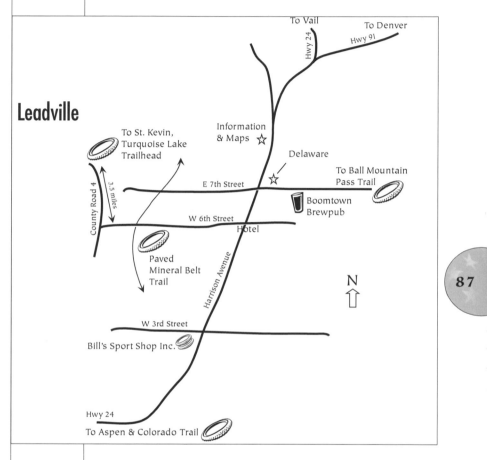

Leadville

To Vail

Hwy 24

To Denver

Hwy 91

To St. Kevin, Turquoise Lake Trailhead

Information & Maps ☆

Delaware

To Ball Mountain Pass Trail

E 7th Street ☆

Boomtown Brewpub

W 6th Street

Hotel

County Road 4

3.5 miles

Paved Mineral Belt Trail

Harrison Avenue

N ⇧

W 3rd Street

Bill's Sport Shop Inc.

Hwy 24

To Aspen & Colorado Trail

Of course, when in doubt about where to ride there is always the **Colorado Trail**. The **Mount Elbert Creek–Pipeline Loop** takes an advanced ride along the base of Mount Elbert, Colorado's tallest mountain. A little ways out of town, this ride can be done either as a loop or shuttle.

Also, recently opened is Leadville's most prized addition, the 12½-mile, paved, **Mineral Belt Trail**. An easy cruise circumventing town, there are many historical stops along the way. Not interested in any more history? Then keep your eyes open for singletrack trails leading off the path at various points. Rumored to be the best singletrack in Leadville, you may want to make friends with some locals who might show you the way.

CONTACTS: The Greater Leadville Chamber of Commerce, 809 Harrison Avenue, Leadville, CO 80461; (719) 486-3900; www.colorado.com/leadville. U.S. Forest Service, San Isabel National Forest, 2015 North Popular, Leadville, CO 80461; (719) 486-0749.

MAPS: Stop by the Greater Leadville Chamber of Commerce in downtown Leadville at 809 Harrison Avenue and pick up the latest *Leadville–Twin Lakes Mountain Bike and Recreation Trails* map. It lists 19 mountain-bike rides in the area with detailed instructions on how to get to the trails, elevation information, and trail instructions.

BIKE SHOP: Bill's Sport Shop Inc., 225 Harrison Avenue, Leadville, CO 80461; (719) 486-0739. The only bike shop in town, Bill's deals with bike rentals, repairs, and sales as well as multiple other sports. This shop is your best bet in town for the local scoop. And, because it is located in a building built in 1895 for Anheuser-Busch and Zang Brewing Companies offices, it's practically a Bike & Brew America brother anyway.

Boomtown Brewpub

115 East Seventh Street
Leadville, Colorado 80461
(719) 486-8297

ATMOSPHERE: Comfortable front dining room with large transom-type windows and a horseshoe bar dominating the carpeted and somehow homelike downstairs. Upstairs, arched windows remind diners and pool shooters that this old building was once an early 1900s church.

THE BREW: In March 2000, Leadville arrived. A historic downtown just begging for a brewpub, Leadville's prayers were answered when Chris and Howard Tucker turned the old church right across from the historic 1886 Delaware Hotel into a brewpub.

Since opening, Boomtown has gradually developed a loyal following, thanks—in part—to the food, the beer, and the restaurant being open seven days a week from 11:00 A.M. to 11:00 P.M., no matter how slow the season may be—a true rarity in a low-profile mountain town. With occasional live music and an upstairs pool room, Boomtown is quickly becoming a local attraction.

The wonderful wooden back bar is from an old Leadville drug store and adds authenticity to the historic surroundings. Also adding authenticity to the place is the brewer, Dave Lawrence. A nine-year veteran from Wynkoop Brewing Company in Denver who was about to throw it all away and enter the welding profession, Chris and Howard got a steal when Dave agreed to make the move to the mountains.

Not a believer that ale yeast makes a good light beer, Dave doesn't even try. The lightest beer he brews, the

Mineral Belt Pale Ale, packs a crisp refreshing flavor into a 5½% alcohol content. Plus, a nickel from each pint sold goes toward maintaining the Mineral Belt Trail. A worthy cause indeed! Moving on to other beers, they each get better. The **Premium Unleaded**—a bit smooth to be called an India pale ale—is about as close as you can get to the real thing without all the hops.

The Bike & Brew America truck parked in front of the former church that is now the Boomtown Brewpub.

The local favorite, the **Moonboot Amber Ale** is a very smooth and very nice amber. Things get even better with an excellent malt monster, **Hilde's Scottish Ale,** and the **Coal Porter** is just packed with chocolate malt. Both are served and carbonated with nitrogen by using a carbonation stone to disperse the nitrogen through the beer, and five cents from the sale of each porter also goes to the Mineral Point Trail, so drink up.

COLORADO

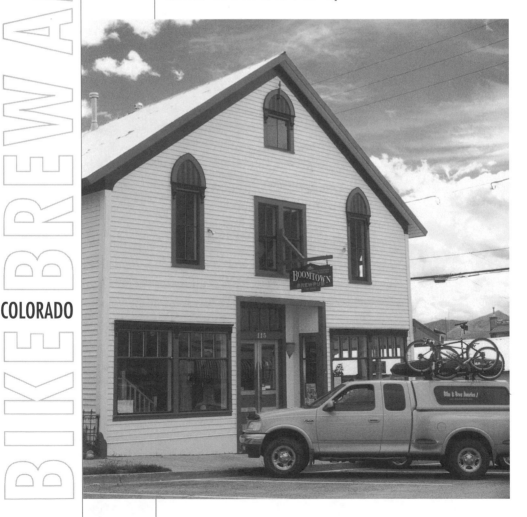

You may also find a **RAM (Raggedy Ass Miner) Stout** or an apple-flavored fruit beer, strangely reminiscent of a cider, on tap.

Regardless of what happens to be brewing, Boomtown has quite a catch in Dave. Now, if the brewpub can just keep him from becoming a welder. Something about staring at a small bright light for many hours. Don't ask.

PRICE OF A PINT: The owners are still tinkering with the idea of a happy hour, but for now it's $3.00 a pint 11:00 A.M. to 11:00 P.M., seven days a week. Boomtown also offers a unique 80-ounce, brown glass, flip-top growler. Although a little pricey at $15.00 for the first fill and $11.00 thereafter, it is 80 ounces of Dave's beer after all.

OTHER BREWS IN THE AREA: No other brewpubs in town, but you do have the touristy **Silver Dollar Saloon**, Doc Holliday's old haunt. For a selection of micros, **Groggy Bottoms** is the other place in town where they might be found.

91

"I don't know what they're gonna do with it, I just hope they don't make it into another brewery."
—TOURIST INFORMATION EMPLOYEE WHEN ASKED ABOUT THE OLD ST. VINCENT HOSPITAL THAT NOW SITS EMPTY ON A HILL OVERLOOKING DOWNTOWN LEADVILLE. SOME PEOPLE HAVE NO IDEA.

Salida

Originally a late-nineteenth-century railroad town, Salida's downtown is now the largest and most significant historic district in the state. After surviving the closing of the local Denver & Rio Grande Railroad line in the 1950s, Salida went through some hard times, surviving, and eventually thriving, on a small mining boom in the '70s and '80s. However, it was in 1984 when Salida's downtown was officially registered as a National Historic District that Salida's future was secured. Since then, tourism has prospered. Even more recently, Salida, though small, has become known as one of the best art towns in America—dozens of art shops and galleries call Salida home.

Salida is located in Chaffee County at an elevation of 7000 feet; this county is truly the heart of the Rockies with more 14,000-foot peaks than any other county in the state. Part of a warm "banana belt" region, Salida enjoys a milder climate than most mountain towns and an incredible 330 days of sunshine per year. The climate variation in the Salida area is so dramatic, however, that if you're lucky, you can literally be skiing at Monarch Pass in the morning and riding your mountain bike in the valley that same afternoon.

Monarch Crest Trail

THE SCOOP: The Continental Divide Trail and the Colorado Trail meet up with the Rainbow Trail to give you up to 40 miles of singletrack smack.

RIDE LENGTH AND TYPE: 35-mile ride from the top of Monarch Pass to downtown Poncha Springs, consisting of 30 miles of singletrack and 5 fast downhill road miles into Poncha Springs. However, a shuttle vehicle is required to get to Monarch Pass and the Monarch Crest Trailhead.

THE BIKE: Bike & Brew America does not typically include shuttle rides, because it's often a drag spending the morning getting cars in position for the eventual shuttle pickup after the ride. Plus, with fresh beer waiting at the end of the day, town-to-town rides are much more B&B friendly. That said, there are always reasons for an exception, and the **Monarch Crest Trail** is just that. During the summer months, the famous Monarch Crest Trail is open. This ride has been written up countless times in those glossy magazines and is considered by many to be the best mountain-bike ride in Colorado and one of the top ten bike rides in the country.

All this fanfare is for good reason. This trail is spectacular in every sense of the word. Once you've ridden it, you'll understand why.

The ride can actually be extended for over 40 miles of singletrack although the entire route is rarely done all at once. There are many access points throughout the ride that allow shorter variations. It just depends on how much roadwork you're interested in after bailing off the singletrack.

The route focused on here is a 30-mile section of singletrack with a 5-mile, all-downhill, road ride to get you back to one of the cars parked in Poncha Springs. Although 35 miles sounds like a lot (and it is), *most* of it *is* downhill. However, contrary to popular belief, this trail is not *all* downhill. In fact, you're in for about 1000 feet of climbing at the start of the ride before getting into an overall elevation loss of 3800 feet. Now don't be worried that you won't be getting a workout with this ride. Those 1000 feet of climbing and the sheer length of the ride will get you good and ready for a beer over at Il Vicino's.

A view of the Continental Divide and Sawatch Mountain Range, from atop the tram running near the 11,386 ft. Monarch Crest Trailhead on Monarch Pass.

The most efficient way to shuttle this ride is by parking one vehicle in Poncha Springs and driving the other one 17 miles up U.S. Highway 50 to the tram parking lot atop Monarch Pass. Gather your group there and proceed up the small service road behind the tram. Not far along this road you will be greeted with a trailhead sign proclaiming you have arrived at the **Continental Divide Trail.** Sign the registry and drop in on one of the best rides Colorado has to offer.

The first 10-mile section of the Continental Divide Trail actually climbs along the Continental Divide on the spines of exposed mountain ridges at elevations of nearly 12,000 feet. This section is above tree line so be prepared for some serious exposure to the elements on a rocky, sparsely vegetated ridge reminiscent of those in the

Money-Saving Tip

Don't buy at regular price. Wait for an item to go on sale.

(answer to Thursday's puzzle:)

1	6	9	5	2	4	3	8	7
7	3	2	6	1	8	9	4	5
8	5	4	3	7	9	6	2	1
2	7	1	8	4	3	5	6	9
6	4	3	7	9	5	2	1	8
5	9	8	2	6	1	4	7	3
3	1	5	4	8	6	7	9	2
4	8	7	9	3	2	1	5	6
9	2	6	1	5	7	8	3	4

DIFFICULTY RATING: ★★★★☆

Scottish Highlands. It's just you, miles of singletrack, naked mountaintops and rock cairns to guide the way.

After this rare treat of alpine tundra riding, you will descend to the **Marshall Pass Trailhead** and your first opportunity to bail. If these 10 miles were all the high-altitude riding you needed to work up a thirst, then take **County Road 200** or **County Road 203** back down the mountain to your waiting shuttlecraft. However, if you're just warming up, then continue south along the combined **Colorado Trail** and **Continental Divide Trail** for the next 5 miles of mixed singletrack and old logging roads to where the **Rainbow Trail** intersects the joined trail. You'll know the intersection because of a multitude of posted signs. Although none of the signs still standing actually says "Rainbow Trail," a metal sign prohibiting motorized travel on the left spur of the trail is a permanent reminder of the correct turnoff.

From here on out, things get a little more technical. Consider yourself warned. This first section of the Rainbow is a steep descent full of loose rock and eroded trail. The increase in technical difficulty is worth it, as you are soon gliding along the valley wall above Silver Creek on a gentle downward grade through pine and aspen forests. After almost 5 miles of this luxury, you cross Silver Creek and your second (and last) chance for a bailout. Simply follow **County Road 201** for 12 uneventful miles down to **State Highway 285** and Poncha Springs beyond.

Once again, if you're not quite ready to give up the good fight, then take the second, 9-mile section of the Rainbow until it drops you out on State Highway 285. The technical difficulty once again increases on this section as you maintain an altitude of about 9500 feet for the first 5 miles, before the trail drops quickly. It spits you out onto State Highway 285 in perfect position for a downhill rocket ride back to your shuttle vehicle. Road riding at its finest, it takes less than 15 minutes to do these last 5 exhilarating miles.

If you're looking for more action than already described, there is always the last section—12 miles—of the Rainbow Trail to tack onto the Monarch Crest ride, which picks up right across Highway 285 and will bring you all the way back to Salida via extremely rough singletrack, which includes another 1100-foot climb before the next of many opportunities to finally break for Salida. Very tired and very, very thirsty.

DIFFICULTY: Intermediate to advanced. Depending on where you decide to bail out, this ride can be an intermediate, but if you decide to go for the "Full Monty" and tackle the whole deal, then you'd better consider yourself an advanced rider or better.

AEROBIC DIFFICULTY (1–5)

3 or 4

TECHNICAL DIFFICULTY (1–5)

3 or 4

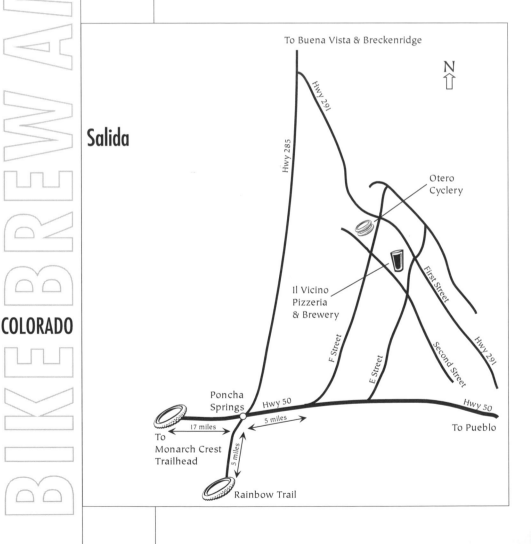

Salida

To Buena Vista & Breckenridge

N ⇧

Hwy 291

Hwy 285

Otero Cyclery

Il Vicino Pizzeria & Brewery

First Street

F Street

E Street

Second Street

Hwy 291

Poncha Springs

Hwy 50

17 miles

5 miles

Hwy 50

To Pueblo

To Monarch Crest Trailhead

5 miles

Rainbow Trail

WARNINGS: This is a popular trail, and for good reason. So don't be surprised if you are preparing for the ride with five or six other groups on a typical Saturday morning. Don't worry, this is a big mountain, and trail users tend to be very friendly. There is a lot of exposure at different parts of the ride, and because you will likely be out there 5 or more hours, be sure to bring a jacket in case a sudden storm comes up.

OTHER TRAILS IN THE AREA: Because of the loose and rocky terrain of the mountain valley surrounding Salida, there are not many easy mountain-bike rides close to town. However, just outside Buena Vista is the grade of the former Midland Railroad, which now makes up the **Midland Bike Trial** with 5½ miles of singletrack and another 2½ miles of dirt road for an excellent beginner to intermediate ride.

CONTACTS: U.S. Forest Service, San Isabel National Forest, Salida Ranger District, 325 West Rainbow Boulevard, Salida, CO 81201; (719) 539-3591. Salida Chamber of Commerce, 406 West Highway 50, Salida, CO 81201; (719) 539-2068.

MAPS: The Salida and Buena Vista newspapers publish a free special edition called the *Chaffee County Mountain Bike Guide* detailing and mapping 15 mountain-bike rides in the area. It's available free at Otero Cyclery in downtown Salida.

BIKE SHOP: Otero Cyclery, 104 F Street, Salida, CO 81201; (719) 539-6704; www.oterocyclery.com. This great shop—right around the corner from the brewpub—has the maps, advice, and bike parts for you to go the distance when visiting Chaffee County. The Otero folks also rent high-end dual suspension bikes and can arrange shuttle service if you forgot your bike or extra car at home.

Il Vicino Pizzeria & Brewery

136 East Second Street
Salida, Colorado 81210
(719) 539-5219
www.ilvicino.com

ATMOSPHERE: Mediterranean café feel with jazz in the background and local art on the walls.

THE BREW: Il Vicino Pizzeria & Brewery inhabits a *circa* 1888 brick building just off Salida's main strip that could easily be mistaken for a small Mediterranean café. Although Salida is now known as an artist's colony, back in 1994 it was anything but. The historic downtown was a couple of stubborn businesses away from becoming a forgotten mountain town. Enter Il Vicino, the first restaurant to come downtown and take up the good fight for finer dining and brewing.

Il Vicino Pizzeria & Brewery is housed in a long, narrow building with scuffed wood floors. Small café tables line one wall, and the bar, kitchen, and brewery take up the other. You place your order at the bar before taking a seat, and your beverage and food will be there shortly. Very shortly. The service is prompt, and the food is excellent.

Il Vicino breweries are a chain. And although chains, as well as shuttle rides, are normally taboo in the Bike & Brew scheme of things, Il Vicino is a well-deserved exception. Il Vicino allows each brewer the artistic freedom to tinker and tweak the beer, as evidenced by the multiple awards Salida's Il Vicino has hanging over the bar.

Each Il Vicino has over a dozen seasonal recipes, and you'll always find three or four of them on tap with the four flagship Il Vicino brews. Of those four, you'll find the crowd-pleasing **Wet Mountain IPA** (India pale ale) an excellent, fully hopped, and sweet version of the brew. Other regulars are the **Tenderfoot Brown,** the 9% alcohol **Loyal Duke Scotch Ale,** and the nicely dry hopped **Ute Trail Pale Ale.** All of Il Vicino's brews are smooth, and even the lightest of the bunch has more character than you've come to expect for a brewery's attempt at pleasing the masses. If you're lucky, **Black Heart Stout** will also be on tap, a cask-conditioned version that is not very carbonated but smooth with a slightly sweet finish.

Another sign that this is not just another chain restaurant is the welcome presence of local art adorning the walls. Paulette Brodeur is one of the artists who commonly has a print or two hanging on the wall. Like Il Vicino, which began the restaurant renaissance, Paulette was the first artist to come downtown and fire the trend that now gives Salida its arty reputation. Paulette does many bike-related pieces, often attracting patrons from Il Vicino to her gallery, The Art Studio, right across the street at 133 East 2nd Street, or www.brodeurart.com.

99

PRICE OF A PINT: True to the four college roomies who founded the Il Vicino Pizzeria & Brewery chain, happy hour is from 3:00 'til 5:30 P.M., and pints are half price, which puts them at $1.25. Not bad at all. . . .

OTHER BREWS IN THE AREA: There are no other brewpubs in Chaffee County, but the **Victoria Tavern** is the other place local mountain bikers go after a ride. With free peanuts and popcorn, Ping-Pong, pool, darts, and shuffleboard, it's fun and close to Il Vicino at 143 North F Street.

Window flowerboxes and wooden benches welcome weary bikers into the Il Vicino Pizzeria & Brewery in historic downtown Salida.

Steamboat Springs

Long before Steamboat Springs was known as a premier destination ski resort, the abundant thermal springs were the main attraction. The 150 natural springs in the area, many of which were believed to have healing and restorative powers, soon attracted bathers to the remote area, and bathhouses were built over some of the warm, relaxing springs. The town was named by three French trappers who thought they heard the chugging of a river steamboat at the edge of town. Instead they found a peculiar chugging spring making the noise. That namesake spring still sits at the end of town; however; the building of the railroad in 1908 damaged the spring's acoustics and silenced the chug forever.

The Yampa River Valley is still a little out of the way, but Steamboat Springs is worth the trip. With a network of trails surrounding the town for all ability levels, plenty of therapeutic hot springs to soak in after the ride, and a brewery that can honestly say it has beaten the King of Beers, Steamboat is a powerful Bike & Brew destination.

Base Camp to Mountain View Trail to Mount Werner

THE SCOOP: Moderately technical singletrack takes you past multiple high-alpine lakes and views of the Gore Range and the Continental Divide.

RIDE LENGTH AND TYPE: 26½-mile out-and-back or shuttle, depending on your luck.

THE BIKE: There are a couple of ways to do this epic piece of singletrack, which stretches nearly all the way from Rabbit Ears Pass to the very bottom of the Steamboat Ski Area. The preferred method is via shuttle vehicle or

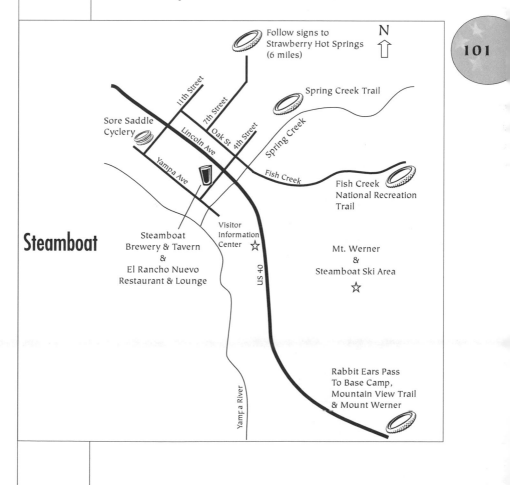

Follow signs to
Strawberry Hot Springs
(6 miles)

N

Spring Creek Trail

11th Street

7th Street

Sore Saddle
Cyclery

Lincoln Ave

Oak St   4th Street

Spring Creek

Yampa Ave

Fish Creek

Fish Creek
National Recreation
Trail

Steamboat

Steamboat
Brewery & Tavern
&
El Rancho Nuevo
Restaurant & Lounge

Visitor
Information
Center ☆

US 40

Mt. Werner
&
Steamboat Ski Area

☆

Yampa River

Rabbit Ears Pass
To Base Camp,
Mountain View Trail
& Mount Werner

drop off at the **Base Camp Trailhead.** From there you can proceed all the way to the "front" (west) side of Mount Werner and down the network of singletrack offered by Steamboat Ski Resort—a 26-mile ride to the brewery where you descend 3400 feet over the last 8 miles! Unfortunately, a shuttle is often hard to find when traveling, so this ride can also be done in the more traditional fashion as a 26½-mile out-and-back from the Base Camp Trailhead to the end of Mountain View Trail. Either way, you're in for a four-star ride with more singletrack riding than is considered healthy.

Though moderately technical throughout, there are no extended climbs as you maintain an elevation right below 10,000 feet the entire way. You're on top of the hills and basically following the Continental Divide as you ride around crystal-clear alpine lakes, meadows, and pine forests.

Mark Stucky looks out on Morrison Divide Trail 1174, more commonly known as "Muddy Slide" in Routt National Forest.
(COURTESY OF MARK KIDDER)

The first 5 miles demand a certain degree of technical awareness but without ever rearing up and knocking you out (or off as the case may be). Just enough to force you to keep your mind focused.

Right around the 4½-mile mark, you come to the first of two important intersections. Straight ahead, the **Continental Divide Trail** will take you all the way to **Buffalo Pass Trailhead.** To the right, **Trail 1134** and to the left, your path, **Fish Creek Falls Trail 1102.**

Tired? This is a nice place to turn around and retrace your steps for a challenging 9-mile ride. Just getting started? Then head toward Fish Creek Falls and Long Lake. Once at Long Lake, skirt around to the right of the lake but keep left when the opportunity presents itself to head to Fish Creek Reservoir. The singletrack resumes on the west side of Long Lake and drops you down quickly to the very important **Mountain View Trail 1032** intersection. Miss this left turn and you are on **Fish Creek National Recreation Trail** proper and the start of the nastiest, meanest, most difficult, gonzo-only downhill in the area. You were warned!

So, take a left at Mountain View Trail and prepare yourself for the apple of Steamboat's eye. Mountain View Trail is the trail everyone is talking about. Here the singletrack smoothes out, and, after a short climb, you follow the contour of Werner Mountain, gliding through views of Yampa Valley, Dakota Ridge, surrounding lakes, and, of course, mountains. Just as the name promises.

One last push almost to the summit of Werner, and Steamboat's lifts come into view. You soon come around to the front of Mount Werner, passing under a ski lift before coming to a trail marker signifying you are now on Steamboat's trails and, among other things, you must wear a helmet.

If you're one of the lucky few with a shuttlecraft, buckle up, 'cause now the real fun begins. Over the next 8 miles, you descend about 3400 feet to Mountain Village and the town of Steamboat Springs. There are many different ways down the mountain, but a particularly tasty way is via **Pete's Wicked Trail** (no relation to the beer), **Cathy's Cutoff**, **Sunshine Trail**, **Huffman's**, and **Valley View Trail**. Ahhh, then it's just a matter of speeding through Mountain Village and taking the bike path on the other side of State Highway 40 along the Yampa River back into town and to the brewery.

However, if no one down below owes you a favor, then this is the end of the line and time to turn around and enjoy the 13 miles of singletrack back to your car. Oh, isn't life unfair?

DIFFICULTY: Intermediate to advanced. Things are technical, but not so technical that you're gonna take a pounding. Just good solid riding. However, 26 miles at almost 10,000 feet is still 26 miles at almost 10,000 feet. So, aerobically, it's advanced.

AEROBIC DIFFICULTY (1–5)

4

TECHNICAL DIFFICULTY (1–5)

3

WARNINGS: You are on the Continental Divide and at the top of mountains for most of this ride. You don't want to get caught out here during a storm. Take extra clothing and try to finish your ride before 2:00 P.M. when the storms usually start rolling in around these parts.

OTHER TRAILS IN THE AREA: As already mentioned, the **Fish Creek National Recreation Trail** is the most difficult trail in the area. On the tamer side, the intermediate, closest-to-town classic is the **Strawberry Hot Springs Trail.** Great if you want to make a day of it and go for a dip in the springs. But, with only 2½ miles of singletrack, the road to dirt ratio is not very favorable. The best novice trail in the area is the **Spring Creek Trail,** which starts out as a doubletrack and makes its way down to singletrack for about 5 miles of dirt each way. You can make it even easier by taking **State Highway 60** to the top and descending the singletrack. Up to you.

CONTACTS: U.S. Forest Service, Hahns Peak–Bears Ears Ranger District, 925 Weiss Drive (off State Highway 40 near Holiday Inn), Steamboat Springs, CO 80477; (970) 879-1870. Steamboat Springs Chamber of Commerce, 1255 Lincoln Avenue, Steamboat Springs, CO 80477; (970) 879-0882.

MAPS: The Visitor Information Center and Chamber of Commerce at 1255 South Lincoln (State Highway 40) (across from McDonalds and Wendy's) has a great *Outdoor Activity Map* that details all the trails. Take this on over to Sore Saddle Cyclery and match it up with the topo on display for detailed trail information.

BIKE SHOP: Sore Saddle Cyclery, 1136 Yampa Avenue, Steamboat Springs, CO 80477; (970) 879-1675. Open year-round, seven days a week. If you're looking for bike-related goodies in Steamboat, this is the place. Located right off the paved bike trail in a unique, dome-like structure that originally did time as a wood chip incinerator. You'll have to see it to believe it.

Steamboat Brewery & Tavern

435 Lincoln Avenue
Steamboat Springs, Colorado 80477
(970) 879-2233

ATMOSPHERE: Friendly and comfortable albeit a bit Eighties with drop ceilings, inset lights, brass décor, and a carpeted dining room.

THE BREW: Steamboat Brewery & Tavern is located right on the main thoroughfare in a building with a ski town façade. You walk into a tiled bar area with the fermentation tanks behind the bar, a couple of TVs on the wall, and a computer for Internet access at the end of the bar. Dining is off to your left in a separate room decorated with beer signs and other beer paraphernalia on the walls.

It's in this setting that Bud takes a second seat as the King of Beers. The number-one–selling beer in Steamboat Springs is Steamboat Brewery's **Alpenglow Strong Ale.** That's right, Alpenglow, a rich and full amber takes top honors as Steamboat Springs' number-one draft beer. This says a lot about the beer and the beer drinkers in Steamboat Springs.

Although Alpenglow may take up four of the five fermentation tanks you see behind the bar, Steamboat is not a one-horse brewery. With over 35 recipes ranging from the "Big Five"—**Whitewater Wheat, Pinnacle Pale Ale, Jane's Brown Ale, Skull Creek Stout,** and the Alpenglow— to an array of beers outside the norm, you never know what may be tapped next. However, if you happen to catch Steamboat brewing **Uncle Kunkel's Dunkelweizen,** order one right up. This is an outstanding German dunkelweizen brewed with a double decoction and true to form.

You'll soon be thinking you're sitting outside a train station somewhere along the Rhine River having a beer while waiting for the next leg of your bicycle tour to begin.

PRICE OF A PINT: Happy hour is from 5:00 to 7:00 P.M. every day of the week, and pints drop from $3.50 down to a buck as long as you keep it only in the bar area.

OTHER BREWS IN THE AREA: Steamboat Brewery actually supplies two connected restaurants, the Steamboat Brewery and Tavern and the **El Rancho Nuevo Restaurant and Lounge** right next door, possibly making this the first and only Mexican brewpub in the Rocky Mountains. The owners of Steamboat Brewery & Tavern acquired the El Rancho and remodeled and renamed the place El Rancho Nuevo. The brewpub now brews three or four Mexican-style beers specifically for El Rancho while keeping Alpenglow Strong and one or two other favorites on tap. This side opens at 5:00 P.M. with the same happy hour as next door. Inside you'll find the front dining area carpeted and cozy with booths, tables, and a large patio out front. In back, you have an open room with skylights over the bar, vinyl-covered metal stools, stainless steel tables, pool tables, and TVs. On tap you will enjoy a more south-of-the-border flavor to the house beers with such names as **Acapulco Gold** and **Panama Red.** A unique brewpub opportunity right next door to tradition.

"Squeeze the lime but hold the rind."
—DAVE, AN OWNER OF STEAMBOAT, RECITES THE MANTRA WHILE SERVING UP A PINT OF ACAPULCO GOLD.

COLORADO

Telluride

Sitting at 8750 feet, surrounded by multiple 13,000-foot peaks and with Bridal Veil Falls as a constant backdrop, Telluride is the most visually striking of all of Colorado's ski towns. A Victorian era mining town with the dubious honor of hosting Butch Cassidy's first bank robbery, Telluride's historic downtown is now a popular destination for tourism and festivals every summer weekend. In fact, there are so many festivals here that one weekend in July has been officially proclaimed the Nothing Festival.

Surrounded by the Uncompahgre National Forest and snuggled right up to incredible mountain scenery, complete with a picturesque waterfall backdrop, Telluride is everyone's image of what a mountain town should be. And although the surrounding mountains may look great to those strolling along Colorado Avenue in the late afternoon sunlight, things might not be so hot sitting behind a set of handlebars. There's no mincing words here. Mountain biking in Telluride is hard. Very hard. However, for someone willing to do the work, the rewards are many and the setting is exquisite with waterfalls, mountain ranges, and a profusion of wildlife. Just make sure you're ready for it when you get here.

In addition to the plethora of other festivals, Telluride has been home to the Telluride Blues and Brews Festival each September since 1994. And ever since 1998, Smuggler's Brewpub and Grille has kept the wort boiling year-round waiting for that glorious September weekend when over 45 breweries descend on the little mountain town.

Mill Creek–Deep Creek Trail

THE SCOOP: A gut-busting singletrack that is the norm for the Telluride area.

RIDE LENGTH AND TYPE: 18-mile town-to-town from Town Park.

THE BIKE: There are many variations of this trail that can be ridden from town, and a good way to get some of the climbing done relatively pain-free is via Mill Creek Road. Prep the rigs at Town Park—only a couple of blocks from the brewery and offering plenty of free parking, a rarity in Telluride—and ride through town to the paved bike path leading west out of town. Follow the path for about 1 mile before turning right onto **Mill Creek Road,** right after passing the Texaco on your left. You'll immediately begin a 600-foot climb over the next 1½ miles where you'll want to catch some quality shots of downtown Telluride before Mill Creek Road ends and the **Deep Creek Trail** singletrack begins. At this point, your Telluride sightseeing tour is effectively over.

About ½ mile into the singletrack, you have a decision to make. Go left up the steep switchbacking singletrack, and you're on your way up a harsh 3-mile climb to where Deep Creek summits. Or, if time is short or you're not interested in coughing up a lung, head to the right over the bridge and enjoy a cruise back into town along the mountain contours on the **Waterline Trail** and **Jud Wiebe Trail.**

Want to put another 2 hours of technical climbing and descending into the log book? Stay on Deep Creek Trail and continue up the mountain through an absolutely picture-perfect stand of aspen intermixed with the occasional pine. You'll top out right around 10,400 feet to views of Palmyra and La Junta peaks above and Mountain Village across the San Miguel River Valley below.

The technical climbing eventually ends, and you are thrown onto a fast-paced descent down a loose and gravelly singletrack that dumps you out onto a doubletrack and the final sweeping singletrack to the **Deep Creek Corral and Trailhead.** From there it's a road ride up **Last Dollar Road** and down the paved **Airport Road** back to **State Highway 145.**

DIFFICULTY: Advanced. Telluride sits at an elevation of 8700 feet, and things go up FAST from there. So unless you're part Himalayan Sherpa, Deep Creek Trail is an advanced ride. By cutting over to Jud Wiebe after the Mill Creek Road climb, the difficulty drops to intermediate and saves you some pain while still getting you out in the saddle.

AEROBIC DIFFICULTY (1–5)

5

TECHNICAL DIFFICULTY (1–5)

4

WARNINGS: In addition to the fact that this is high-altitude riding and should only be attempted by someone in great condition, the area abounds in wildlife. Be cautious of and courteous to the bears, bighorn sheep, mountain lions, and elk in the area. Also, afternoon thunderstorms are common in the mountains. Be prepared and bring extra food and clothing.

Telluride

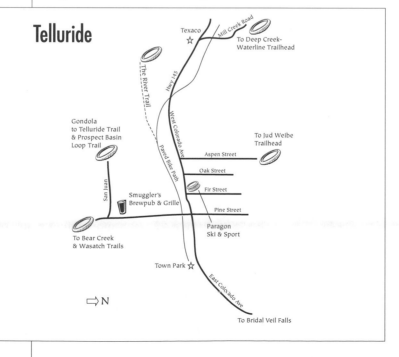

OTHER TRAILS IN THE AREA: Despite being a high-altitude destination, Telluride does offer a trail or two on the novice side. The **River Trail** offers 4 miles of easy (but sometimes muddy) singletrack right along the San Miguel River. It can be combined with another 2 miles of more difficult singletrack riding on the **Ilium Valley Trail** for an out-and-back total of about 12 miles.

Looking for more trouble? The next step up is **Bear Creek Trail,** actually a 2¼-mile dirt road with a 500-foot-per-mile incline and enough loose rock to keep things interesting. It ends with a ¼ mile hike to Bear Creek Falls. The next step up involves taking the free Telluride Gondola to the top of the mountain and downhilling on the **Telluride Trail.** Also starting at the top of the gondola is the **Prospect Basin Loop;** another advanced ride that will keep you out in the mountains 4 or 5 hours on a vast array of trails. Anyone can get around with a couple of instructions from the bike shop, but for the true Tour de Basin, have a local show you the singletrack secrets that await. Want even more than Deep Creek can give? The already-mentioned Bear Creek Trail turns into the **Wasatch Trail,** 16 miles of technical singletrack complicated by altitude. The Wasatch has been called "the most difficult ride in the United States" by one of those glossy bike magazines.

CONTACTS: U.S. Forest Service, Norwood Ranger District, 1760 Grand Avenue, Norwood, CO 81423; (970) 327-4261. Telluride Visitors Services, 700 West Colorado Avenue, Telluride, CO 81435; (970) 728-3041.

MAPS: Paragon Ski & Sport right downtown on Colorado Avenue has free maps of all the trails listed here. Stop in, pick one up, and get the lowdown on the local trail scene.

BIKE SHOP: Paragon Ski & Sport, 213 West Colorado Avenue, Telluride, CO 81435; (970) 728-4525. Right downtown, this locally owned shop is fully equipped with a staff knowledgeable about the local trails and conditions. They also have a free trail map listing many of the area's more popular trails. Well worth a stop before hitting the trails, and it's only a couple blocks from the brewery.

Smuggler's Brewpub and Grille

225 South Pine Street
Telluride, Colorado 81435
(970) 728-0919

ATMOSPHERE: An old tin warehouse two blocks off the main drag with patio seating wrapping around the front and side of the building. A true frontier town building with rough-hewn planks making up the interior walls and floor.
THE BREW: Located in an old warehouse that originally did time as an electrical supply house, much of the original interior has been salvaged to add character to the pub. Read the graffiti on the walls, and it won't be hard to imagine what it was like in the 1890s when Telluride was home to 5000 folks seeking their fortunes in the gold, silver, copper, zinc, and lead mines that still riddle the mountains on the valley's east end.

Walking past the outdoor patio with tables constructed from old ski-lift chairs and offering views of the ski mountain, you are reminded that snow is now the main reason Telluride thrives. Inside you'll find the long building divided lengthwise; one half is occupied by tables for dining, and the other half is filled by a long wooden bar. Casual all the way around, Smugglers is the perfect après-ride hangout after a tough day on Telluride's trails.

After taking in the ambiance inside and out, the next question is beer. With seven taps for the regulars and two more taps rotating for the brewer to play with, there's always plenty to choose from. Of the standard seven, the **Wildcat Wheat**—an American wheat with a surprisingly

full flavor—comes highly recommended for those hot mountain days. The real beer gems are **Ingram's IPA** (India pale ale; it's what the folks who work here drink, always a good sign) and the **Two Planker Porter,** which has a great chocolate aroma and smooth, wonderful flavor. Honorable Mention goes out to **Smuggler's Strong Scottish Ale** and the **Shred Betty Raspberry Wheat** if you like those kinds of beers.

Look for German beers to fill up those other tap slots real soon. There's a new brewer in town, and he hails from the excellent H.C. Berger microbrewery out of Fort

Collins, Colorado. His specialty is German—ever had that excellent H.C. Berger Kolsch?—and it won't be long before it's Smuggler's specialty as well.

PRICE OF A PINT: Whatever the pint of the day happens to be will ring in at $2.00 (down from the ski-town usual of $3.50) between 3:00 and 5:00 P.M. daily.

OTHER BREWS IN THE AREA: Smuggler's is "Telluride's Only Brewpub" and the place to go after a ride. However, if you happen to end up in Mountain Village, then give **Leimgrubber's** a go for authentic German beer and food.

Vail

An Interstate 70 town located almost geographically in the center of the Rockies, you won't find the kind of authentic historic charm so often associated with mountain towns. However, what you will find is world-class accommodations and a ski resort that was voted the best ski resort in America by *Ski Magazine* readers. Designed like an overpriced amusement park for the wealthy, Vail Village has a charming Austrian Alps façade that hosts hundreds of top-quality shops, galleries, restaurants, and bars. With such a reputation for class, few can resist the pull to this mountain retreat, and everyone eventually comes to Vail, at least for a day.

Surrounded by the White River National Forest, all riding in Vail Valley starts around 8000 feet, and no matter which direction you go, glorious singletrack awaits just minutes from town. It's never easy, but using the dirt service roads can take the edge off the incline and elevation. The Hubcap Brewery & Steakhouse gives you a comfortable place to relax and enjoy Vail Village's quality of life after a day in the saddle without the outrageous price tag often associated with this world-famous destination.

Lost Lake–Buffehr Creek Loop

THE SCOOP: Views of the Gore Range mingled in with technical singletrack and a Lost Lake.

RIDE LENGTH AND TYPE: 20-mile loop from downtown Vail.

THE BIKE: There are two advanced must-do rides in Vail. Benchmark to Two Elk to Minturn and Lost Lake–Buffehr Creek. Either way, you can't go wrong. Lost Lake, a touch more technical but with the added reward of a pristine alpine lake, is where you'll start.

What begins as a 7-mile, 1½-hour dirt road climb gradually turns into a rocky, root-filled, technical singletrack as you make your way to Lost Lake. You can break up the grind with breathtaking views of the Gore Range and a road that slowly deteriorates to something slightly better than a 4x4 trail. This "road" takes you to the **Lost Lake Trailhead** and well on your way to the lake where you can grab a log, have a snack, and look out onto the clear calm waters. If you're lucky, you may see a moose having lunch, but—regardless of your luck—you can definitely see the Gore Range rising up over the trees surrounding the lake.

Eventually you have to continue. Follow the dispersed trails around the lake to the right for some more technical singletrack and a bit more climbing. After this couple of miles, you begin a nice descent. Not quite as technical, the trail smoothes out for a B&B Hotmile as you coast along the pine-shrouded ridge before arriving at the **West Lost Lake Trailhead,** the side most commonly used by hikers to achieve the lake and **Forest Service 700 Road.**

Here you can end the work, hang a left and follow Forest Service 700 all the way back down to Vail Valley, or you can hang that left and then an immediate right and follow Red &

White **Forest Service 734 Road** on your way to the single-track **Buffehr Creek Trail**. Buffehr Creek starts out as a sweeping ride through stands of aspens and pines and more views of the Gore Range. A mix of singletrack, sheep(!), and doubletrack turns into an extremely steep and technical, switchbacked singletrack descent onto the new **North Trail**. The North Trail smoothes things out considerably and gently drops you out just north of Interstate 70 and the Frontage Road and your way back to the Hubcap Brewery.

Vail

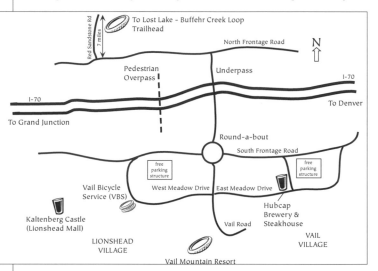

DIFFICULTY: Advanced. Although most of the climbing is on dirt road, the distance and time in the saddle—not to mention a fair bit of technical climbing once you get to the Lost Lake singletrack—give this ride an advanced aerobic rating. Technically, things don't get any better as Buffehr Creek finishes with a very demanding descent before dumping onto the North Trail and then pavement. If you cut the Buffehr Creek singletrack off the end, the ride would drop to intermediate aerobic with some challenging technical riding around the lake.

AEROBIC DIFFICULTY (1–5)

4

TECHNICAL DIFFICULTY (1–5–)

4

WARNINGS: This loop has a reputation of being hard to find (which may have something to do with the name). Things have improved recently, with some of the roads mistaken for the way now blocked off. Regardless, make sure you have a map AND perfect directions. Also, this is the Rockies, and what may be hot and sunny down in Vail could turn cold and rainy up in the hills. Be prepared.

OTHER TRAILS IN THE AREA: The other classic advanced mountain-bike ride in the area is **Benchmark to Two Elk to Minturn Trail.** A true epic 26½-mile ride, it's longer and not quite as technical as Lost Lake, but still very demanding. It's also easier to find and follow and, by all counts, another one of Vail's must-do rides. The most casual singletrack in the valley is the fast and winding North Trail, which runs along the north side of Interstate 70 up and down Vail Valley. An intermediate ride to get you—and your quads—pumped after a day in the car is **Son of Middle Creek,** a ten miler that'll have you home in time for a couple of brews over at the Hubcap. A mix of trails can be found on **Vail Mountain** as well. The resort supplies free maps, and you'll find everything from gonzo downhill tracks to a multitude of lower loops perfect for casual cruising and good conversation.

CONTACTS: U.S. Forest Service, Holy Cross Ranger District, 24747 Highway 24, Minturn, CO 81645; (970) 827-5715. Vail Chamber of Commerce; (970) 477-0075.

MAPS: Fortunately you're in Vail, where rides surround every valley drainage. Unfortunately you're in Vail, where nothing is free (except parking in the summer). The best source of maps is either the Forest Service Office in Minturn or by stopping by Vail Bicycle Service and picking up the local trail bible, Laura Guccione's book, *Vail Mountain Bike Trails,* for $10.50. Not cheap, but at least you're guaranteed to find what you're looking for.

BIKE SHOP: Vail Bicycle Service (VBS), 450 East Lionshead Circle, Vail, CO 81657; (970) 476-1233. If you're preparing for a ride in Vail, go to VBS for trail directions and maps. It's conveniently located right below the free public parking structure on the Lionshead Village (south) side of town. If you are staying in Minturn or plan on going to the Forest Service Office there, the people to talk to are at Mountain Peddler, 474 Main Street, Minturn, CO 81645; (970) 827-5522.

"You could ride in Vail every day for a month and not do the same trail twice."
—TIM YOUNG OF VAIL BICYCLE SERVICE, TALKING UP THE TRAILS IN THE AREA.

117

Hubcap Brewery & Steakhouse

143 East Meadow Drive
Vail, Colorado 81657
(970) 476-5757
www.hubcapbrewery.com

ATMOSPHERE: Comfy and low key, a nice change from the contrived authenticity of Vail Village. The below-ground location in what used to be a Burger King is the perfect place to come and snuggle up to a pint of beer after a long day on the trail.

THE BREW: Tucked away beneath Vail Village and just visible from street level is the Hubcap's wooden patio. Large glass doors stand open to the lower deck connecting the interior with the exterior. Bike racks are perfectly situated within touching distance of your beer. Vintage hubcaps hang from the ceiling inside and lie under the glass bar top. An upscale dining area is separated from the bar where locals hang out shooting pool, playing video games, and watching TV.

Although Hubcap went through a brief identity crisis as Lakota Chops & Hops, ownership has now stabilized, and big things are again on the horizon. They have resumed bottling operations and revived past recipes that have garnered Great American Beer Festival medals. In fact, that is a prerequisite for all of Hubcap's bottled products. Any Hubcap beer you find in the store has medaled at the GABF at some point in the past. Not a bad standard of quality to live by.

The **White River Wheat, Beaver Tail Brown, Vail Pale Ale,** and **Rainbow Trout Stout** have all earned bottling status and make very fine draft choices, with the Vail Pale Ale (an India pale ale) weighing in with a 6.9% alcohol content. The heir apparent to this long-time favorite is the **JR's Extra Special Bitter,** an almost perfect example of an English-style ESB: low carbonation, heavy on the malt, and with the bitterness in all the right places. Not afraid to give customers what they want, the Hubcap keeps 24 taps on hand, of which 8 to 12 offer house beers and the others are filled with complementary imports, micros, and domestics.

Don't let Hubcap's Burger King roots fool you. The owners are serious about the entire dining experience and boast an extensive wine list and top-shelf alcohol. Just because they buck the trend and offer an affordable menu does not mean the food is anything less than gourmet.

PRICE OF A PINT: The good news is you're a mountain biker and that means you'll be visiting during the summer when all house beers are only $2.00 all the time. Food incentives are offered in the bar area and change regularly. Ask your server for the current specials. If you happen to stop by when Vail is a full-swing ski town, expect the price of a pint to increase to $3.50. Hey, as much as you might forget it while sipping a pint with a dog's eye view of the surrounding bustle, this is Vail, and you just may be sitting in the most expensive brewpub, per square foot, in the United States.

OTHER BREWS IN THE AREA: Just as there are two must-do rides in Vail, there are also two must-do brewpubs in Vail. The other brewpub, located on the Lionshead Village side of Vail, is **Kaltenberg Castle Royal Bavarian Brewhouse.** Known locally as "The Castle," it is actually owned and operated by a Bavarian prince and is plastic Bavaria at its best. The brewing system comes straight from Germany and so do the beer styles. The **Prince Leopold Pils** and **King Ludwig Dunkel** are both excellent.

119

CHAPTER TWO

IDAHO

The state of Idaho earned the International Mountain Bike Association's only *A* in the recent nationwide mountain-bike trail-access report card. An excellent example of these quality trails is found in Idaho's "Panhandle" where—of the 20,000 miles of singletrack, doubletrack,

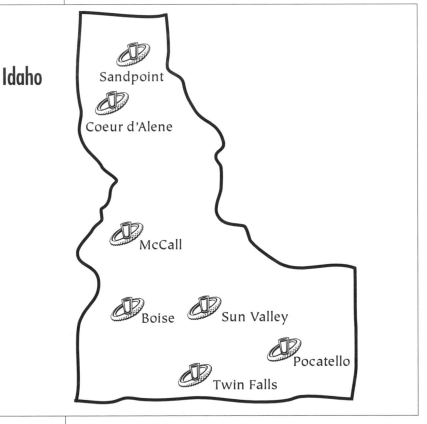

Idaho

Sandpoint

Coeur d'Alene

McCall

Boise

Sun Valley

Pocatello

Twin Falls

and dirt roads available—only 50 miles are closed to mountain biking. With these kinds of numbers, and virtually no user conflicts, it's no wonder Idaho earned such a high mark from mountain biking's governing body. And this quality biking is matched by Idaho's devotion to beer. Though lacking the population to support as many brewpubs as Colorado, a beer savvy influenced by the Pacific Northwest more than makes up for this lack of quantity.

The northern Rocky Mountains cover about one-half of Idaho; most of the high mountains are in the central and north-central region of the state. Thus much of Idaho's riding is mountainous, but in most cases, it doesn't have the extreme altitude often associated with the rest of the Rockies. In fact, alpine riding in the Panhandle region generally begins right around the 3000-foot mark, which means you get all the excitement of pine-lined singletrack 2000 feet lower than you're used to in other Rocky Mountain states, leaving you with more oxygen and more energy to ride longer and farther.

The southern regions offer the very arid climate of the Snake River Plain; a vast treeless expanse of hardened lava flows and volcanic craters—easily some of the most desolate land in the northwest and a stark contrast to the numerous lakes and forests of the northern Panhandle region. However, all is not lost in Idaho's southern reaches. Pocatello, Twin Falls, and Boise offer extraordinary riding practically within shouting distance of a brewpub. You may have to climb a little higher to escape the summertime heat and dust (as the pines and aspens start closer to 5000 feet), but these lower-elevation areas are often rideable early in the season while northern trails are still knee-deep in snow.

So, no matter where you go—from the panhandle vacation towns of Sandpoint and Coeur d'Alene, to the central Idaho ski towns of Sun Valley and McCall, or to the cities of Boise, Pocatello, and Twin Falls—Idaho consistently offers up great biking and fresh brews in unique and different atmospheres for the weary Bike & Brew America traveler.

Boise

Idaho's capital and largest city, Boise is the state's only metropolitan area and its hub of commerce, banking, and government. Home of Boise State University and located in the southwestern corner of the state at the foot of the Rocky Mountains, Boise is one of those cities that have it all. Itself very arid and sitting at 2842 feet above sea level, Boise is minutes away from mountains, rivers, lakes, and alpine skiing. The dry and warm climate means nearly year-round riding practically butting up to a brewpub. An active, cyclist-friendly town, it's not uncommon to see mountain bikers in full regalia making their way to or from the trails and pubs on the crowded city streets.

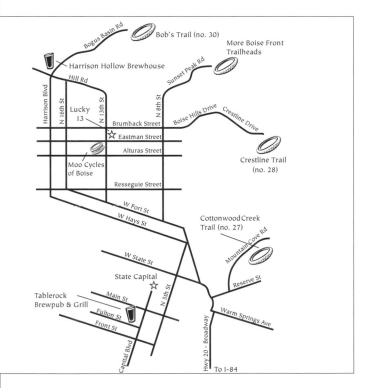

Boise

The Boise Front

THE SCOOP: Miles of singletrack just out of down-town Boise.

RIDE LENGTH AND TYPE: 12-mile loop.

THE BIKE: Right out Boise's back door, the southern end of the Boise Range slows urban sprawl and provides miles of singletrack-filled bliss. Looking up at these foothills known as the Boise Front, you're faced with treeless, arid hills, not exactly inspirational alpine conditions. However, these very conditions are also the Boise Front's strengths. They make for great visibility for remarkable views of the surrounding countryside and city below, and dry, almost desert-like conditions that allow year-round riding.

What may appear faceless and featureless from below becomes creeks, ridges, hollows, and singletrack upon closer inspection. Plus, starting at an elevation of only 2700 feet, the Boise Front is a great way to experience Rocky Mountain hill climbing without the usual lack of oxygen. However, if the only things that make you happy are depriving your brain of oxygen among conifer-filled forests, there are plenty of rides nearby that will take you through the terraced (to prevent erosion and mudslides) Front up and over 5000 feet and into the forests beyond.

A great introduction to Boise Front riding, and one that's easily accessible from the downtown, is the loop composed of Cottonwood Trail (no. 27) to Ridgecrest Trail (no. 20) to Crestline Trail (no. 28) to Bob's Trail (no. 30). The biking experience starts out along a tree-lined creek bed **(Cottonwood Trail)** that soon turns to prairie before eventually heading up into the hills. A couple of extended climbs along **Ridgecrest Trail** put you onto **Crestline,** a smooth piece of trail that eventually gets you to the intersection and parking lot for **Bob's Trail**. Bob's is a fast and fun downhill with a couple of technical spots that'll keep your mind on business.

Unfortunately, as is all too common, it ends much too soon, and you pop out onto a residential street. Unless you want to go around again, the only consolation for continuing downhill on asphalt is the Harrison Hollow Brewhouse waiting for you at the bottom.

DIFFICULTY: Intermediate. There are many variations to the trails listed here, and nearly all trails can be ridden in both directions.

AEROBIC DIFFICULTY (1–5)

3

TECHNICAL DIFFICULTY (1–5)

3

WARNINGS: Boise is Idaho's largest city, and it's growing by leaps and bounds. Not only does this mean more riders, hikers, and horses on the trails, it also means fewer trails as private land is sold to developers and trail systems become inaccessible. Please stay on posted trails and ask before crossing private property. The access rights to these urban trails depend on your actions. Also, be aware that the Boise Front is prone to flashfloods. If you hear sirens and it's not noon on the first Saturday of the month (that's when Boise tests the system), get to higher ground. Fast.

OTHER TRAILS IN THE AREA: Sticking to the Boise Front, the easiest trail is **Crestline Drive** to **Crestline Trail (no. 28)**. A steady paved road climb from town, it eventually turns into a fun, nonthreatening doubletrack. The ride can be done as an out-and-back or as a connector to the more technical singletrack, **Hull's Gulch Trail (no. 29)**. If you're looking for more adventure, then the **Hard Guy Trail** is for you. An epic ride that leaves right from the brewery, this ride takes you from 2700 feet all the way to 6000 feet and Boise Ridge Road. Turn around and prepare yourself for one of the best downhills around or find any of a dozen other routes down the Boise Front.

CONTACTS: Bureau of Land Management, Boise District Office, 3948 Development Avenue, Boise, ID 83705; (208)

384-3300; www.trailsandtread.com. Boise Chamber of Commerce, 250 South Fifth Street #800, Boise, ID 83702; (208) 344-5515.

MAPS: Because each trail spur has its own name, most loops consist of two, three, four, or more trails, which is no problem once you're familiar with the area. Until then, get a good map. The *Ridge to Rivers Trail System Map* lists all the trails mentioned here and many more. It's usually available at Moo Cycles and the Bureau of Land Management District Office. Call (208) 384-3360 for the current locations and price.

BIKE SHOP: Moo Cycles of Boise, 1517½ Thirteenth Street, Boise, ID 83702; (208) 336-5229. This well-appointed local shop is right in the heart of cool, historic Hyde Park. Run by Jake Hawkes, this guy lives, breathes, and eats bikes of all types. From cutting-edge road to mountain-bike classics (yes, there is such a thing), this guy loves, and knows, about them all. His shop is also one of those rare breeds that specializes in the latest bike-fit techniques and methods. Well worth a stop to pick up the *Ridge to Rivers Trail System Map,* and anything else you may need, before getting after it on the Boise Front.

Harrison Hollow Brewhouse

2455 Harrison Hollow Boulevard
Boise, Idaho 83702
(208) 343-6820

ATMOSPHERE: Cozy, down to earth, with a neighborhood-tavern feel. A remodeled pizza joint with a large circular fireplace in the center, this pub features limitless coasters, copies of *Guitar Magazine,* and 78-rpm records plastered to anything that didn't move quick enough when the place was being turned into a brewpub back in 1992.
THE BREW: An inconspicuous little building right at the base of the Boise foothills but one you can't miss on your way down the hill at the conclusion of Bob's Trail. So close in fact, you'd be committing a crime if you didn't stop to sample the wares after a dusty day on the trails.

Harrison brews about 12 different beers with 6 or 7 of them on tap at any one time. Its signature beer, and number-one seller, is the English-style pale ale known simply as **Fiegwirth.** A rich, tasty, copper-colored beer, it's easy to see why this is the Hollow's staple. If you're interested in a little more body and creamy flavor, then give the **Western Ale** a try. It's a dark beer—lighter than a porter but with more malt flavor than a pale and another crowd favorite. The 6-4-3 **(Double Play) Porter** has a nice coffee aroma, and the **Picabo Wheat** is a light crisp beer honoring the local hero Picabo Street, who won the gold medal in the women's super-giant-slalom race at the 1998 winter Olympic Games. Regardless of which flavor you choose, all of Harrison Hollow beers are unfiltered for a pure, flavor-rich experience.

Slated for summer 2000 construction is a new patio area. Sitting right at the base of the Boise Front, it's hard to believe this has not been done long before now as patios are a necessary characteristic for any B&B main attraction.

Bring an appetite because this place is known for its large, large portions of fresh food. In fact, the brewer is so confident of his kitchen he's been known to boast, "If you can get a better meal for the price, I'll buy it for you." This line may just have been the couple pints of his finest talking, but he sure did sound confident.

PRICE OF A PINT: Finish your ride and make it back here between 5:00 and 7:00 P.M. and you can knock 50 cents off the $3.00 price of a pint.

OTHER BREWS IN THE AREA: There's always the upscale **Tablerock Brewpub & Grill** downtown, which has a nice collection of house brews including **The Bird.** Though not really one of the brewery's best (that honor goes to its incredible 7½% alcohol by volume **Tablerock IPA**—India pale ale—or, for real hop heads, the **Double Gnarly IPA**—a double-hopped version of the same beer), you still just gotta love the name.

The place in town that attracts the cyclists because of its generous patio seating (hear that, Harrison?) is **Lucky 13**, also in Hyde Park and right across from Moo Cycles bike shop. Nothing upscale here except the selection of regional micros on tap. You order inside and sit outside where dogs are welcome. There's even a water bowl set out for your furry friends.

127

Coeur d'Alene

On the northern shore of beautiful Lake Coeur d'Alene is the town of Coeur d'Alene, named after the Native American people originally from this area. It seems that they were considered by the French trappers to be sharp-witted traders, and Coeur d'Alene translates to "heart of an awl" or "sharp hearted."

Once primarily a mining community, the historic downtown is now a thriving tourist destination surrounded by three national forests (the Coeur d'Alene, Saint Joe, and Kaniksu National Forests) and, of course, the 24-mile-long, 2-mile-wide lake.

Relaxing vacation towns make for great B&B destinations, and Coeur d'Alene is no exception. Park downtown at the city beach, and do a town-to-town ride up onto Canfield Mountain. Soak in the climbs, singletrack, and views before heading back off the mountain for a quick dip in Lake Coeur d'Alene and a nice stroll over to the brewery and pub in time for happy hour. Very relaxing indeed.

Canfield Mountain Trail System

THE SCOOP: Well-developed trail system with fantastic views of the area.

RIDE LENGTH AND TYPE: Variable—25-mile town-to-town loop ride.

THE BIKE: Used by motorcycles since the 1950s, and recently redeveloped into a managed trail network for motorcycles and mountain bikes, the Canfield Mountain Trail System offers more than 30 miles of single and doubletrack trails. Although some of these trails are eroded and rocky from motorized use, many are still perfectly groomed sections of singletrack. Thanks to various grants allocated to the project over the years, the whole trail system is well posted, and free maps are available at the local bike shop and Fernan Ranger Station.

Of the trails in the park, the best ones for mountain biking are the 8½-mile Trail A and the 4-mile Trail B. These two trails generally follow the contours of the mountain, so you don't experience the steep inclines like most of the other trails in the system. You'll still need to use these other trails to make connecting loops, but you can usually take them coming down the mountain.

You can explore on your own or go straight to Vertical Earth Bicycle & Ski (right around the corner from the brewery), get a free map, and have the owner, Mark Beattie, give you turn-by-turn instructions for a 25-mile circuit of the mountain. This particular ride leaves right from his shop and avoids most major washouts and other gnarly trail conditions.

If you follow Mark's directions, most of your climbing will be on dirt roads, first on **Nettleton Gulch Road** up to the initial turnoff onto **Trail A** and later on **Forest Service**

Road 1562 to regain lost altitude and the connector to **Trail B.** However, no matter which way you go, there are many scenic views of Lake Coeur d'Alene, the town, surrounding mountains, and, of course, the Coeur d'Alene Brewing Company way down below.

DIFFICULTY: Intermediate to advanced. Even if you stay on Trails A and B, there are a couple spots that challenge even the best riders. If you start exploring on your own, it gets even dicier with trail erosion and washouts in many areas on the mountain.

AEROBIC DIFFICULTY (1–5)

3

TECHNICAL DIFFICULTY (1–5)

3

WARNINGS: As already mentioned, motorcyclists use this trail system, so watch out and always yield to them. Also, some unmarked trail spurs wander off into private land. Please be aware of this possibility, and be prepared to backtrack if you get off course. The logging activity that created most of these trails still goes on here, so be aware of trail closures and on the lookout for forest-industry vehicles.

OTHER TRAILS IN THE AREA: For another great intermediate ride not far from town, **Beauty Bay** offers 23 miles of cool singletrack and epic downhilling. Vertical Earth also carries topographic maps of this trail for a nominal cost.

Then 20 miles north of Coeur d'Alene is **Farragut State Park**—including a well-developed network of over 30 miles of trails ranging in difficulty from beginner to advanced. Located on the southern end of Lake Pend Oreille, a swim at one of the many park beaches after your ride should cool you off. A $2.00 park entrance fee also buys you a color map of all the trails.

CONTACTS: U.S. Forest Service, Fernan Ranger District, 2502 East Sherman Avenue, Coeur d'Alene, ID 83814; (208) 664-2318. Coeur d'Alene Area Chamber of Commerce, P.O. Box 850, 1621 North Third Street, Coeur d'Alene, ID 83816; (208) 664-3194; www.coeurdalenechamber.com.

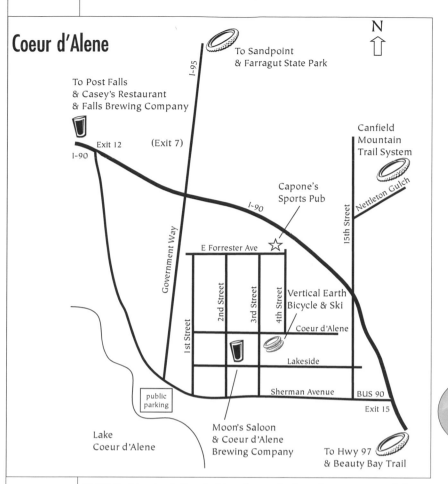

Coeur d'Alene

N

To Sandpoint
& Farragut State Park

I-95

To Post Falls
& Casey's Restaurant
& Falls Brewing Company

Exit 12   (Exit 7)

I-90

Canfield
Mountain
Trail System

Nettleton Gulch

Capone's
Sports Pub

I-90

Government Way

E Forrester Ave

15th Street

2nd Street

3rd Street

4th Street

1st Street

Vertical Earth
Bicycle & Ski

Coeur d'Alene

Lakeside

Sherman Avenue

BUS 90

Exit 15

public
parking

Moon's Saloon
& Coeur d'Alene
Brewing Company

Lake
Coeur d'Alene

To Hwy 97
& Beauty Bay Trail

MAPS: Vertical Earth Bicycle & Ski has free copies of the Canfield Mountain Trail System map. These folks also know which trails to take, and not to take, once you get there. It's worth the time to stop by and let them give you the lay of the land.

BIKE SHOP: Vertical Earth Bicycle & Ski, 206 North Third Street, Coeur d'Alene, ID 83814; (208) 667-5503. Not only can Mark Beattie and his employees get you squared away with maps and directions, they've been doing shop rides up to Canfield and back since 1989. They go on Tuesday and Thursday evenings at 6:00 P.M. According to Mark, the Tuesday night rides are, "fairly hardcore and not for the faint of heart," but the Thursday night gigs are at a much more relaxed pace. After the rides, they often stop at **Capone's Sports Pub**, a local joint featuring 31 taps, most of which are micros.

Moon's Saloon and the Coeur d'Alene Brewing Company

209 Lakeside Avenue
Coeur d'Alene, Idaho 83814
(208) 664-BREW(2739)
www.cdabrewing.com

ATMOSPHERE: Moon's Saloon is a smoky blue-collar bar with animal heads mounted on the wall.

THE BREW: Coeur d'Alene is northern Idaho's primary lakeside vacation town although most of these vacationers, and the seasonal workforce, come from nearby Spokane, Washington. Lake Coeur d'Alene creates a nice resort-town feel with a downtown beach and park on the lake. And, it's only two blocks from the brewery. In this setting, it's not surprising to hear tales of the Jacuzzi parties that used to be held in the brewery's mash tun not too many years ago.

TW Fisher's Brewpub (the 6-foot-tall eternally filling beer mug sign is still hanging out front) recently sold the brewery part of the business to Coeur d'Alene Brewing Company and renamed itself Moon's Saloon. Not to fear. The two are still attached, and one of TW Fisher's original brewers has returned to the scene after a long hiatus. Brew tanks are visible behind a glass wall, and Moon's serves up many of the excellent Coeur d'Alene beers.

There's now also the bonus of having the brewer's own tap room right next door where you can sample the wares for free before committing to a pint or two over at Moon's. However, if the taproom is closed when you get there (its hours are Wednesday to Sunday, 11:00 A.M. to 5:00 P.M.) and you can't try 'em all for yourself, whatever you do, don't miss a pint of **Centennial Pale Ale.** The gold medal winner at the 1987 Great American Beer Festival, this beer has withstood the test of time, and any visitor here would be remiss without at least one pint of this historic ale.

And things just get better from there. Once you're ready for something darker, the **Lakeside British Ale** (the head brewers' favorite by the way) is an excellent example of a smooth full-flavor nut brown ale. Huckleberry beers are common in this region of the country because of the berries' availability and popularity (it's Idaho's state fruit), and the Coeur d'Alene Brewing Company claims to have brewed it here first. The **Huckleberry Ale** is a light and refreshing ale with just a hint of northwest huckle-berries throughout.

All told, Coeur d'Alene brews nine beers year-round plus a brewer's whim whenever he, well, feels like it. In addi-tion to the three already mentioned, Moon's also serves the **Mike's Picnic Pilsner** and the award-winning **Polar Bear Stout**. The Bear is a very dark, very rich beer with hints of chocolate and espresso for you coffee lovers, whereas the Pilsner uses the same recipe as the Centennial Pale Ale, but substitutes lager yeast for ale yeast. It's amazing how much this change affects the beers' characters, so be sure to compare the two.

Pick your favorite at the tap room and head over to Moon's patio, which sits out back, order up a pint and count the kegs as they get shuffled around at the brewery next door.

PRICE OF A PINT: Moon's Saloon runs a happy hour between 5:00 and 7:00 P.M. every day where pints are only two bucks each.

OTHER BREWS IN THE AREA: Casey's Restaurant & Falls Brewing Company in Coeur d'Alene's neighboring town of Post Falls is a modern, comfy, family place brewing all lager beers. The brewers were able to find a lager yeast that ferments out in only 3–4 weeks, making this unique concept practical. Falls Brewing Company does a very nice **Detonator Doppelbock.** Also, some of the brews are lagered in used bourbon and red wine barrels that impart their distinct aroma and flavor to the resulting beers.

"No true beer is a twist off!"
—GAGE STROMBERG, PRESIDENT, COEUR D'ALENE BREWING COMPANY. WITH TRADITIONAL PHILOSOPHY LIKE THAT, COEUR D'ALENE BREWING COMPANY WILL BE AROUND FOR A VERY LONG TIME INDEED.

133

McCall

Perched in the heart of central Idaho, McCall is the first sizable vacation destination town north of Boise. It has a resort-like feel enhanced by beautiful Payette Lake, which reflects distant mountaintops from its deep blue waters rumored to be home to Sharlie, McCall's version of the Loch Ness Monster. Harbors, marinas, beaches, restaurants, shops, and art galleries await idle window shoppers and form the bulk of downtown business, and the popular Brundage Mountain Ski Resort offers winter skiing and summer biking a few miles from town.

However, McCall's biking experience is not limited to Brundage Mountain. There are dozens of trails in this area, and you can spend a week riding them all. Multiple hot springs offer a great way to keep the body loose from all this activity before heading over to the McCall Brewing Company where the main attraction is the upstairs patio. Sitting there, overlooking Payette Lake, you've got it all: mountains, water, sunshine in your face, and, of course, good beer.

That is, we can be hopeful there will be good beer. The winter of 2001 saw a change of ownership at the McCall Brewing Company. Or rather, a switch back to previous ownership. The new old owners are scheduled to reopen in time for biking season in 2001, but you'd better give them a call just to make sure. If the restaurant's number still isn't working, don't worry, they may have changed it. Call Gravity Sports and ask for Travis. He'll know the scoop about the brewpub just up the street.

Loon Lake

THE SCOOP: Singletrack, a rushing river, alpine lake, mountain views, and the obligatory crashed World War II airplane.

RIDE LENGTH AND TYPE: 10-mile loop or 11-mile out-and-back if the river is running high.

THE BIKE: Although it takes a little longer to get here than is the B&B norm, the Loon Lake Trail is the first trail in the area cleared each summer by the Forest Service. Because forest fires ravaged most of the trails in the area back in 1994, they often have more than their fair share of deadfall each spring, making them all but unrideable until cleared.

The Chinook Campground and the **Loon Lake Trailhead** are 30 miles north (almost an hour by car) of McCall. The trail can be ridden in either direction. Clockwise is the most popular because the Secesh River is the first obstacle on the trail in the counterclockwise direction. Why get your feet wet before you have to, right?

So, running clockwise on **Trail 080,** the first 3½ miles roll along the Secesh River valley and pretty much define a perfect section of singletrack trail. A couple of rocks here and a few roots there keep advanced riders happy and other riders challenged.

At the 3½-mile mark, the trail branches; Trail 080 continues along the river, and **Trail 084** crosses the river on an impressively constructed foot bridge. Cross the river and prepare for a ½-mile lung-burning climb out of the valley before the trail levels off and continues to Loon Lake.

If you have the time, it's worth a side excursion to the shore of Loon Lake where you're likely to find a mixed bag of horses, lamas, motorcyclists, mountain bikers, and hikers hitched up, camped out, and/or sunning on the rocks surrounding the beautiful alpine lake. You can join them on your own rock, swim, or walk the 20 minutes around the lake to the wreckage of a downed B-23 bomber that lies just off the south shore.

Todd Mercer poses on the wing of a rare B-23 bomber that crashed near Loon Lake in 1943. (COURTESY OF SOME FRIENDLY CANADIAN HIKERS)

Storyboards tell how the plane went down on a courier mission in 1943 and the heroics and eventual rescue of all eight crewmembers aboard. The entire town of McCall closed up shops and schools to welcome the men home after their 16-day ordeal.

Once you've finished your history lesson, take **Trail 081** north away from the lake where the climbing resumes at a much more comfortable rate, topping out right around 6000 feet—only about 400 more than where you started. Stay on Trail 081 and enjoy a fast descent back down to Chinook Campground and a crossing of the Secesh River, which, at times, can get quite interesting (see warnings).

DIFFICULTY: Intermediate. The climb at elevation out of the river valley is gonna be painful for most riders, and there are enough roots, rocks, and ruts elsewhere to keep the whole ride interesting.

AEROBIC DIFFICULTY (1–5)

3

TECHNICAL DIFFICULTY (1–5)

3

WARNINGS: The Secesh River is running at its highest in the spring. If it's over knee deep, you may want to ride this one as an out-and-back to and from Loon Lake using Trail 080 or plan on going for a swim.

OTHER TRAILS IN THE AREA: There are many other great rides in the McCall area, the closest and easiest being at **Ponderosa State Park.** Riding to and from the park and incorporating the 2½ miles of mountain-bike trails would make for a pleasurable afternoon. Plus bikers are allowed in free whereas cars are charged $3.00. Only about 10 miles east of McCall is the challenging **East Fork of Lake Fork** ride. A 4.6-mile out-and-back with a 1000-foot elevation gain, downed trees, and steep switchbacks make an advanced ride that's a real favorite. Other rides in the area include the trails at **Twentymile Lakes** and the **Brundage Mountain Ski Resort.** The resort has a good

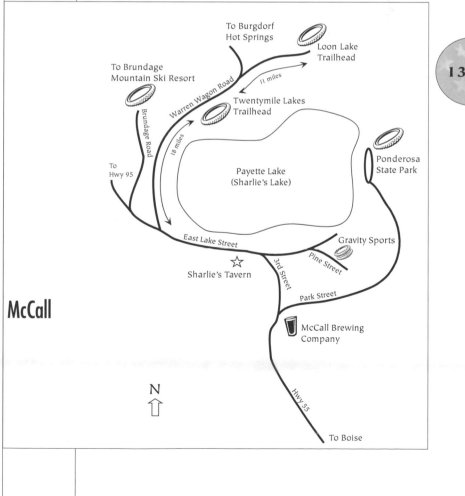

To Burgdorf
Hot Springs

Loon Lake
Trailhead

To Brundage
Mountain Ski Resort

11 miles

Warren Wagon Road

Twentymile Lakes
Trailhead

Brundage Road

18 miles

To
Hwy 95

Payette Lake
(Sharlie's Lake)

Ponderosa
State Park

East Lake Street

Gravity Sports

Pine Street

Sharlie's Tavern

3rd Street

Park Street

McCall Brewing
Company

McCall

Hwy 55

To Boise

N

trail system with chairlifts running during July and August for those who like the downhill part of mountain biking more than the uphill.

CONTACTS: U.S. Forest Service, McCall Ranger District, 102 West Lake Street, McCall, ID 83638; (208) 634-0400. McCall Chamber of Commerce, 1001 State Street, McCall, ID 83638; (208) 634-7631.

MAPS: Gravity Sports has a topo map on the wall and can give directions to all the trails listed here. In Loon Lake's case, the trail is well marked with a map at the trailhead and signs posting all intersections. Because this trail is one of the more popular trails in the area, there is usually someone to ask if you think you took a wrong turn somewhere.

BIKE SHOP: Gravity Sports, 503 Pine Street, McCall, ID 83638; (208) 634-8530. Stop in for directions and current trail conditions before setting out into the woods. The folks there are the first to ride the trails each year, so they know which have been cleared and which have not.

Todd Mercer reloads the Bike & Brew America truck at the trailhead, after riding the incredible Loon Lake Trail.

IDAHO

McCall Brewing Company

807 North Third Street
McCall, Idaho 83638
(208) 634-2333

ATMOSPHERE: A wood-timbered building with bikes, kayaks, paddles, and snowboards hanging from the walls and ceiling, offering cozy downstairs dining and an open rooftop patio.

THE BREW: Sitting on a hill overlooking Payette Lake, McCall's upstairs patio offers breathtaking views of the town, the lake, and the surrounding mountains. Inside, you'll find comfortable wooden décor and the brew house behind the bar. Because this is a resort town, expect early afternoon crowds buying T-shirts and growlers of beer to go, sipping a pint, or trying a sampler of house beers served uniquely on the back of a retired skateboard deck.

McCall's has about a dozen different beers on tap, and the upstairs selection differs from that downstairs. Not all the beers here are as perfect as the setting, but the dark trio of **McCall Oatmeal Stout**, **McCall Porter**, and the **Powdertrail Ale** all make very nice companions. The **Osprey Pale** is another good beer offering a perfect balance of malt and hops, and, if you absolutely must go lighter, the **McCall Hefeweizen**—the best seller—isn't bad on a hot afternoon. The **Freeride Brown**, **Secesh Scotch**, and **Jughandle Amber** are average, but the **Old Nick English Ale** is just plain off.

PRICE OF A PINT: Monday through Friday between 4:00 and 6:30 P.M., pints are discounted a buck down to $2.25 and pitchers are only five bucks each!

139

OTHER BREWS IN THE AREA: **Sharlie's Tavern** is a local joint with a nice selection of northwest micros on tap. Be sure to ask the folks at Sharlie's about their namesake, the monster of the lake, Sharlie, whose sightings seem to mostly be concentrated around one of the more popular late-night-party beaches. Maybe she just has a taste for McCall Brewing Company's **Payette Pils?**

"Oh yeah, there's something out there all right."
—A LOCAL'S RESPONSE WHEN ASKED ABOUT SHARLIE, PAYETTE LAKE'S LOCH NESS MONSTER.

IDAHO

Pocatello

Sometimes called the Gate City, Pocatello was founded in 1882 as a railroad center and even now serves as a commercial hub with Interstates 15 and 86 forming a T in her midst. Pocatello sits at an elevation of 4448 feet on the western foothills of the Rocky Mountains. If driving in from the north or east, you'll think Idaho may have been

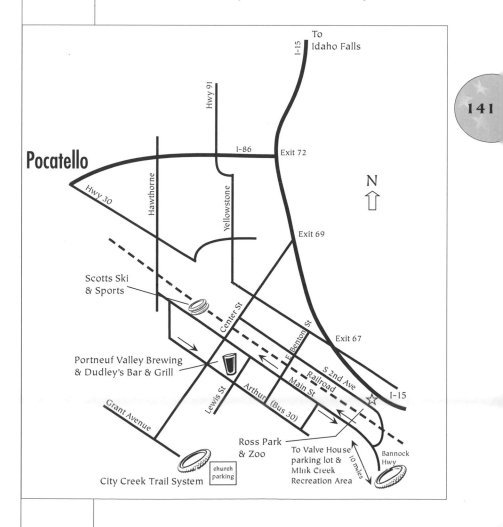

leveled off and that green conifer forests were turned to arid plains, scrub, and black lava fields. Just as hope begins to wane, you pass American Falls Reservoir and up pops Scout Mountain, rising to more than 9400 feet and serving as a beacon of singletrack paradise.

Also called the Mink Creek Recreation Area, it's just minutes from downtown Poky, as the local Pocatellans proudly refer to their town. And, although Scout Mountain looks almost barren from a distance, that illusion will be dashed as soon as you make some progress into the heavily forested hills and river-lined valleys. Scout Mountain's southern location and relatively warmer climate also make it an early-season destination for folks higher up in the Rockies. Those willing to drive a few hours south will find Poky's trails open and waiting.

Historic downtown Poky is a thriving business district and, just as Mink Creek's exterior fools, don't let the rough interior of Dudley's Bar & Grill fool you either. Home to the fantastic Portneuf Valley Brews, a.k.a. Penny's Beer, Dudley's is the place local mountain bikers, hikers, and climbers come for Penny's famous Nut Brown Ale, and you should too.

Mink Creek Recreation Area

THE SCOOP: Nearly limitless miles of alpine singletrack just minutes from town.

RIDE LENGTH AND TYPE: Loops from Valve House parking lot range from 8 miles to as far as you can go.

THE BIKE: A good place to begin your exploration of Scout Mountain, also known as the Mink Creek Recreation Area, is at the **Valve House Trailhead.** Here you're sitting at 5100 feet of elevation, and you can take off to explore the **Valve House–South Fork Trail** to the south or the **West Fork–Gibson Jack Trail** off to the, well, you guessed it, west. Both of these loops are just a small part of the trail system running throughout the mountains, so expect to find many trails intersecting and branching from your path throughout your explorations.

No matter which way you go, be prepared for conifer-supplied shade, babbling creeks making their way down to the Portneuf River, and miles of tight singletrack, rock-star doubletrack, and dirt-road connectors. The higher you climb, the better the views of the Portneuf River Valley (hence the brewery's name), the more loamy the soil, and the denser the vegetation. Thus the rewards at the higher elevations are great, but so is the climb to get to them. Just be prepared to earn those reward points.

DIFFICULTY: Intermediate to advanced. Venturing up into Mink Creek means elevations over 5000 feet and intermediate to advanced riding throughout. Some easier riding is available closer to town.

AEROBIC DIFFICULTY (1–5)

3

TECHNICAL DIFFICULTY (1–5)

3

WARNINGS: A multiuse trail system close to civilization always means traffic of some sort. Please be prepared to meet other cyclists, equestrians, and hikers and always give way.

OTHER TRAILS IN THE AREA: Don't have the time, transportation, or desire to drive up onto Scout Mountain? Then the classic after-work town-to-town ride is the **City Creek Trail System** waiting for you right on the West Bench and only about 1 mile from Dudley's. Expect narrow singletrack along City Creek with plenty of cottonwoods, aspen, and maples. Rated as a beginner trail, you can form loops as short as 2 miles to as long as you wish because the trails reach over the Bannock Range to the **West Mink Creek Trail** and **Elk Meadows Trail.**

CONTACTS: U.S. Forest Service, Westside Ranger District, 250 South Fourth Avenue, Pocatello, ID 83201; (208) 236-7500. Greater Pocatello Chamber of Commerce, 343 West Center Street, Pocatello, ID 83204; (208) 233-1525; www.pocatelloidaho.com.

MAPS: Scotts Ski & Sports carries the *Pocatello Area Trail Map*, a topographic map of the area with trails labeled and marked in various colors according to difficulty level. Well worth the $6.95 price tag it bears.

BIKE SHOP: Scotts Ski & Sports, 224 North Main, Pocatello, ID 83204; (208) 232-1449. Scotts is a three-story biking, climbing, hiking, x-c skiing, and general outdoor sports shop, but don't let the nonspecificity scare you away. Besides carrying the *Pocatello Area Trail Map*, Scotts has a well-appointed bike shop with a basement dedicated solely to the wrenches. Plus the shop is just a block from the brewery, so drop off the rig and go fetch yourself a pint of Penny's finest.

Portneuf Valley Brewing and Dudley's Sports Bar & Grill

150 South Arthur Avenue
Pocatello, Idaho 83204
(208) 232-1644

ATMOSPHERE: No yuppie haven here. This is a dark, musty place with neon beer signs, pool tables, video trivia, big-screen TV, electronic darts, and, of course, a Pop-A-Shot basketball machine. This place is cavernous with huge rooms for banquets, a piano bar, and bands. The later in the evening, the livelier it gets. Not to fear, squished into one corner of the bar area is the glass-surrounded brewery and the real reason for a visit.

THE BREW: Since 1996 Penny Pink and her son Cody have been brewing Portneuf Valley beers, also known simply as "Penny's Beer," at Dudley's Sports Bar & Grill for on-premises consumption as well as Poky-wide distribution.

Dudley's and Portneuf are housed inside Pocatello's old U.S. Post Office and Court House. This accounts for the shear mass of the building and the fact that Penny mills her grain in an old Post Office vault. Not only is this the safest grain in Idaho, Penny does not disturb Dudley's patrons if she decides to mill during business hours behind the nearly foot-thick soundproof steel that makes up the vault's door.

All of Penny's beers are good—from her best seller, the flavorful **Sunshine Pale Ale,** to her dark and robust **Scout Mountain Stout.** But it's the **Nut Brown Ale** that gives this place a star on the map. This is a big brown with lots of nutty malt flavor and an absolutely perfect cream head. Penny's Brown has what it takes to go the distance at any beer festival out there. It's that good.

There's more going on here than just beer and games. Penny, a former analytic chemist, is also on the city council, so don't be surprised if you find her discussing city matters such as the Portneuf Greenway Foundation (a cooperative effort between the City, County, and U.S. Park Service to link various historic sites and parks along the Portneuf River with a paved bicycle path). How's that! Penny's a brewer and bike philanthropist—need any more reasons to visit?

Although Dudley's may not be a place for fine dining, you can get some decent pub grub, and as this is where Poky comes to play, be prepared for a rowdy crowd and plenty of fun. In the spirit of the old courthouse, let's all raise a pint to the honorable Penny Pink!

PRICE OF A PINT: Every day of the week, Dudley's offers a different drink special, so check the table tents before placing your order and hope you're there on Monday for $1.00 pints of Penny's finest.

OTHER BREWS IN THE AREA: Penny's is currently the only game in town, but be on the lookout for her and Cody to open up a brewpub of their own down in Pocatello's old brewery district. They have already purchased the old Aero Club Brewery's building on South First Street, and plans are underway to turn the place into a brewpub. And, because there are no plans to pull the current brewery out of Dudley's, this may mean there will be two places to drink fresh beer in Poky before all is said and done.

"My husband started blowing up carboys, so I took over the family's homebrewing responsibilities."

—PENNY PINK, DESCRIBING HOW SHE GOT INTO THE BREWING INDUSTRY. JUST GOES TO SHOW, A FAMILY WHO BREWS TOGETHER STAYS TOGETHER.

Sandpoint

Sandpoint is surrounded by the natural beauty of the
Coeur d'Alene Mountains and the shores of Lake Pend
Oreille (pronounced Pond-O-Ray), which is French, meaning "ear pendant," and may have been named after the
ear ornaments worn by the Kalispell Native Americans.
Either that, or as you'll notice, the lake just happens to be
the shape of a rather large ear. Whatever, the lake is big
(111 miles of shoreline), deep (1158 feet; the fifth deepest
natural lake in the nation), and a worthy namesake for
the Pend Oreille Brewing Company located only a few
blocks inland.

Founded in 1880 as a mining town, Sandpoint now
caters to the kinder things in life. Whether you're participating in the annual Long Bridge Swim, skiing down the
slopes of Schweitzer Mountain, or peddling across the
1.76-mile pedestrian Long Bridge spanning Lake Pend
Oreille on your way to Gold Hill Trail 3, you're sure to
realize that Sandpoint is the Panhandle's crowning jewel.
Still mostly undiscovered, this is where mountain bikers
who live in Idaho's Rocky Mountains come to ride when
they're not riding at home. It's like putting the star on
Idaho's Bike & Brew America Christmas tree.

Gold Hill Trail 3

THE SCOOP: 44 perfectly designed singletrack switch-backs leading to views high above Sandpoint and Lake Pend Oreille.

RIDE LENGTH AND TYPE: Either an 11½-mile out-and-back from the trailhead or a 25-mile town-to-town ride.

THE BIKE: This trail can be ridden as an out-and-back jaunt leaving from the developed trailhead just off of Bottle Bay Road, or as a 25-mile town-to-town from downtown Sandpoint. The town-to-town ride uses the **North Idaho Bike Path** and pedestrian bridge that crosses the lake before turning at the Budweiser (of all things) distribution warehouse onto **Bottle Bay Road.**

From the trailhead, 4½ miles from the turn onto Bottle Bay Road, **Gold Hill Trail 3** rises more than 1600 feet above the shores of Lake Pend Oreille. The trail immediately starts out with a switchback turn and continues in this fashion for the next 4 miles. In fact, there are a total of 44 switchbacks snaking up the hill—all perfectly designed and all perfectly rideable by mere mortals.

Although you are climbing a pretty steep grade (about 400 feet/mile), the switchbacks make for a very doable ride and give plenty of opportunity to polish your switch-backing skill set, that is, power up, come around, ease it back down anticipating, and resting up for, the next one.

Concentrating on the trail this way, it won't be long until you pop out of the dense forest and catch a couple of postcard-quality views of Sandpoint, its bridges, and Lake Pend Oreille spreading out below you. Not long after these views disappear behind you, the trail empties out onto **Forest Service Road 2642.** Hang a right and continue uphill for ½ mile to where the maintained road ends in a doubletrack. Stay left, and this eventually becomes a ripping singletrack descent, ending once again on Road 2642, only this time downhill of Gold Hill Trail 3. Crank back up the hill on the road and dip back into the lush forest so that you can practice a downhill session of Switchbacks 101.

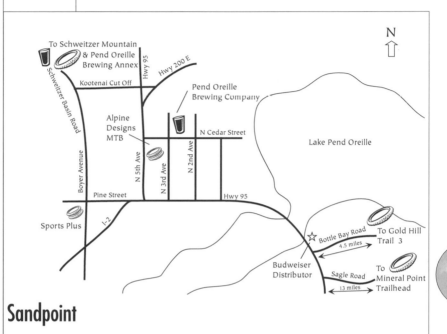

Sandpoint

DIFFICULTY: Intermediate to advanced. The elevation starts out right around 2200 feet, so that's not much of a consideration. However, it is still an extended climb with many switchbacks. Even though these switchbacks are incredibly designed and maintained, they may intimidate a less experienced rider. Riding from town obviously makes this a more aerobically demanding ride and raises the difficulty closer to advanced.

AEROBIC DIFFICULTY (1–5)

3

TECHNICAL DIFFICULTY (1–5)

3

WARNINGS: This beautifully constructed trail leading to incredible overlooks of the surrounding countryside is very popular with both mountain bikers and hikers. Always yield, say *Hi*, and check those brakes so you don't scare people on your way back down.

OTHER TRAILS IN THE AREA: On the other side of Gold Hill from Sandpoint is the **Mineral Point Trail,** a kinder, shorter, and even more scenic version of Gold Hill Trail 3. This trail can be done as an out-and-back from the Green Bay campground or as a loop by climbing on the campground-access dirt road and descending the Mineral Point Trail. The second option makes this an even easier ride as you don't have to contend with the singletrack while ascending the trail at 200 feet/mile. Although the Mineral Point Trail is only 2½ miles long, the **Lost Lake Trail** (whose trailhead is across the parking lot from the upper trailhead for the Mineral Point Trail) can add another 2½ miles plus the chance to spot a moose having brunch in Lost Lake.

Another B&B destination is **Schweitzer Mountain Resort.** The chairlifts run daily from June 25 to September 6 and cost $12.00 for a daily pass. More important is the fact that the Pend Oreille Brewing Company performs a public service by opening up its satellite brewpub on the mountain during special summer events. Call to see if today happens to be one at (208) 255-4557.

CONTACTS: U.S. Forest Service, Sandpoint Ranger District, Federal Building, 1500 Highway 2, Sandpoint, ID 83864; (208) 263-5111. Sandpoint Chamber of Commerce, 900 North Fifth Avenue, Sandpoint, ID 83864; (208) 263-2161.

MAPS: Maps for Gold Hill Trail 3 are almost unnecessary if you follow the directions previously given. Alpine Designs keeps a stock of the free Sandpoint Ranger District Travel Map, which will give you a good idea of the territory surrounding Gold Hill.

BIKE SHOP: Alpine Designs MTB, 312 Fifth Avenue, Sandpoint, ID 83864; (208) 263-9373. Not only is this the only year-round bike shop in town, it keeps stacks of all the Forest Service, state park, and topo maps of the area, and the employees aren't afraid to show you how to use them. These are also the folks behind Alpine Designs mountain bikes, and this is where the bikes are built. Right around the corner from the brewery, stop by and check out the facilities or find the company on the web at www.alpinedesignsmtb.com.

Another cool shop in town is Sports Plus, 102 South Boyer Avenue; (208) 263-5174. A little harder to find, this shop is known for its racing team. A top northwest team with many past members who have turned pro, these racers train by "riding the hell outta Gold Hill" from the shop. Interested in that kind of a group ride? Give 'em a call.

IDAHO

Pend Oreille Brewing Company

**220 Cedar Street
Sandpoint, Idaho 83864
(208) 263-SUDS(7837)
www.idahobeer.com**

A mural on the outside wall of the Pend Oreille Brewing Co. depicts the creation of beer from farm field to beer barrel.

ATMOSPHERE: Comfortable downtown pub where locals and vacationers both feel welcome.

THE BREW: The Pend Oreille Brewing Company is right on the main drag of downtown Sandpoint in a building originally used to sell tractors back in the 1950s.

Nowadays, thirsty B&B travelers can't miss the life-sized mural on the brewery's outer wall depicting the life cycle of beer. Showing beer from wheat field to wooden cask, the mural is a testament of the quality of beer waiting for you inside.

Pend Oreille offers a variety of ways to stay entertained as you enjoy Sandpoint's finest. A game room offering pool, shuffleboard, and video games and a separate cigar room reminds one of an old-fashioned card house and offers a comfy place to kick back with couches, arm chairs, and tables—with or without a stogie. Of course, the bar and shaded patio are readily available if a good pint of beer is all it takes for you to pass the time discussing the day's trails.

Once you've found a place to get more comfortable, a tasty array of beers will be your next quandary. And a pleasant one it will be with eight beers to choose from, all of them good, but some of them spectacular.

One of the two that you cannot leave town without trying is **Pend Oreille's IPA**—that's Idaho pale ale if you read the fine print. A multiple gold medal winner and local favorite, you may not even bother trying another beer the entire time you're here. Resist being so loyal because the **HooDoo Porter** is described as "a chocolate truffle in a glass." I'm not sure what that means, but it sure does sound tasty, though not nearly as tasty as the HooDoo really is.

PRICE OF A PINT: Happy hour is 4:00 to 6:00 P.M. when pints drop from $3.00 to $2.50, but for the real fun, there's "Over the Hump Wednesday" when pool is free, the music is live, and pints are only two bucks each. So from 8:00 P.M. until midnight on Wednesdays, just "get over it" at the Pend Oreille Brewing Company.

OTHER BREWS IN THE AREA: As mentioned, Pend Oreille has another brewpub on Schweitzer Mountain Resort. Although it's open all winter, it's only open for special events during the summer, so you better call (208) 255-4557 before making a day of it up there. The other beer place in town, named **Eichardt's,** is right next door to the Pend Oreille Brewing Company. It's not a brewpub but is renowned for a nice selection of quality micros.

153

Sun Valley

Named for the stretch of land surrounding the towns of Ketchum, Hailey, and Bellevue, picturesque Sun Valley is surrounded by the Sawtooth Mountain Range and National Forest. And, it's loaded with over 1100 miles of maintained singletrack at last count. Once a major sheep migration route, the town still holds the Trailing of the Sheep Festival each autumn when the sheep are herded though town to winter pastures. The town of Ketchum retains much of its historic charm and is now home to the internationally renowned Sun Valley Ski Resort. Only 8 miles south of the Sawtooth National Recreation Area, Sun Valley is a haven for outdoor sport enthusiasts year-round, the most recent addition being the mountain biker.

For a long time, Sun Valley successfully hid from the roaming eyes of traveling mountain bikers, and although Sun Valley still isn't as well known as other biking desti-nations in the Rockies, it offers what is probably Idaho's best riding. Throw in the Sun Valley Brewing Company down in the town of Hailey, and the set is complete. A true B&B mecca.

Greenhorn Gulch

THE SCOOP: Incredible loop on perfectly maintained trails. Great climb and even better descent.

RIDE LENGTH AND TYPE: 15-mile loop with many other variations available.

THE BIKE: The trail system to begin your indoctrination to this paradise lies right between Hailey (and the Sun Valley Brewing Company) and the posh resort town of Ketchum. You'll get a feeling for some of the wealth hidden in this valley as you drive past the ranches and homes along Greenhorn Gulch Road and to the waiting trailhead. Better yet, get the legs moving with a 6-mile warm-up along the paved bike path connecting Ketchum and Hailey.

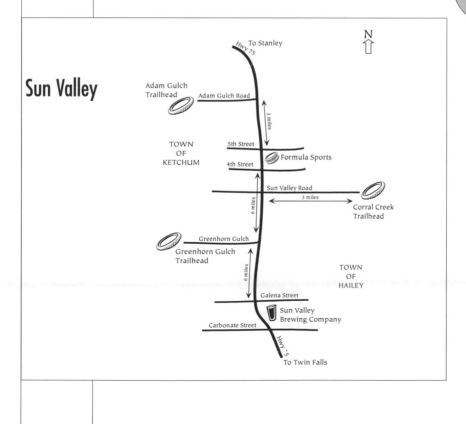

Sun Valley

The Sawtooth Mountain Range fades into the distance, looking south from the Mahoney Trail peak in the Greenhorn Gulch Trail system.

If this is your first time to Greenhorn, and you don't mind a little climbing, then the Greenhorn to Mahoney to Lodgepole to Mahoney and finally back to Greenhorn loop is for you. Sound confusing? It's really not. The trails are perfectly maintained (by Formula Sports), and all intersections are well posted.

The **Greenhorn Trail** begins with a moderate, well-trodden climb, but you soon find yourself on **Mahoney Trail,** where things get a little steeper, before intersecting with the **Lodgepole Trail**. Take the Lodgepole Trail, shift into your middle ring, and ride for the next couple miles while surrounded by lodgepole pines. You'll still be climbing, but it's at such a perfect grade, you'll hardly even know it. So many of these pines have become deadfall over the years that they look like giant match sticks strewn about the hillside. You will soon realize that this trail would become impassable without constant maintenance.

To get to the summit, you're gonna have to back down to the little ring and dig in a bit, but it's well worth it. Both the view of mountaintops stretching off into the distance in every direction and the impending descent will plaster a smile on your face and some drool on your chin.

Once you've taken in enough scenery, buckle up the chin strap and prepare for a 4-mile, 2000-foot descent of switchbacks, stream crossings, and choice singletrack all the way to the original Greenhorn Trail–Mahoney Trail split and the 1½ miles back to your car. Ahhhhhh!

DIFFICULTY: Intermediate to advanced. There's nothing easy about a more than 2000-foot climb at high elevation. The saving grace is the perfect construction and immaculately maintained trails that make this an unforgettable ride indeed.

AEROBIC DIFFICULTY (1–5)

4

TECHNICAL DIFFICULTY (1–5)

3

WARNINGS: The Sun Valley area weighs in right around 5900 feet in elevation. That means the oxygen is gonna be thin no matter where you decide to bike.

OTHER TRAILS IN THE AREA: A great little town-to-town ride, known as **Adams Gulch Loop**, leaves right from Ketchum. A 3-mile (mostly on paved bike path) ride north of Ketchum puts you at the trailhead. Ridden clockwise, the Adams Gulch Loop offers a quick 7 miles of dirt riding before the trip back to town for a total of 13 miles. If you have all day, then the **Adams Gulch Trail** is for you. An extended version of the Adams Gulch Loop, Adams Gulch Trail is a 22-mile ride from the trailhead with plenty of options for more exploration on the nearby **Fox Creek Trail** system.

Crazy mountain climbs make up the majority of the riding here in Sun Valley, but a kind and gentle ride can be found on the **Corral Creek Trail**. Corral Creek is a 7-mile bike path, the last 4 miles of which are dirt singletrack, with very little elevation gain throughout. This is as close a thing to a novice dirt ride as you'll find anywhere in the Rockies.

CONTACTS: U.S. Forest Service, Ketchum Ranger District, 206 Sun Valley Road, Ketchum, ID 83340; (208) 622-5371. Ketchum–Sun Valley Chamber of Commerce, 411 North Main Street, Ketchum, ID 83340; (208) 726-3423.

MAPS: Located back in the far reaches of Formula Sports is an area known as "The Library." It has free copies of write-ups for popular trails in the area and a topographic map under glass for all to look at and discuss the day's impending activities. The staff will be more than happy to help you find whatever trails you happen to be looking for.

BIKE SHOP: Formula Sports, 460 North Main, Ketchum, ID 83340; (208) 726-3194. No visit to Sun Valley would be complete without a stop in Ketchum, so you may as well make that stop at Formula Sports. The employees there will take care of you; they have a completely outfitted bike shop, "The Library" (as already described), and a prime location right on Ketchum's high-rent Main Street.

Where does Will Hamill, owner of Uinta Brewing Company in Salt Lake City, Utah, ride when he's not brewing beer? Greenhorn Gulch, that's where.

157

Sun Valley Brewing Company

202 North Main Street
Hailey, Idaho 83333
(208) 788-0805

ATMOSPHERE: An old car dealership turned brewery with a friendly light-wood décor, a separate family dining area around back, and a patio out front.

THE BREW: Sun Valley has been brewing its High Flying Beers since 1986 and added the restaurant in 1992. The brewpub now has this game down to a science with a nicely timed (and priced) happy hour, award winning beers, and great food—all in a casual user-friendly atmosphere (although the owners did have to remodel a couple of years ago to keep the tavern's rowdies from spilling over into the dining area.)

As for the brews, Sun Valley rotates through a selection of three or four seasonal beers but you'll always find the brewery's 1986 flagship and gold-medal winning **White Cloud Ale** on tap. It's an excellent, medium-bodied amber that makes for a perfect post-Greenhorn hydrator. If you want a little more kick in your diet, check out the **Y2K IPA** (India pale ale) (or whatever the brewer'll call it next year) for an excellent, nicely hopped India pale ale.

The locals know this place as much for the food as the beer. And there's a reason why. It's good. And fun. The Tiger Won Tons—won tons with a mixture of crab and cream cheese served with a sweet and sour sauce—may sound bizarre, but are really somehow perfect with a pint of White Cloud.

PRICE OF A PINT: Happy hour is from 4:00 to 6:00 P.M. every day of the week as long as you are at the bar, where the chips and salsa are free and the pints drop from $3.00 down to $2.00.

OTHER BREWS IN THE AREA: Sun Valley is not the only micro game in town. There is also a self-proclaimed "stealth brewery" known as the **River Bend Brewing Company.** You can't visit the premises, and the company doesn't bottle its wares but you can find River Bend beers around town at various restaurants or, get this, give the company a call and have a 2¼-gallon Party Pig delivered right to your door. Or bike. Or tent. Well, maybe not your bike, but just about anywhere in the valley with an address. Only $24.00, plus a refundable deposit on the Pig, and you get the same amount of beer as a case without all the hassle of bottles. You can't go wrong if hearty, real, unfiltered draft ale is what you want while discussing the day's trails around the fire. River Bend brews up five different recipes including the **'Round the Bend Pale Ale, Big Wood Bitter, Pica Pica Porter, Mere's Stout,** and a brown by the name of **Powder Pig Large Ale.** Yum, yum. So put in a call to (208) 788-8087 and find out what's in stock.

Twin Falls

As you near Twin Falls, dry, barren plains give way to the spectacular crossing of the Snake River Gorge on the Perrine Memorial Bridge—an impressive sight with the rushing Snake River surrounded by deep green golf courses on either side hundreds of feet below you. Just keep in mind that Evil Knievel attempted to jump this span in 1974 and was saved only by his parachute. Founded in 1904 and named for the nearby Snake River Double Falls (now but a single fall because of the hydroelectric plant since installed), the community was originally an irrigation center for the surrounding land. In fact, the area is nicknamed "Magic Valley" from the way these irrigation channels turned once barren scrub into some of the most productive farmland in the nation. Still an agricultural region, Twin Falls also serves as a perfect launching pad into the nearby Sawtooth National Forest.

The riding is a little way from town, but well worth the 30ish-minute drive it takes for real alpine riding. When you're done, it's just enough time to work up a thirst for the fine brews back in Twin Falls at Mugger's Brewpub. And what a brewpub Mugger's is! From the moment you walk through the door, you'll appreciate the pride taken in every aspect of the dining process: the surroundings, the service, the beer, and the food.

Third Fork of Rock Creek

THE SCOOP: A mountain oasis riddled with buffed-out singletrack.

RIDE LENGTH AND TYPE: 14-mile out-and-back, 14-mile loop, or 7-mile shuttle.

THE BIKE: About 30 miles southeast of Twin Falls, the Cassia Mountains (known locally as the South Hills) rises out of the arid southern Idaho plains. Inside this 303,000-acre mountain reserve is the longer than 50-mile multiple-use trail system known as the **Rock Creek Trail Complex.** This system contains trails ranging from slightly above novice all the way to advanced depending on which trails you ride, the direction you ride, where you start, and how long you decide to remain on them. Whatever you decide, you'll be riding through a creek valley that goes from high desert shrubs to lush aspens and conifer-shaded trails as you gain the higher reaches of the mountains.

The most popular ride in the area is along the **Third Fork of Rock Creek Trail.** This ride can be done as an out-and-back or as a loop with the return trip on pavement, making it considerably less challenging. The trail itself is 7 miles long, so if climbing at elevation isn't your cup of beer, drive your car or truck to the top of the mountain, descend to the **Third Fork Trailhead,** and save the 7-mile uphill return trip for the paved road leading back to your car. Or, better yet, have someone else climb back up to the car for you while you wait in the shade beside the creek!

If you're here for the workout, then start your ride from the Third Fork Trailhead, which sits at an elevation of 5200 feet, and start climbing singletrack to the 6800-foot summit near Magic Mountain Ski Resort. From the lower trailhead, you're looking at narrow singletrack for the first 3½ miles before Third Fork meets the **Little Fork Trail (no. 163)**. Take the Little Fork Trail, which is used by 4x4s, meaning the trail will widen a bit as you get closer to the top. Not to fear, the black soil here is very forgiving and, rather than a rutted and rocked-out mess, you have a smooth widetrack that only slightly loses its attraction for mountain bikers. Truth be told, novices will find it a very forgiving trail.

DIFFICULTY: Beginner to Intermediate. By parking at the top and descending to the Third Fork Trailhead, the ride is almost for novices. Start at the bottom and climb to the top, and you're looking at a straight intermediate ride.

AEROBIC DIFFICULTY (1–5)
Downhill 2
Uphill 3
TECHNICAL DIFFICULTY (1–5)
Downhill 2
Uphill 3

WARNINGS: This is a multiuse trail system, so you will encounter motorcycles, horseback riders, hikers, 4x4s, and other mountain bikers. Be careful going around the blind corners and downhill at speed. The Rock Creek Trail Complex has many, many spurs, branches, and loops all

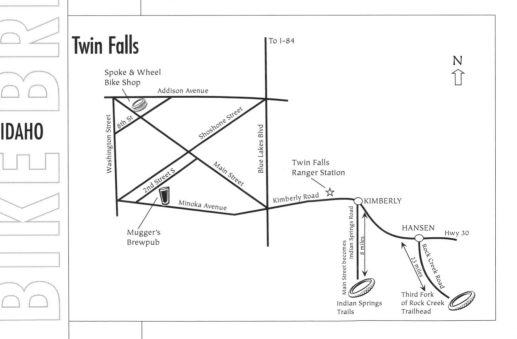

Twin Falls

To I-84

N

Spoke & Wheel Bike Shop
Addison Avenue
Washington Street
8th St.
Shoshone Street
Blue Lakes Blvd
Main Street
2nd Street S
Minoka Avenue
Kimberly Road
Twin Falls Ranger Station
KIMBERLY
Mugger's Brewpub
HANSEN
Hwy 30
Main Street becomes Indian Springs Road
8 miles
Rock Creek Road
23 miles
Indian Springs Trails
Third Fork of Rock Creek Trailhead

going someplace else, so be sure to secure a free map from the Ranger Station in Twin Falls.

OTHER TRAILS IN THE AREA: For a more advanced variation of the Rock Creek Trail, take the **A-H Creek Trail (no. 167)** to the **Wahlstrom Hollow Trail (no. 238).** These trails will have you climbing up a much steeper incline before dumping you back into the Third Fork Trailhead. Also, during cooler months, a desert area known as **Indian Springs** (under the purview of the Bureau of Land Management) offers many miles of desert-type riding. Free maps created by the Southern Idaho Fat Tire Association are available at local bike shops.

CONTACTS: U.S. Forest Service, Twin Falls Ranger District Office, 2647 Kimberly Road East, Twin Falls, ID 83318; (208) 737-3200. Twin Falls Chamber of Commerce, 858 Blue Lakes Boulevard North, Twin Falls, ID 83301; (208) 733-3974.

MAPS: Whatever way you decide to tackle Rock Creek, make sure you stop by the Twin Falls Ranger District Office. It has free trail maps of the Rock Creek Trail Complex along with other valuable information about the surrounding national forests.

BIKE SHOP: Spoke & Wheel Bike Shop, 148 Addison Avenue, Twin Falls, ID 83301; (208) 734-6033. Located right at the old downtown outskirts and not far from the brewpub, the folks at this shop will make sure you arrive at the trailhead with everything you need except you still have to go to the Ranger's Station for copies of the Rock Creek Trail Complex map.

Mugger's Brewpub

516 Second Street South
Twin Falls, Idaho 83301
(208) 733-8159
www.muggersbrewpub.com

ATMOSPHERE: With one of Al Capone's Prohibition Era brewing tanks out front and his copper brewkettle still in use in the brew house, you know you're in for a treat as you walk into this building. On the National Historic Register, it originally did time as a flour distribution center.

THE BREW: This place is the perfect setting for a little relaxation after a long day on the trails. It has everything you want in a brewpub: historic character, comfortable atmosphere, sitting room and library, separate dining area, fireplace, shaded patio, real darts, free pretzels, fine cigars, and, most important of all, lots and lots of good beer on tap.

At any one time you're gonna find about 10 beers on tap, but with 30 different styles brewing throughout the year, the exact flavors change weekly. However, you'll always find the **Fall Down Brown** and **Honey Blonde** on tap as they are the locals' favorites. And because Mugger's employees regularly receive well-warranted death threats whenever they run out, **Mugger's India Pale Ale** is also a sure bet.

In addition to these staples, you'll usually find at least one Belgian-style beer on tap. As true to form as a Belgium beer can be when brewed here in the United States, the **Trappist White**, the **Belgian White**, and the very popular **Belgian Strong** all make the rotation regularly.

The screened-in outdoor patio, shrouded in hop vines, is also a real treat. With old industrial silos as an odd but scenic backdrop, the patio features an outdoor pool table and attracts nationally touring bands throughout the summer.

PRICE OF A PINT: Finish your ride and make it back here between 5:00 and 7:00 P.M., and you can knock 50 cents off the $3.00 price of a pint.

OTHER BREWS IN THE AREA: This is one of the few B&B pairs with no other brews in the immediate area, and to be honest, no others are needed—Mugger's is that good.

CHAPTER THREE

MONTANA

As the largest Rocky Mountain state with over a quarter of its 147,000 square miles of landmass being national forest lands, Montana was a sure bet to be a biking and brewing bonanza. Unfortunately, for all the Bike & Brew potential Montana promises on paper, all is not well in the Big Sky State. A powerful Tavern Association, afraid of what a few barrels of fresh beer might do to the market, is giving Montana a microbrew struggle similar to what other states go through for mountain-biking trail access.

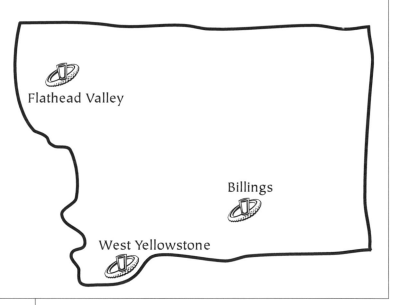

Flathead Valley

Billings

West Yellowstone

As such, Montana is the last remaining state yet to legalize brewpubs as the rest of the country knows them. State law still prohibits a brewery from owning a restaurant even though a recent law change allows a brewery to offer 48 ounces (3 pints), or less, per patron. But only if the establishment closes by 8:00 P.M. Some view this as the first logical step to eventual brewpub legalization, while others believe this new law will soon be repealed.

Thus far, only the Wolf Pack Brewing Company in West Yellowstone operates under this new law. Other microbreweries have gotten around the law by joining forces with a restaurant entity and setting up what, for all intents and purposes, are brewpubs—that is, they offer craft beer brewed on the same premises where food is being served. The problem with this arrangement is the lack of long-term commitment between the two businesses. As soon as any differences arise, or space becomes an issue, one of the businesses will move out. End of brewpub.

Currently, there are three exceptions that look like they will stand the test of time—and meet Bike & Brew's stringent criteria of great beer near great riding. These establishments are in Bigfork, West Yellowstone, and Billings. Places to look for a brewpub in the near future are the popular college towns of Missoula (Iron Horse and Bayern Brewing recently split) and Bozeman (long-time Bozeman fixture, Spanish Peaks, recently moved to California). Helena, the state's capital, already has the Sleeping Bear Brewing Company in place, but the attached restaurant is undergoing a change of ownership. Still, all three of these towns are ripe for a brewpub and already offer plenty of great riding.

On the riding front, Montana has no shortage of trails thanks to the extensive national forests. Unfortunately, few of these trails are set up and maintained with mountain biking in mind. The result usually is that the trails are steep and technical. But, not to fear, the bike shops are very accommodating, and everyone involved can suggest somewhere, regardless of your ability, for you to go and get in the dirt.

Billings

The old Montana Power Company is now home of the Montana Brewing Company in downtown Billings.

As the largest city between Minneapolis and Portland, Billings is a major commerce hub with a thriving historic downtown business district. Not the mountain paradise often associated with the Rocky Mountain states, Billings sits in the Yellowstone River Valley on the Great Plains. Still, Billings serves as gateway to Yellowstone National Park, the Battle of Little Bighorn National Monument, and the ski and resort town of Red Lodge. And, even though Billings is Montana's largest city, it's not so large that you can't get in a good town-to-town ride from the brewery.

Fittingly enough, Montana Brewing Company is also the state's largest brewpub, and the folks involved make it look so easy and natural you'll wonder why there just aren't more like it in the state. It almost brings a tear to the eye. The riding in Billings is plentiful and, if you have the time to journey south to the Red Lodge area, you're in for a whole new world of fun.

Rimrock Trail

THE SCOOP: Slickrock, arid desert, and cliff-top riding—no, not Moab, rather Billings, Montana.

RIDE LENGTH AND TYPE: Variable—16 miles out-and-back town-to-town as described with another 6 miles of dirt possible.

THE BIKE: Rising from the middle of downtown Billings are the sandstone cliff walls known locally as the Rimrocks. Winding along the edge of these cliffs is the **Rimrock Trail** and some 9 miles of singletrack overlooking downtown Billings. Three main sections of trails compose the Rimrock Trail System: the 3-mile Boothill Trail; the 31/2-mile Zimmerman Trail East; and the 21/2-mile Zimmerman Trail West. All three trails follow the Rimrock cliffs, but each has very different characteristics.

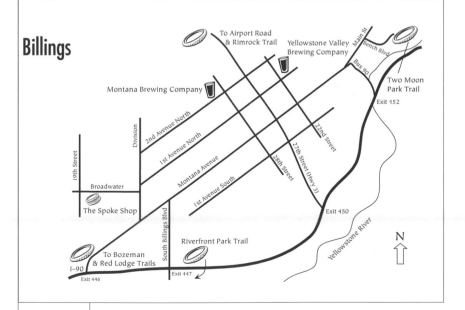

The Boothill section—named after the Boothill Cemetery where most of its occupants were buried with their boots still on—sits on the eastern end and is the least developed of the three **Rimrock Trail** sections. The trail runs through Swords Park, a popular teenage make-out and party locale. And despite a prohibition against motorized off-road vehicles in this area, there are still plenty of indicators showing that this prohibition is pretty much ignored. The trails in this area are harder to follow, and signs of past parties such as broken glass and garbage are a constant problem.

The middle section, Zimmerman Trail East, is much better. The trail is more developed and although there is still a lot of broken glass lying about, the trail in this area is very entertaining with more than half of the trail traversing sandstone slickrock.

The third and shortest section, Zimmerman Trail West, is the best. You have left civilization behind, and the trail becomes more challenging, offering tight turns, plenty of short challenging climbs, and some spectacular cliff-hugging riding. In fact, it's reminiscent of the Fruita section of the famed Kokopelli's Trail, only overlooking the town of Billings instead of the Colorado River.

The recommended way to bike these trails is a town-to-town route leaving from and returning to the brewery. (What did you expect? This is Bike & Brew America after all!) From the brewery downtown, head north on **Twenty-Seventh Street** toward the towering Rimrock cliffs. About 2 miles of pavement and a 400-foot climb finds you at the top of the sandstone bluffs and at **Zimmerman Trail East,** which begins immediately to your west. Carefully make your way off Twenty-Seventh Street, climb over the guardrail and to the cliff side. You will almost immediately spot the trail snaking off along the top of the Rimrocks.

Follow this trail, which never strays far from the cliff's edge and alternates between bumpy slickrock and hard-packed singletrack. This middle section crosses some private property (quite literally through people's backyards, so please—by riding courteously through these areas—respect the landowners who have graciously allowed this activity). The farther west you travel, the more scenic the trail becomes and the farther you leave civilization behind. By the time you reach Zimmerman Trail West, you are in uninhabited woods and about to enter a mix of county parkland and undeveloped private land.

Press on across Zimmerman Trail Road to **Zimmerman Trail West,** and you will be winding through huge boulders, trees, cliff outcroppings, and fantastic views of the Yellowstone Valley—all on a mix of slickrock and dirt trails. The ride ends much too soon when you come to a mesh fence signifying the private property of an underenlightened landowner. Please turn around and try not to think about what you're missing as you retrace your tracks back to the brewpub and a pint of cheer.

DIFFICULTY: Intermediate. The trail is tight and winding in a few spots, enough to keep everyone interested but nothing that will stump the careful intermediate rider.

AEROBIC DIFFICULTY (1–5)

3

TECHNICAL DIFFICULTY (1–5)

3

WARNINGS: No matter how you decide to follow the trail, you will be biking along a cliff edge that is hundreds of feet above the valley's floor. Be very careful when near the edge, and never ride when it's wet. This warning has nothing to do with trail erosion. This type of sandstone slickrock gets very slippery when wet, and one wrong move can send you over the edge. Aside from possible more permanent damage, you could be late for happy hour.

OTHER TRAILS IN THE AREA: Also, right in Billings are two short loops reachable by bike from the brewery, just perfect for beginner mountain bikers working up a thirst. **Two Moon Park Trail** offers riding unique to the area, with singletrack following the Yellowstone River among tree coverage and abundant wildlife. And probably the easiest trail in the area is **Riverfront Park Trail,** which offers 5 miles of mild river-bottom trails along the Yellowstone River.

The best ride in the Red Lodge area is a 22½-mile ride called **Sykes Ridge Trail.** Way out of the normal B&B

range, being well over 2 hours from the nearest brewpub (not to mention the hour or so of shuttle time), it's still worth the effort if you have the time. Just make sure you pick up a copy of the *South Central Montana Mountain Biking Trail Guide* mentioned in the Maps paragraph to help get you there. You will descend almost 5000 feet, cross through the Pryor Mountain Wild Horse Range, take in beautiful vistas of Big Horn Canyon, and pass by no less than six caves on your way to the waiting shuttle vehicle.

CONTACTS: Billings Department of Parks & Recreation, 510 North Broadway, Suite F14, Billings, MT 59101; (406) 657-8371. Mountain Bike Adventures, P.O. Box 1706, Billings, MT 59101. Billings Chamber of Commerce, 815 South Twenty-Seventh Street, Billings, MT 59101; (406) 245-4111.

MAPS: The Spoke Shop carries free copies of *South Central Montana Mountain Biking Trail Guide,* which gives detailed directions to 18 mountain-bike rides in the Billings and Red Lodge area, including all the trails mentioned here.

BIKE SHOP: The Spoke Shop, 1910 Broadwater, Billings, MT 59102; (406) 656-8342. Rated as a Top 100 Shop in the country by *Bicycler Retailer and Industry News* and *VeloBusiness,* this is the place to come for service when in Billings. Not only can you pick up a free *South Central Montana Mountain Biking Trail Guide* and get trail advice to go with it, the proprietor and employees also place your welfare as a traveling cyclist on top of the list when it comes to road repairs. Just be sure to tell them what you're up to. The Spoke Shop is your bike's home away from home when you're on the road.

Montana Brewing Company

113 North Broadway Avenue
Billings, Montana 59102
(406) 252-9200

ATMOSPHERE: Large glass windows along the front keep the place bright and cheery while offering views of downtown Billings.

THE BREW: Since December 1994, an area staple has been the Montana Brewing Company. Located in the old Montana Power Company building, Montana Brewing Company has a great location right on North Broadway Street with plenty of outdoor sidewalk and patio seating to take in the prospect of Montana's largest city.

Inside this Montana marvel you'll find a large, open, dining area. Behind glass along the dining room wall is the elusive 10-barrel brewing system belonging to the Billings Brewing Company.

Billings brews up some fine beers beginning with the multiple Great American Beer Festival medalist, the **Sharptail Pale Ale.** Very, very hoppy, almost an IPA (India pale ale), this beer is the local favorite and Montana's flagship brew. Not quite in it for that much hop? The **Blind Boar Amber** is an excellent English mild ale with a low alcohol content, making this one an excellent "session beer" with which to discuss the merits of the day's trails. Montana Brewing Company also pours its **Custer's Last Stout** off nitrogen, making for a very smooth, very creamy, very drinkable stout.

Montana Brewing Company recently hired a new brewer, Sheldon Scrivner, away from Prescott Brewing Company down in Arizona. He's just getting his feet wet, but his first beer, a German hefeweizen, proved to be an excellent example of a German wheat beer and a sign of great things to come. Expect more German recipes from Montana Brewing Company in the future as they are Sheldon's preferred style of beer. If the hefe is any indication, Billings is in for a real treat.

PRICE OF A PINT: Happy hour pints are only $2.00 from 4:30 to 6:30 P.M., Monday through Friday, so please time your rides accordingly.

OTHER BREWS IN THE AREA: If you happen to be in town Thursday or Friday evening, then **Yellowstone Valley Brewing Company** has a place for you. Located in a warehouse just east of downtown Billings, Yellowstone opens its doors to the public for sampling on Thursday and Friday afternoons. With names like **Wild Fly Ale, Renegade Red, Black Widow Stout,** and **Wooley Bugger Root Beer**—you'll soon realize that the owner and head brewer, George Moncure, is a passionate fly fisher and names his libations accordingly.

Not only is George a fly fisher and mountain biker, he was a Ph.D. geochemist in a former life and uses a spectrometer to measure the shelf life of his beers. You'll never have to worry about dead beer when you choose Yellowstone Valley. Operating since 1997, Yellowstone is in seven states with plans for expansion. He distributes by keg and bottle so stop by, try the flavors, talk about fish or trails, and pick up a six-pack or growler to go.

Finally, a cool little mountain town called Red Lodge, about an hour southwest of Billings, is loaded with mountain biking. It even had its own brewpub for a while. Unfortunately, a parting of the ways left the **Red Lodge Ale House** safely in its downtown location and **H&H Brewery and Tap Room** down the road in a sheet-metal warehouse. Both are worth checking out if you make the drive down for some trail time.

Flathead Valley

Surrounded by the Whitefish, Swan, and Mission Ranges and taking up 191 square miles, breathtakingly beautiful Flathead Lake is the largest natural freshwater lake west of the Mississippi. The lake lies in the Flathead Valley, which starts about 60 miles north of Missoula and is home to the Flathead Indian Reservation, resorts, and many, many campgrounds. This region of Montana is an outdoor playground and offers access into the surrounding state forests, national forests, wilderness areas, Glacier National Park, and the ski town of Whitefish.

Flathead Valley

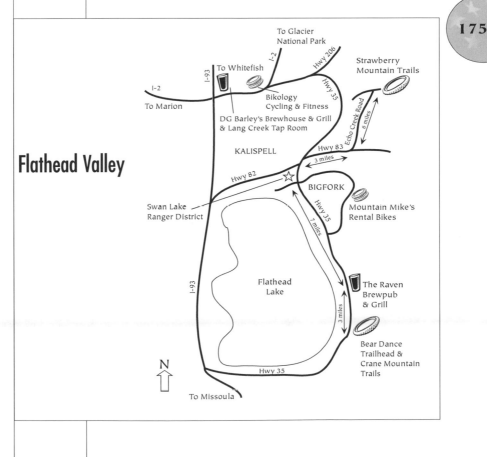

Strawberry Mountain

THE SCOOP: Miles of mountain trails to explore with epic ride potential.

RIDE LENGTH AND TYPE: Variable—interconnecting trail system or 20-mile Loop-N-Berry epic.

THE BIKE: Located right on the northern edge of the Swan Lake Ranger District in the Flathead National Forest is the **Strawberry Lake Trail System.** Names like **Cheeseburger with the Works Trail, Pickle on the Side Trail, Downhillers' Demise Trail,** and **One-Way Trail** prepare riders for what's in store as they approach the range of mountains circling Flathead Valley.

The lower reaches of the mountain are filled with a dark, conifer and fern-filled forest. This place is densely vegetated and collects moisture like a sponge, but the rocky soil ensures that the trails drain well and are still very rideable after a storm.

Most trails on Strawberry Mountain stay between the elevations of 3200 and 4000 feet. The exception is the **Loop-N-Berry** ride that takes you over and around the top of Strawberry Mountain. A 20-mile epic, plan on a full-day excursion with a 2-mile stretch on **Trail 37** where you'll be climbing at close to 1000 feet/mile. Not exactly a fun thought. But once you're over the 6400-foot summit, you'll be rewarded with a screaming downhill, Strawberry Lake, and unforgettable views of the Flathead Valley. This is definitely an advanced ride and should only be attempted after mid-July by experienced back-country riders.

By sticking to the network of trails lower on the mountain, you'll find plenty of singletrack, short but challenging climbs, killer downhills, and memorable views of the

Flathead Valley and Flathead Lake. This last option is definitely the recommended way of visiting Strawberry Mountain unless, of course, you like pain, suffering, and trails covered in snow until the end of July.

DIFFICULTY: Intermediate to advanced. By sticking to the lower reaches and reading the map's trail descriptions to find out what a trail offers, you'll be fine. But if you start thinking about Loop-N-Berry, crank the difficulty to advanced and the aerobic and technical ratings to 5 each.

AEROBIC DIFFICULTY (1–5)

3

TECHNICAL DIFFICULTY (1–5)

3

WARNINGS: This is bear country. In fact, you are only about 15 miles from the most bear-infested area in the lower 48 states—the Great Bear Wilderness—where seeing a bear is about as common as seeing an antelope in Wyoming. So this is the one time it's considered cool for your bike to squeak, rattle, and clang. In fact, noise is a good thing, so the addition of bear-bells, handlebar ringer, or clown horn would not be considered foolish. Standard procedure in bear country is the more noise you make the better; give the bears plenty of warning and hope they head in the other direction. Regardless of what you remember from Grizzly Adams, they really don't want to encounter you any more than you want to encounter them.

OTHER TRAILS IN THE AREA: Flathead Valley is filled with trails. Nearest to The Raven Brewpub & Grill, and a very nice pub-to-pub ride, is **Bear Dance Trail (no. 76)** to **Phillips Trail (no. 373)**. Bear Dance and Phillip's are both steep and technical (still nothing compared to Trail 37 on Strawberry Mountain), but constitute the only national forest dirt access to Crane Mountain near the pub. A 3-mile road ride south on State Highway 35 from The Raven takes you to the Bear Dance Trailhead. Take Bear Dance about ½ mile to the well-maintained and marked Phillips Trail (no. 373). Phillips is about the most moderately inclined trail on this side of Crane Mountain and will take you up to a multitude of old logging roads. You'll find miles of exploring possibilities on these dirt roads before heading back down the hill and the 3-mile cruise back to the pub for some much needed B&B recreation.

Another great resource for mountain biking in the area is **Mountain Mikes Rental Bikes** located in downtown Bigfork. Not only does Mike bartend at The Raven on Monday nights, he also owns a tour company and can lead you onto some of the sweetest trails in the area. Agreements with many of the landowners in the area allow him to take you to trails on Crane Mountain generally unknown or inaccessible to others. He can make these as easy or as demanding as you, the customer, would like.

CONTACTS: U.S. Forest Service, Swan Lake District Office, 200 Ranger Station Road, Bigfork, MT 59911; (406) 837-7500. Bigfork Chamber of Commerce, 8155 Montana Highway 35, Bigfork, MT 59911; (406) 837-5888. Kalispell Chamber of Commerce, 15 Depot Loop, Kalispell, MT 59901; (406) 758-2800.

MAPS: Detailed maps of Strawberry Mountain are available free from Bikology Cycling and Fitness in Kalispell. The rangers at the Swan Lake District Office in Bigfork also have a free *Open Roads Map* that gives a fairly detailed view of the major roads and trails used for hiking, biking, and horseback riding in their district. They also have a "Swan Lake Ranger District Trails Inventory" pamphlet that gives detailed directions to the trails in the area. Just remember; the ranger station information is geared more toward hikers than bikers, and even though bikes are allowed on most hiking trails in the district, what makes a good hiking trail does not always make a good mountain-biking trail. Steep grades and deadfall keep many promising hiking trails from cutting the mustard. However, good singletrack is out there; you just need to know where to look. Strawberry Mountain's trails will get you started and Crane Mountain will keep you going.

BIKE SHOP: Bikology Cycling and Fitness, 428 East Idaho Street, Kalispell, MT 59901; (406) 755-6748 or (888) 755-BIKE. Located in the nice town of Kalispell, this is a full-service bike shop just down the street from DG Barley's Brewhouse & Grill. This is also where to come if you're looking for a free map and directions to the Strawberry Lake Trail System. If you're sticking to the Big Fork area, check out Mountain Mikes Rental Bikes, 1063 Swan River Road, Bigfork, MT 59911; (406) 253-BIKE(2453). Need to rent a bike or looking for a guided tour of Crane Mountain, give Mike a call or stop by his bike hut on Mill Street in the little hip downtown of Bigfork, home of the world-famous "Wild Mile." An extreme kayaker's delight, paddlers travel from all over the world to try their hand at this stretch of whitewater surf.

The Raven Brewpub & Grill

25999 Highway 35 South
Bigfork, Montana 59911
(406) 837-2836

"Beer education takes a dive when hunting season starts."

—NEAL BROWN, BREWER AND OWNER OF RAVEN BREWING, LAMENTING THE START OF HUNTING SEASON AND HOW HUNTERS WOULD RATHER SPEND THEIR MONEY ON BULLETS AND GAS THAN GOOD BEER.

ATMOSPHERE: Caribbean cool meets western lakeside restaurant and brewery. Excellent cask-conditioned beer and exotic cuisine, including sushi on Thursday nights, keep the regulars coming back again and again.

THE BREW: A funky little Caribbean Blue building right on the shores of the immense Flathead Lake. You walk past seashell Christmas lights into a mismatched and brightly colored collection of tables and stools. The whimsical interior conveys an attitude of Bob Marley, beaches, and warm oceans, a feeling that is only enhanced by the huge three-pane glass windows overlooking the lake's crystal-clear water.

Outside, the bar has both an upper balcony with heat lamps for those cool mountain evenings and a lower patio with seating at picnic tables and colorfully painted cable-spool tables within touching distance of the rocky beach. The restaurant's dock butts right up to the lower patio, bringing in water-bound patrons and making room for a nice stroll out over the water to watch the western sunset (or to get a better view of the famous Polar Bear Plunge held January 1 each year).

The Raven Brewpub keeps four beers on tap at all times. Although the flavors change at the whim of the brewer, Neal Brown, you can expect a lighter beer for the masses and a mix of big beers just waiting for the enthusiasts to sink their teeth into. All of Raven's beers are unfiltered cask-conditioned ales. They are still served from regular

The Raven Brewpub & Grill sits on the shores of Flathead Lake, the largest natural fresh-water lake west of the Mississippi. Crane Mountain, a likely fat tire destination, rises beyond.

CO_2 taps, but the barrel conditioning gives them the "less fizzy" taste you're more likely to equate with an English pub than a brewery from the lakeshores of northern Montana.

Again, though you never know what may be on tap, Brown brews the unforgettable **Raven Bock**, which he cask conditions for up to 6 months! It's a real treat, very smooth and very dark, just like bocks were meant to be. His **Raven Stout** is a chocolate malt monster that offers plenty of raw flavors without any kind of lingering after-taste. In addition, he brews an excellent **Raven Scotch Ale** that also sees considerable time in the cask before making an appearance. All these beers just get better with age and, because he does a good deal of brewing during the slow winter months, by the time you'll be settling onto a bar stool, these beers will be just about perfect.

PRICE OF A PINT: There's no happy hour here to ease the $3.00 price per pint, and the place doesn't even open until 5:00 P.M. on the weekdays and 1:00 P.M. on summer weekends. These inconveniences seem minor once a pint is in hand and your feet are dangling in the cool blue water of Flathead Lake.

OTHER BREWS IN THE AREA: DG Barley's **Brewhouse & Grill**, 285 North Main Street, Kalispell, MT 59901; (406) 756-2222; www.barleysbrewhouse.com and www.langcreekbrewery.com. If you're not in the mood for a laid-back Caribbean atmosphere while visiting the Big Sky State, the opposite end of the spectrum awaits in Kalispell. What's the opposite of Reggae skewed views of Flathead Lake? How about a brand new, upscale, country-western–themed brewpub by the name of DG Barley's? Located in downtown Kalispell on the corner of State Highway 93 and State Highway 2, DG's sits in a strip mall sandwiched between two casinos. This is a modern, clean, family restaurant with old cowboy movies playing on the gift shop TV and country music playing over the stereo. An open doorway even leads from the bar area straight into the casino next door.

Even if the country-western scene isn't for you, the beer will be. Two doors down the strip mall is the **Lang Creek Brewery's Tap Room and Brewery.** Situated with its brewery right next to DG Barley's restaurant and with its brewhouse visible behind the bar, Lang Creek brews eight house beers for DG Barley's in addition to the six regular Lang Creek ales. Lang brews for the masses as well as the connoisseurs, and you'll find quality in all the DG prod-ucts, the most notable being the exceptional India pale ale called **Whitetail IPA** (India pale ale).

Also proving this is a beer joint, as well as a great restaurant, is the welcome presence of both nitrogen taps and hand pumps serving up both DG and Lang beers. The DG's **Pistol Packin' Porter** is usually available, as well as

Lang's **Scudrunner Dark** on nitro, hand pump, and CO_2, a great way to try all three serving methods and taste how each affects the flavor, smoothness, and character of the beer.

A visitor this close to the source would be remiss without giving a pint of Lang Creek's flagship beer, the **Tri-Motor Amber,** a test flight. Named after the 1930s classic Ford aircraft of the same name, this beer is an excellent example of an English amber ale. This brew has even won praise from noted beer expert Michael Jackson and should be on everyone's sampling list when in Montana.

West Yellowstone

Literally located at the western gate of the world's first national park, Yellowstone, West Yellowstone caters to the more than 3 million visitors who annually make this park their travel destination. As such, souvenir shops, ice-cream parlors, restaurants, and motels make up the bulk of downtown West Yellowstone. However, this influx of tourists also supports one more very important business: the Wolf Pack Brewing Company.

Because of the strange and restrictive Montana laws now starting to change, this is the only true brewpub in Montana where both restaurant and brewery have the same owners and operate under the new 48-ounce law. Beer lovers can only hope that it won't be long until someone with the necessary legal background (like Wolf Pack's owner Dan, who happens to be a retired judge) makes it a personal project to bring Montana's brewing laws up to speed with the rest of the United States.

Mountain biking is not allowed on Yellowstone National Park trails, but the Gallatin National Forest spreads out to the west of West Yellowstone and offers miles of legal trails including a section of the famous **Continental Divide Trail.** So, the next time you're visiting Yellowstone, bring your mountain bike, go for a ride of the Divide, and stop by the Wolf Pack Brewing Company to see what all those beer-loving Germans are coming over here to see. It sure ain't just Old Faithful anymore!

Lionshead Loop

THE SCOOP: "Ride the Divide" on steep, rocky trails offering up views of two national parks.

RIDE LENGTH AND TYPE: 15-mile loop or out-and-back more than 11 miles long.

THE BIKE: The **Lionshead Loop** offers close-up views of Hebgen Lake, Lionshead Mountain, Yellowstone National Park, and distant images of the Teton Range. The loop also offers steep and rocky, singletrack and doubletrack trails to reach these views.

A short detour from Lionshead Loop offers views of Hebgen Lake and Yellowstone National Park in the distance.

The first 1¾ mile stretch is a grueling 1100-foot climb left rutted and rocky from motorized travel. Oxygen will be in high demand, as you begin climbing at an elevation of over 6600 feet, so be sure to start the ride properly hydrated. You'll be hard-pressed to get a drink in edgewise during this demanding ascent. After that initial push, things eventually get a little better, and you'll soon be

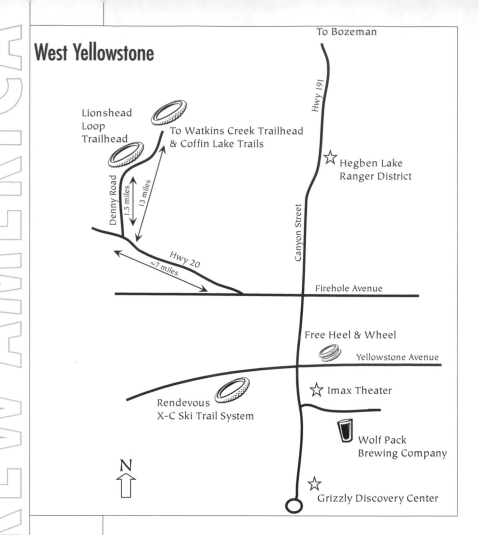

To Bozeman

Hwy 191

Lionshead
Loop
Trailhead

To Watkins Creek Trailhead
& Coffin Lake Trails

Hegben Lake
Ranger District

Denny Road

1.5 miles

13 miles

Canyon Street

Hwy 20

~7 miles

Firehole Avenue

Free Heel & Wheel

Yellowstone Avenue

Imax Theater

Rendevous
X-C Ski Trail System

Wolf Pack
Brewing Company

Grizzly Discovery Center

N

rolling through alpine forest with occasional views of both Hebgen Lake and Yellowstone National Park.

It won't be long until you round the mountain and see the bald, cliff-faced summit of Lionshead Mountain. After a quick descent and a chance to catch your breath, a final switchback climb brings you up to flowering mountain meadows at elevations of over 8200 feet. Straight ahead is the trail marker signifying the intersection of **Lionshead Trail** and the **Continental Divide National Scenic Trail** and your chance to "ride the Divide" so to speak.

By heading south (left) at the trail marker, you will be on the Continental Divide Trail with Lionshead Peak towering over you on your right (to the west). Hebgen Lake

MONTANA

and Yellowstone will be below on your left (to the east) and, on clear days, the Teton Range will be visible straight ahead, way off to the south.

If you prefer an out-and-back ride, anywhere along here is a good place to turn around and return the way you came. The Continental Divide Trail marker is 5½ miles from the Lionshead Trailhead, making for a nice cool 11-mile ride. Or you can continue along the Continental Divide Trail for a white-knuckle descent on some pretty rough doubletrack (in fact, most of the Continental Divide Trail is pretty rough doubletrack), where you'll take the first dirt road you see for a fast descent back to **State Highway** 20. The road branches a few times but as long as you keep heading down, you'll be fine. Even if you miss the turnoff to the dirt roads, the Continental Divide Trail eventually drops you out on State Highway 20 up on Targhee Pass. Just head east, and after a blistering fast downhill off the pass you'll be back to **Firehole Avenue** and on your way back to the Lionshead Trailhead.

DIFFICULTY: Advanced. Some hardcore climbing on less-than-ideal trails give this one a very difficult rating.

AEROBIC DIFFICULTY (1–5)

4

TECHNICAL DIFFICULTY (1–5)

4

WARNINGS: This is bear country so travel with some friends and make lots of noise. However, chances are that the most vicious creatures you'll encounter are the black flies. These critters are tough and can bite right through your shorts so bring plenty of Deet insect repellant, or you'll have more to worry about than just altitude on those climbs.

OTHER TRAILS IN THE AREA: A true novice trail, a rarity in the Rockies, is right on the edge of town. Called the **Rendezvous Cross-Country Ski Trail System,** its primary use is for cross-country skiing, but these trails make for an excellent afternoon of easy riding from town. Expect gently rolling hills through pine forests with trail markers and maps at every intersection.

Maybe the nicest intermediate trail in the area is the 6-mile out-and-back **Coffin Lake Trail (no. 209)**. Farther from town than all the others, this trail begins at the **Watkins Creek Trailhead** and follows an old dirt road for 2½ miles before becoming a singletrack trail and leading to Lower Coffin Lake at 7500 feet. A ½-mile footpath makes a great side excursion to Upper Coffin Lake. You're still gonna be climbing to get to these lakes but not nearly as harshly as on the Lionshead Trail. There's also a way to connect the Coffin Lake Trail with the Lionshead Trail to create a truly epic ride, but just make sure you have a current forest service map with you before you try that one.

CONTACTS: U.S. Forest Service, Hebgen Lake Ranger District, P.O. Box 520, State Highway 191, West Yellowstone, MT 59758; (406) 823-6961. West Yellowstone Chamber of Commerce, 30 Yellowstone Avenue, West Yellowstone, MT 59758; (406) 646-7701.

MAPS: The Hebgen Lake ranger's office has a free campground map showing the location of the Lionshead Trailhead and Watkins Creek Trailhead. The office also has free trail maps of the Rendezvous Cross-Country Ski Trail System right outside downtown West Yellowstone. Detailed national forest maps are available here for around $5.00.

BIKE SHOP: Free Heel and Wheel, 40 Yellowstone Avenue, West Yellowstone, MT 59758; (406) 646-7744. Located right across from the IMAX Theater's parking lot and the brewpub (and just about the last thing you see before entering Yellowstone Park), Free Heel and Wheel is the place to go in West Yellowstone for maps, directions, bike repairs, and java. That's right, bike shop meets Mocha Mamma's coffee house. Now you have it all: java, directions, and beer, all within a block.

Wolf Pack Brewing Company

111 South Canyon Street
West Yellowstone, Montana 59758
(406) 646-PACK(7225)
www.wolfpackbrewing.com

ATMOSPHERE: A corner joint tucked away between the IMAX Theater and Grizzly-Wolf Discovery Center with picnic-table seating outside and a small, but friendly, pub inside.

THE BREW: West Yellowstone is a T-shirt–wearing tourist town where a bag of ice costs almost $2.00 and a McDonald's dinner for two will top $25.00. However, among the western-style façade buildings, a little off the main drag, with an indoor seating capacity of only 48 persons, the Wolf Pack Brewing Company seems the antithesis of everything that is West Yellowstone. In fact, the 20-barrel brewery takes up more space than the rest of the restaurant and really leaves room for only three things—great food, great German beer, and you. So, whether you're being served by the brewer, his wife, or the joking Frenchman who tends bar when he's not working as a bear-handler next door, you'll instantly feel at home and welcome right next to one of the largest tourist attractions in America.

In January 2000, Dan and Sherry Abraham opened the Wolf Pack Brewing Company. It's the only brewpub in Montana owned and operated by the same family. The Wolf Pack is run under the already-mentioned recent Montana law allowing a brewery to sell up to 48 ounces of beer to patrons for on-premises consumption. This may sound extremely prohibiting (and legally it is), but when all of Wolf Pack's beers weigh in between 4.9% and 5.5% alcohol by volume, three pints usually does the trick. Of course, if you're still thirsty, a 64-ounce growler to go is always available.

Dan brews only German ales and lagers in the tradition of Reinheitsgebot, the German Purity Law that allows only water, malt, hops, and yeast to be used in the brewing process. Dan takes this one step further by using only German malts, hops, and yeast. Although this doubles the cost of ingredients for Wolf Pack, this attention to detail is a veritable treat for you and earns praise for Wolf Pack's beers from both German tourists and fellow brewers.

The bar and brewery at the Wolf Pack Brewing Co. (COURTESY OF WOLF PACK BREWING CO.)

During the summer mountain-biking months, Wolf Pack keeps three or four different styles on tap including the **Lone Mountain Alt,** the **No. 10 Kolsh,** and the **Jim Bridger Marzen.** All of these beers are true to form, down to the glass they are served in. Close your eyes, take a sip, and you may as well be in Deutschland for all the difference you'll taste.

Brewpubs are generally a place for a somewhat more exotic cuisine than your typical chain restaurant. Wolf Pack embodies this characteristic with Sherry working the grill behind the bar. She starts off serving up an assortment of hot dogs, including Sabrett brand (New York City's finest), Polish sausage, and, of course, German brats. It doesn't stop there. Not only is Wolf Pack known as the only place in town for a real hot dog, it also has the reputation as the best place in town for sandwiches. Throw on some of Dan's homemade Wolf Pack ale mustard, and you'll forget all about the three-beer rule.

PRICE OF A PINT: Pints are $3.25 all day, and the pub stays open until 8:00 P.M. or so. Come in after 8 o'clock, and they'll still serve you up a cup of beer to go. You can sit right out on their patio while they clean up inside. How's that for a relaxed and friendly, downright German, attitude?

OTHER BREWS IN THE AREA: There are no other brewpubs in the area, but many fine microbreweries abound. The **Big Hole Brewing Company,** located in the vicinity in Belgrade, Montana, bottles and distributes an outstanding pale ale.

"Whenever he gets thirsty!"
—DENNIS, A.K.A. "PEPE," THE FRENCH BARTENDER–BEAR-HANDLER'S ANSWER WHEN DAN WAS ASKED HOW OFTEN HE HAS TO BREW.

191

CHAPTER FOUR

UTAH

Ranging from the seemingly barren but spectacular rock canyons and plateaus of the south to the alpine forests of the north, Utah may have the most diverse terrain in the Rocky Mountain states. Utah's broad range of landscapes makes for virtually every kind of mountain-bike riding imaginable and takes you from the dark loamy alpine singletrack of Park City to the desert of Moab and the famous Slickrock Trail with everything in between. And, though it's true that Utah offers some of the best riding anywhere, the land that brings you slickrock has some problems of its own.

What most people do not know about is the beer. Without special licenses, taverns in Utah can only serve 3.2% alcohol by weight (a.b.w.) beer, and brewpubs can only brew 3.2% a.b.w. brews. Although the 3.2 beer is still 4.0% alcohol by volume, and the breweries are always trying to maximize, it still prohibits really big beers and, for that matter, most medium beers as well.

Therefore, while traveling in Utah, you're often better off with beer styles that are traditionally brewed within this limit. American ales and lagers, American wheat beers (including the very popular fruit varieties), English milds, oatmeal and sweet stouts, bitters, and Scottish ales are all fairly common and can all be brewed true to style within this limit. However, you won't find any true porters, India pale ales, American pale ales, extra special bitters, English or American browns, doppelbocks, . . . and the list goes on. Nevertheless, you will find some clever simulations that are very tasty in their own right.

The best way to deal with the 3.2 law, as it's known locally, is by sticking to the traditionally lighter beers, as already mentioned, or by trying different serving methods offered by most of the brewpubs. Many brewpubs will serve a couple of their beers by using nitrogen instead of CO_2 or slightly warm and cask conditioned through a hand pump or "beer engine." Either method gives low-alcohol beers (or any beer for that matter) such a smooth and full flavor that you'll soon forget all about some silly 3.2 law. And although that law can be daunting to those seeking great beer, just remember Utah's microbrewed beers are still fresh and unique, and they will easily give even the most hardened Bike & Brew traveler something to smile about.

Utah

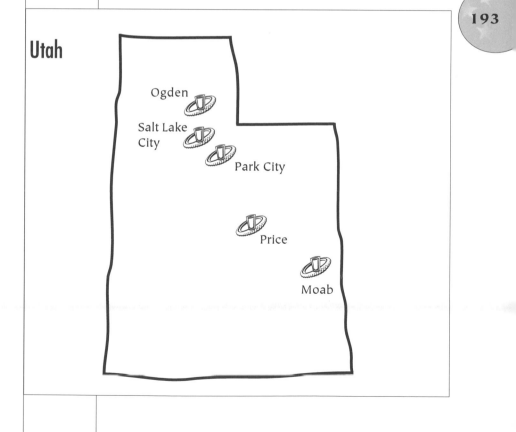

Moab

A land of box canyons, red rock towers, and delicate arches, Moab is certainly a place like no other on Earth. With Arches and Canyonlands National Parks for hikers and sightseers, the famous stretch of "Wall Street" for climbers, the Colorado River for rafters, and uncounted miles of the precious commodity known as slickrock for the mountain bikers, Moab sees over a million visitors each year. Say what you want: touristy, discovered, over-crowded, it's not like it used to be. You can say all that, but you know what? Who cares! Sure there are more peo-ple here now than ever before, but (for the most part) they're the kind of people you want to be around: healthy, athletic, hikers, climbers, rafters, and, of course, cyclists. You name it and they're here, and Bike & Brew America says, "Welcome!"

However, all things seem to level out in some strange way. Although Moab riding is second to none, its beer is prevented from equal greatness by the appalling statewide 3.2 law already described. So make the best of things and do more riding. Then do yourself a favor and go to Moab Brewery where the folks make the most of an uncomfort-able situation by putting out some darn good suds.

Klondike, Amasa Back, Porcupine Rim

THE SCOOP: The Mountain Bike Capital of the World needs no introduction.

RIDE LENGTH AND TYPE: Klondike Bluffs is a 15-mile, less than 2-hour, out-and-back. Porcupine Rim, a town-to-town trail with a splash of the Slickrock Trail, is a 34-mile, more than 5-hour loop. Amasa Back can be done as a 10-mile out-and-back, as a 10-mile loop, or as a 20-mile loop via Hurrah Pass and Jacob's Ladder.

THE BIKE: Moab has the reputation as a hardcore mountain-bike destination, and it's well deserved; no matter what direction you head out of town, endless miles of trails await. Sure, there are epic rides like the 100-mile **White Rim Trail** or the 140-odd-mile **Kokopelli's Trail**, but there are also kinder, gentler trails to introduce one to the splendors of slickrock, mesas, and red rock canyons— all that is Moab.

And that's where you might like to start—with the kind and gentle **Klondike Bluffs Trail** ride. If you like what you find here, then bigger, longer, and tougher trails are available. A great way to introduce yourself to Moab slickrock, this is as novice as a trail gets here at 4000 feet. You start out on a moderate dirt-road climb that leads to a large rock hill, which is the trail. Be sure to keep your eyes peeled for dinosaur tracks fossilized right in the rock you're riding on. Also, the trail terminates at the Arches National Park border. Stash your bike and hike the last ¼ mile to sit on the bluffs overlooking the park's canyons below. A very nice place to contemplate the world.

Now that we mountain bikers are veterans, it's time to move on to **Porcupine Rim Trail.** If you only have time for one ride in Moab, make it Porcupine Rim town-to-town if you can handle it. This is not a ride for the timid or weak of leg. Plan on at least 5 hours of desert biking, so bring a LOT of water, that is, camelback and two water bottles. Most of the climbing is on **Sand Flats Road** heading out of town about 7 miles. Bring a couple of bucks with you because there is a $2.00 per bike (or $5.00 per car) usage fee for the Sand Flat area. Once through, and as you've paid your fee anyway, you may as well stop off at the famous **Slickrock Trailhead** and do the 3-mile practice loop to get the flavor of pure slickrock. Then it's onward and upward to where the true goods lie.

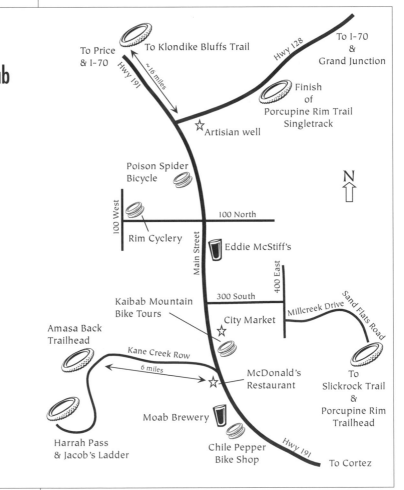

Moab

To Price & I-70

To Klondike Bluffs Trail

Hwy 191

~16 miles

Hwy 128

To I-70 & Grand Junction

☆ Artisian well

Finish of Porcupine Rim Trail Singletrack

Poison Spider Bicycle

N ⬆

100 West

100 North

Rim Cyclery

Main Street

Eddie McStiff's

400 East

Kaibab Mountain Bike Tours

300 South

Millcreek Drive

Sand Flats Road

Amasa Back Trailhead

City Market ☆

Kane Creek Row

6 miles

McDonald's Restaurant ☆

To Slickrock Trail & Porcupine Rim Trailhead

Moab Brewery

Harrah Pass & Jacob's Ladder

Chile Pepper Bike Shop

Hwy 191

To Cortez

Once at Porcupine's trailhead it's onto an old double-track for some fairly technical climbing. At the top, take a break and look out over Castle Valley spreading out to the northeast. Rehydrate, snap some photos, then prepare yourself for the descent of a lifetime. Technical difficulty, heat, speed, rock ledges, and continuous motion will dull the senses to the point where your mind may start drifting, and what looked like a perfectly fine piece of trail will have you belly up wondering what happened. Just when you think you've seen and conquered it all, the double-track becomes single, and the true technical riding begins. You'll be more than 3 hours into the game at this point, so drink some more of that water you were told to bring and have a snack. This next piece of singletrack is not the time to bonk.

Then with one last jump, you're on **State Highway 128** on your way back into Moab. Be sure to stop at the artisan well at the junction with **State Highway 191** for a water break, or emergency fill if you've run dry. Then it's on to the Moab Brewery to complete the rehydration process. To ease up on the difficulty of this ride, take a shuttle up to the trailhead.

Been here, done this? Make it a bit more difficult and ride the Porcupine in the opposite direction by starting at the singletrack of Hwy 128 and riding up!

And then there is **Amasa Back Trail**, a local's favorite. There are about as many ways to do Amasa as Moab has trails. Here are three classics. Well, two anyway, the third is bound to be classic soon. One, you can do the basic out-and-back. Time tested and true, everyone's first introduction to the slickrock shelves of Amasa should be as a straight out-and-back, or up-and-down, as the case may be. Two, recently, a way down the backside has been created to make Amasa a loop. Take the right-hand trail just after you cross over the old water pipe on the main trail. This section gets into some nice singletrack with sections of intense difficulty. Three, try Amasa Back via **Jacob's Ladder.** Got all day? Take **Hurrah Pass** out for about 10 miles. That should put you up on top of the pass looking down into **Jackson Hole**. Take the dicey-looking double-track down. Be sure to take the two right turns (one right at the bottom of the pass and the other 4.6 miles after you have started the loop around the Hole.) This leaves you

197

looking up at a 400-foot hike-a-bike up (Jacob's Ladder) onto Amasa Back; follow an old water pipe most of the way up. It looks pretty bad from the bottom, but once you get started you'll be up in no time. Then it's all downhill via Amasa Back. The whole way is moderate in technical difficulty, but is definitely rated as an advanced ride because of its sheer length.

DIFFICULTY: Klondike is beginner and both Porcupine Rim and Amasa Back are intermediate to advanced: intermediate riders will survive, advanced riders will thrive.

AEROBIC DIFFICULTY (1–5)
Klondike Bluffs 2

Porcupine Rim 4

Amasa Back 4

TECHNICAL DIFFICULTY (1–5)
Klondike Bluffs 2

Porcupine Rim 4 (singletrack finish is a 5)

Amasa Back 3

WARNINGS: Is it just me or is Moab a desert? Please, remember your water and always bring more than you think you can drink. Trust me. Also, cryptobiotic crust is everywhere. Beware of the dark thin mineral crust on much of the soil out here. It's a critical part of the desert soil-building process so be careful not to step, ride, or urinate on it. And Moab is not an amusement park. Trails are rarely marked, and an infinite number of trail spurs exist on all trails. Go to Chile Pepper bike shop, get good directions, buy or copy maps, bring a compass, and know how to use these tools or ride with someone who does.

OTHER TRAILS IN THE AREA: Unlimited. The Chile Pepper bike shop will take care of you once you've exhausted the three trails already described.

CONTACTS: Bureau of Land Management, Grand Resource Area, P.O. Box 970 or 885, South Sand Flats Road, Moab, Utah 84532; (435) 259-6111 (District); (435) 259-8193 (Resource Area). Moab Chamber of Commerce, 805 North Main Street, Moab, UT 84532; (435) 259-7814.

MAPS: There are many, many maps of the Moab area. These range from locally copied hand-drawn maps of specific trails to waterproof, tear-proof, 100% plastic topographic maps. These range from $8.00 on up, but if you plan on biking here for any length of time, be sure to get one. This is a big dry desert, and you want to know what's out there if you happen to take a wrong turn at the big rock that looks like a donkey.

BIKE SHOP: There are a multitude of excellent bike shops in Moab. The closest to the brewery happens to be Chile Pepper, 702 South Main Street, Moab, UT 84532; (435) 259-4688 or (888) 677-4688; www.chilebikes.com. A nice laid-back atmosphere, plus the shop sells pint glasses. Buy one and take it next door to fill up at the Moab Brewery while your rig gets straightened around after a long day on the trails.

However, with so many shops to choose from, make sure you find the shop you're most comfortable with as all carry different manufacturers, stock different parts, and deliver a different atmosphere. If you feel you're being treated as just a number, go somewhere else. Three other great bike shops include Rim Cyclery (very friendly), Poison Spider (showers!), and Kaibab (good all-around shop). All are close to the Moab Brewery, and all offer expert service and sales.

Moab Brewery

686 South Main Street
Moab, Utah 84532
(435) 259-6333

ATMOSPHERE: Moab Brewery greets you with a large, noisy, tavern feel. The dining room and kitchen are off to the right, bar and brewhouse off to the left. A Chile Pepper Moab Schwinn hanging between. The bar offers TV and pool; a comfortable porch out front allows you to watch the hustle and bustle of Moab's main drag.

THE BREW: Okay, Bike & Brew America is going against the grain on this one (pun intended). Eddie McStiff's is the hands-down traditional favorite and most well-known brewery in town. McStiff's features over a dozen beers with everything from a **Pure Desert Wheat** to a **Black & Blue Blueberry Stout.** But, as so often is the case in both biking and beer, quality means so much more than quantity. So move over Stiffy's 'cause there's a new kid in town. Enter Moab Brewery.

Although the Moab Brewery is the relative new comer to Moab (established in 1996) and it only has 6 or 7 beers on tap (compared to 12 or 13 at Stiffy's), what it does have is quality. Remember you're dealing with the insidious 3.2 law, so what you can't get in alcohol you better be getting in taste. Moab delivers a fuller, more complete flavor in even its lightest beer, the **White Water Lager,** than the Stiffer does in some of its stouts! Want a little more punch for the buck? The **Scorpion Tail Ale** is the best pale in town and, if you're a red drinker, the **Derailleur Red Ale** smacks the barley and hops outta anything Stiffy keeps on tap. The Moab Brewery even takes advantage of brewing technology to spice up this alcohol desert we mountain bikers all pay homage to by putting its **Black Raven Stout** on nitrogen. Not usually a high-alcohol beer to begin with, Black Raven on nitrogen will have you thinking friendly thoughts about Utah beer in no time.

PRICE OF A PINT: During regular business hours you're looking at $2.75 a pint.

OTHER BREWS IN THE AREA: The time-tested and traditional favorite **Eddie McStiff's** is right down the street from Moab Brewery and sports the famous Eddie McStiff image above the door. Where McStiff's gives you a cozier feel with fun little rooms done in a desert motif and a relaxed biker, come-as-you-are atmosphere, it does not give you much in the way of quality beer. However, if you happen to fall into the same-old-thing trap, order up the **Chestnut Brown Ale.** A good beer, it has more flavor and a better finish than most, so you won't have to start pouting.

Ogden

Originally laid out by Mormon leader Brigham Young in 1850 and incorporated in 1851, Ogden has come a long way. Located on the thin strip of land between the Wasatch Mountains and the Great Salt Lake, Ogden is perfectly situated to take advantage of both the high-alpine mountains to the east and the recreation available on the Great Salt Lake to the west, including the popular Antelope Island, home to a herd of buffalo and 25 miles of single-track and doubletrack hiking and mountain-biking trails.

Just minutes up the road from Salt Lake City, you'd be doing yourself a huge disfavor by not hitting Ogden for a little Bike & Brew adventure. B&B pairs this close to each other are unusual, but in this case, an exception seemed warranted. Stop in and see why.

Ogden

UTAH

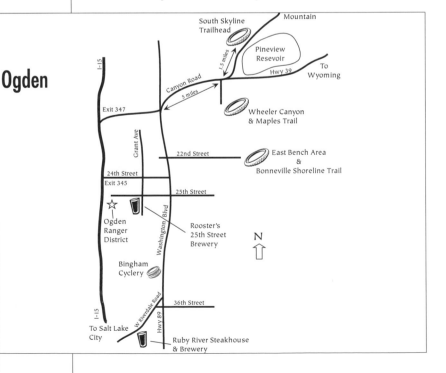

South Skyline Trail to Lewis Peak

THE SCOOP: Epic riding, out-of-this-world descent.

RIDE LENGTH AND TYPE: 20 miles out-and-back or, more accurately, up and down.

THE BIKE: Don't mind a little work? Then how does climbing almost 3000 feet to the summit of 8031-foot Mount Lewis sound? If you're still interested, Ogden has got the trail for you! After parking at the **South Skyline Trailhead** at Pineview Reservoir, you cross the street, and the trail will immediately begin switchbacking above the reservoir. Bring your climbing legs and settle into a comfortable routine, as this is pretty much your life for the next 2 hours. As the reservoir dwindles below, you get your first glimpse of why this is called Skyline Trail— Mount Ogden and the rest of the Wasatch Front Range are right there staring you in the face! Intermixed with the incredible views are trees, hawks circling *below* you, lizards, and wild flowers everywhere. But it's the Wasatch peaks you won't be able to keep your eyes off of— especially after you've climbed to a point where you're almost level with them.

The trail itself is superbly maintained, so it's hard to get lost. Just stay on the main trail by going left at all intersections until a sign to Lewis Peak specifically tells you to go right. FYI, around the 7-mile mark there is a branch in the trail that goes to the north. This is the way to the more technical **North Skyline Trail** and the way to make a complete day of it with an additional 15 miles of single-track (those are one-way miles).

Also at the 7-mile mark, the trail begins to roller-coaster a little, giving those climbing muscles a break before the final push to the summit. When you see the summit marker, dig in and dig it! Now you can just sit back and enjoy about as much of the Salt Lake Valley and Wasatch Front Range as it is possible to see by bike. And, if you look real hard, you can see Rooster's 25th Street Brewery down below off to the southwest—but that's getting ahead of ourselves, now isn't it?

After taking in the view, hop back on the ride and begin enjoying all those hard-earned miles. Got brakes? Check, 'cause you're gonna need 'em. You'll probably have to stop just to repressurize your ears, and it's then that you'll realize you're only halfway down. . . . Yeah!!

DIFFICULTY: Intermediate to advanced. Skyline Trail is no place for beginners. Intermediate riders willing to take a breather every once in awhile will have a great ride.

AEROBIC DIFFICULTY (1–5)
4
TECHNICAL DIFFICULTY (1–5)
3

The fruits of your labors at the top of Skyline Trail. The 8031 ft. summit of Lewis Peak with 9572 ft. Mount Ogden rising beyond.

WARNINGS: Trees, shrubs, and the contour of the mountain make for limited trail visibility. On your way back down, please ride in control and keep an eye out for upward-bound traffic.

OTHER TRAILS IN THE AREA: For a kinder, gentler ride, check out **Maples Trail** (also called **Wheeler Canyon**). The trailhead is located just below Pineview Reservoir dam, on the south side of the road. Park here and you're looking at a 2-mile climb on a hard-packed dirt road. Another 2½ miles of easy singletrack can be added once you get to the top for an out-and-back easy-going 9-mile total.

Closer to home is the East Bench area, Ogden's part of the **Bonneville Shoreline Trail** (described further under Salt Lake City). This trail can be reached straight from the brewery by following Twenty-Second Street east until it dead ends. Expect a mix of trails in the area with something for everyone right on the edge of town.

CONTACTS: U.S. Forest Service, Ogden Ranger District, 507 Twenty-Fifth Street, Suite 103, Ogden, UT 84401; (801) 625-5112. Ogden Chamber of Commerce, 2393 Washington Boulevard, Ogden, UT 84401; (801) 621-8300.

MAPS: A free trail guide is available at the Ogden Ranger District that outlines these trails and more.

BIKE SHOP: Bingham Cyclery, 3259 Washington Boulevard, Ogden, Utah 84401; (801) 399-4981. These folks know the trails and how to get you to them. Plus the owner, Joel Bingham, rides with Steve Kirkland, the brewer over at Roosters. Need I say more?

Rooster's 25th Street Brewery

253 Twenty-Fifth Street
Ogden, Utah 84401
(801) 627-6171

ATMOSPHERE: Historic brick building with a casual yet stylish bistro atmosphere. The outdoor patio is a real treat with plants covering everything, umbrellas to keep the heat off, and only a wrought iron fence between you and the action out on historic Twenty-Fifth Street.

THE BREW: Built in 1890, the building's first business was the Kansas City Liquor House. Destiny has now come full circle, and libations are once again top priority at this address. Walking into the two-story building, you'll face a stairway to the second floor and a bar continuing down the length of the main floor. If you're just in for a beer, settle right there and order yourself a cold one. If you have food on the brain, then head immediately to Rooster's incredible patio. Just remember, you have to order food if you're planning to drink out there. Don't ask, it's just Utah. Besides, Rooster's not-to-be-missed Chile Verde appetizer makes everything okay anyway, so all you have to do is sit back and enjoy.

Once you're settled in, it's time to order up a brew. All the regular house beers are nice, but the seasonals are what'll turn your head. Check what's on tap when you arrive. If you can't find a seasonal to sink your teeth into, the **Polygamy Pale** is a nicely hopped beer with a curious name and is always a good place to start. Got a hankering for a little mocha flavor, then check out the **Junction City Chocolate Stout,** a flavorful beer with a nice coffee finish.

PRICE OF A PINT: No happy hour when last checked, so expect a $2.95 price tag.

OTHER BREWS IN THE AREA: Ogden is also home to **Ruby River Steakhouse & Brewery** at 4286 Riverdale Road if you're looking for a little variety.

Park City

A silver mining town from the mid-nineteenth century, Park City survived three devastating fires during the first 30 years of its existence, the last of which completely destroyed the small mountain town. By 1920, Park City was completely rebuilt with a mind on its original character. Today the town appears to be the same alpine mining town of old. In 1963, Park City became home to its first ski resort, which was followed by two more, and is known worldwide as a premier ski destination.

Even more recently, Park City has become a destination for another sort of sport, mountain biking. This place was one of the first ski towns to embrace mountain biking as THE summertime alternative. And, after 20 some years of mountain biking on the slopes of Park City Mountain, and being home to the Wasatch Brewing Company since 1986, this place has bikes and beers down to a science. This is a major Bike & Brew destination, and any trip to the Wasatch Mountains should include it.

Park City Mountain Resort and Deer Valley Resort

THE SCOOP: Miles and miles of singletrack all leaving from the brewery's front door.

RIDE LENGTH AND TYPE: Variable—about 3½ miles to the 9000-foot summit; then get as creative as possible on your way back down.

THE BIKE: Before there was Bike & Brew America there was Tour des Suds, a historic sprint up Park City Mountain Resort's ski slope where a keg of beer awaited the victor—and anyone else who happened to make it up there. The keg is no longer there, but the trail that inspired such

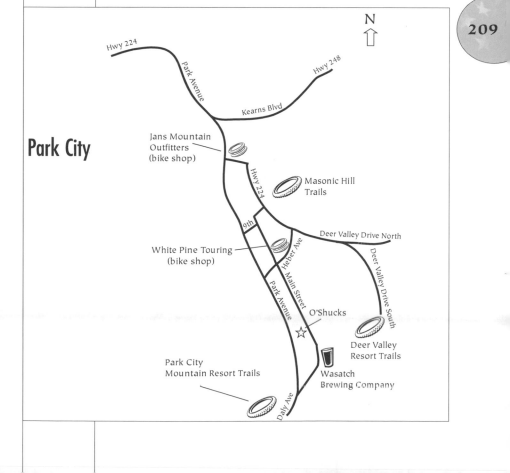

Park City

heroics still is. And, even though the trail is now just one of dozens crisscrossing the mountain, it's a perfect way to induct yourself into Park City culture and relive a little mountain-bike history at the same time.

You can park right behind the Wasatch Brewing Company to make the eventual transition from mountain biker to beer connoisseur that much less painful. From this prime locale, head south on **Main Street**, which soon becomes **Daly Avenue,** which soon turns to dirt. Continue past the gate and old silver mining ghost town until you see a line of huge boulders. Hang a left here, and orange trail directional signs will light the way up the historic **Tour des Suds Trail**, a switchbacked singletrack ascent of the mountain. Of course, there are easier ways up the hill—dirt roads, paved roads, even chairlifts—but to really earn the title of Sud's Master, you gotta suck it up and take the singletrack.

The author takes a break for some much-needed bike maintenance.

After this acclaimed ascent through pine and aspen forests, make a game out of finding as many singletrack miles as possible on the way back down. Some classics to look for when out on the mountain are **T.G. 1, Spiro Trail, John's Trail, Sweeny's Switch Backs,** even **Twist and Shout** over on the Deer Valley side—all classics, all singletrack, and all downhill from here. And the best part? No matter how you come down, there it is—the brewery's patio calling you in to add a little Suds to your Tour at the Wasatch Brewing Company.

DIFFICULTY: Novice to advanced. When the Deer Valley lifts are running (or with a friendly shuttle up to the top of Guardsman Road), any level of biker can enjoy the scenery and descents offered by both Park City Mountain and Deer Valley ski resorts. Intermediate riders can bike up the dirt roads, and advanced riders can get their fill on any of the singletrack snaking up the hill. Be sure to pick up the latest copy of the free *Hiking-Biking Trail Map* available at all Park City bike shops as well as at the Visitors Bureau for a complete listing of trails and their difficulty levels.

AEROBIC DIFFICULTY (1–5)
Going up the hill 4

Coming back down 2

TECHNICAL DIFFICULTY (1–5)
Going up the hill 4

Coming back down 3

WARNINGS: Watch for uphill-bound trail users on your way back down.

OTHER TRAILS IN THE AREA: In addition to the infinite number of variations on the resort's slopes, there are the **Masonic Hill Trails** and the **Gambel Oak Trail**. These are beginner to intermediate rides on two parallel trails—a newer, wider trail right above the older, more technical (but still only moderately so) trail.

For the easiest way up the mountain, check out the Sterling lift ticket packages offered by **Deer Valley Resort,** ranging between $7.00 and $16.00 per rider. This may be just the ticket you were looking for.

CONTACTS: Park City is rare in the fact that most of the trails are on private land. Contact numbers therefore vary accordingly, but the following are all good bets. Park City Chamber and Visitors Bureau, 1910 Prospector Avenue F11, Park City, UT 84060; (435) 649-6100 or (800) 453-1360. Mountain Trails Foundation, (435) 649-6839. Deer Valley Lift Ticket Information, (800) 424-3337 or (435) 649-1000.

MAPS: In conjunction with various interest groups, Park City publishes a free *Hiking-Biking Trail Map* of the area.

Outlined, by level of difficulty, are Park City Mountain Resort, Deer Valley Resort, and various other local trails.

BIKE SHOP: There are two great bike shops in Park City. The first one you will come to is Jans Mountain Outfitters, 1600 Park Avenue, Park City, UT 84060; (435) 649-4949. Talk to the guys in back who will hand you a copy of Park City's *Hiking-Biking Trail Map,* grab a marker, and proceed to outline the must-do trails of Park City.

The other shop is just as good and a bit closer to the brewpub. And you know how B&B America likes to keep things close to the brewpub! Check out White Pine Touring, 201 Heber Avenue, Park City, UT 84060; (435) 649-8710. From here, map in hand, it's a half-mile to the brewery and not much farther from there to the trails.

"No self-respecting beer guide would leave it out."
—ANONYMOUS, CONCERNING THE MERITS OF THE TOUR DES SUDS TRAILS.

Wasatch Brewing Company

250 Main Street
Park City, Utah 84060
(435) 645-9500

ATMOSPHERE: Surely designed with Bike & Brew America in mind, Wasatch caters to thirsty bikers like that place with the golden arches caters to hungry preschoolers. (No references to mentality here, just enjoyment level.) Housed in a relatively newly constructed, open wood building on the edge of Park City's cool historic downtown business district, the Wasatch Brewing Company offers another perfect B&B location just waiting for you to finish your day on the slopes.

THE BREW: Located right at the base of the mountain, Wasatch is the last business you pass on your way up to the Park City Mountain Resort trails and the first to greet you on your way back into town from them. With an outdoor patio just off the street, this place is perfect to watch other deliriously happy bikers descend from a day of carving fresh turns on the slopes. Just remember; to enjoy such a fine seat, you don't need to palm the host or hostess a ten spot, but you do have to order food. It's The Law.

However, if you're not quite ready to break the fast with anything other than barley and hops, then stay put at the downstairs bar or head to the second floor where pool tables, TVs, another bar, and another deck are all just waiting for you to drink beer without wasting your palate on food. Confused and haven't got the Utah drinking laws down yet? Don't worry, neither has anyone else.

Regardless of where you settle, you'll be enjoying Utah's first brewpub's handcrafted beers in a comfortable, casual wood-timbered setting. As per usual with Utah brewpubs, Wasatch brews up excellent wheat beers—including the insanely popular "Number 1 Microbrew in the Country" **Wasatch Raspberry Wheat.** From the wheat beers, go directly to whatever happens to be today's cask-conditioned beer, regardless of what it actually is. The cask-conditioning process and serving technique lower the level of carbonation, temperature, and beer filtration. These changes combine to give the lighter Utah 3.2% alcohol by weight beers a fuller, more-rounded flavor. A much better beer. Don't believe it? Try a sampler of the regular tap beer head to head with the same recipe cask conditioned—Wasatch carries both. The difference is truly amazing and will make a cask lover out of you.

PRICE OF A PINT: The happiest hours are from 3:00 to 5:00 P.M. when the cost of a pint goes down from $3.50 to $2.50. Not bad for a ski town with a perfect network of trails within spitting distance of the brewpub.

OTHER BREWS IN THE AREA: Park City is home to only one brewpub, but a fun place to hang with the biking crowd is **O'Shucks** just down Main Street from Wasatch. Don't expect much in the way of fine dining here, but do expect good prices on the beer and a lively crowd.

Price

Since the railway between Salt Lake City and Colorado was completed in 1883, over a billion dollars in coal has been extracted from this region of Utah. To support this industry, Price, known for its ancient Fremont Culture rock art and for dinosaur fossil discoveries, is now the agricultural, mining, and tourism center for Carbon and Emery Counties, collectively known as "Castle Country." Located on the cusp of the Wasatch Plateau, visitors to this area can experience everything from desert and canyon conditions to mountains within minutes of each other.

About 120 miles southeast of Salt Lake City and about halfway between Salt Lake City and Moab, this is the perfect place to stop, stretch those legs with a ride, and have a beer during one of your regular pilgrimages. What's classic about these rides are the history, scenery, and location. For the most part, the roads are a little too smooth to make these technical rides, but Castle Country is still an excellent opportunity for anyone looking for some dirt miles in a remote area that offers the unique opportunity to glimpse American history from the seat of your bike.

Harvey Trestle Loop and Consumer Road

THE SCOOP: Mostly dirt roads with great scenery, archaeological ruins, and lots of history.

RIDE LENGTH AND TYPE: A loop ride from Pinnacle Brewing Company totals out at 22 miles of dirt and paved-road riding.

THE BIKE: If dirt-road riding is your thing or you happen to be traveling through and need to get in some nonthreatening dirt miles, Price has just the thing for you. Within an hour (or so) drive of Price are almost 20 mountain-bike rides. Although most of these are dirt roads or double-tracks—they all offer fantastic views of the area known as Utah's Castle Country.

One ride, perfect for working up a little thirst, covers the **Harvey Trestle Loop.** This ride begins just outside of Price, so you can park downtown or save yourself the trip later and park right at Groggs Restaurant and Pinnacle Brewing Company. Traveling south from the brewery for 1½ miles on **North Carbonville Road,** you soon cross Highway 6 and turn onto residential roads. These become dirt as you follow the sporadically placed brown scenic biking symbols and find yourself in Pinnacle Canyon (coincidentally, also the brewery's namesake). As you climb out of the canyon, it's not hard to imagine Butch Cassidy making his getaway after robbing the Castle Gate mine in 1897.

Following the road above the canyon, you soon come to railroad tracks. Cinch down your helmet strap because this is where the ride gets a little rougher as you descend into the Gordon Creek gorge. If you're inclined for a little exploration, upstream from the railroad bridge are waterfalls and downstream are Fremont Culture petroglyphs. Once you decide to climb out of the gorge, cross under the trestle and climb up the opposite side. Following more dirt roads, you soon come to the paved **Consumer Road** and a downhill high-speed ride all the way to **Highway 6, North Carbonville Road**, and your seat on Pinnacle Brewing Company's patio.

DIFFICULTY: Beginner to intermediate. The total distance of the ride is 22 miles, which may put this out of the reach of some beginner cyclists. The terrain itself is mostly groomed dirt and paved roads. Things get a little dicey as you descend into the gorge, but nothing that can't be navigated on foot if need be.

AEROBIC DIFFICULTY (1–5)

2

TECHNICAL DIFFICULTY (1–5)

2 (because of the descent
into the river gorge)

WARNINGS: The Harvey Trestle Loop and Consumer Road sees significant mining and energy company vehicles

Price

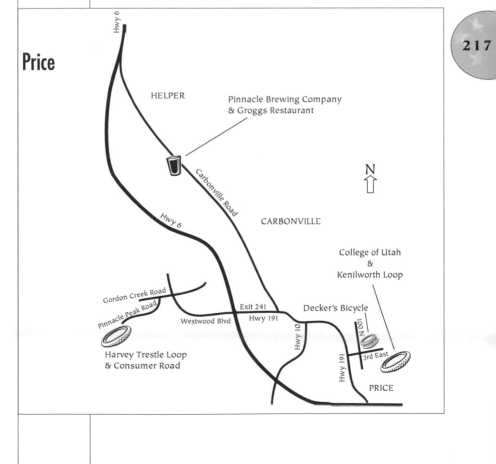

Hwy 6

HELPER

Pinnacle Brewing Company
& Groggs Restaurant

Carbonville Road

Hwy 6

CARBONVILLE

College of Utah
&
Kenilworth Loop

N

Gordon Creek Road

Pinnacle Peak Road

Exit 241

Decker's Bicycle

Westwood Blvd   Hwy 191

Hwy 10

Hwy 191

100 N

3rd East

Harvey Trestle Loop
& Consumer Road

PRICE

so be aware that on graded dirt roads and paved roads you may see motorized vehicles. Summer in Castle Country frequently sees temperatures climb over 100 degrees. Get your ride in early and bring lots of water. Also, the American Artifacts and Antiquities Act protects the ruins in these regions. Don't disturb them, and you won't have to go to jail.

OTHER TRAILS IN THE AREA: The **Nine Mile Canyon Trail,** located about 30 miles northeast of Price, is known for its concentration of Fremont Culture ruins, petroglyphs, and pictographs. At the brewpub, pick up the self-guided tour book covering the canyon called *9 Mile Canyon: A Guide* and head out for rides that can be as long as you like. The canyon is actually much longer than implied by its name, which is due to a government mix up when deciphering the maps of the area presented by explorer John Wesley Powell. Again, prepare yourself for more dirt-road riding through some of the area's most remote and unique regions.

Closer to home is the **Kenilworth Loop.** About 14 miles in length, this one leaves right from the bike shop in Price and, after a mild climb, offers excellent views of the town and surrounding areas.

CONTACTS: Utah's Castle Country Travel Region, P.O. Box 1037 or 90 North 100 East, Price, UT 84501; (435) 637-3009 or (800) 842-0789. Carbon Counties Chamber of Commerce, 90 North 100 East, Price, UT 84501; (435) 637-2788.

MAPS: *Utah's Castle Country Mountain Biking Guide* is a free publication that contains step-by-step instructions on all the riding in Carbon & Emery Counties including the rides listed here. It's available at Decker's Bicycle, but one note of caution: even though the turn-by-turn instructions are invaluable, the distances listed in this guide are sometimes a little off, so individual creativity may be required.

BIKE SHOP: Decker's Bicycle, 279 E100 North, Price Utah 84501; (435) 637-0086. This is the place to go to pick up your copy of *Utah's Castle Country Mountain Biking Guide* as well as the place to take care of any last-minute repairs or questions.

Pinnacle Brewing Company and Groggs Restaurant

1653 North Carbondale Road
Helper, Utah 84526
(435) 637-2924

"Looks like you're gonna have to get out there and do a little riding."
—COMMENT BY DECKER'S BICYCLE EMPLOYEE WHILE DISCUSSING THE MERITS OF DIFFERENT TRAILS IN THE AREA.

ATMOSPHERE: Located in a small, inconspicuous building between Price and Helper on Carbonville Road, Pinnacle Brewing Company is known by the locals for its excellent food and relaxed family dining. All you really need to know is that there's riding outside and fresh beer inside.

THE BREW: Kind of out on its own between the towns of Helper and Price, ask anyone to point you in the right direction. You walk into a hearth room and dining room having light-wood décor with farm implements hanging on the walls. The bar serves and separates the two, so settle there or head right out to the patio and order yourself up one of the five regular beers on tap. This is hot country in the summer months, as reflected by the beers offered. The menu lists two fruit wheat beers, and they both offer what you have come to expect out of Utah; tasty and light, something you could drink all day out in the hot sun. The local favorite is **Pinnacle's Amber,** a nice caramel-colored beer with low carbonation and a pleasant malt taste. It's an excellent companion while sitting out on the deck listening to the trains go by on the nearby tracks. **Pinnacle's Pale** is where to go if you're looking for a little hop bite, and **Pinnacle's Porter** is perfect after the sun goes down. Stop in for a beer, make yourself comfortable, and order some food, 'cuz the locals already know what you're about to find out.

PRICE OF A PINT: No happy hour here, but you're still only looking at a reasonable $2.75 a pint.

OTHER BREWPUBS IN THE AREA: You'll have to look at Pinnacle as an oasis in the desert all mountain bikers know and love as Utah. It's open Sundays, and you can even drink beer out on the patio without having to order food along with it. How novel. There aren't any other brewpubs in the area; however, you can still pick up Utah's Uintah and Wasatch beers at the local stores.

Salt Lake City

Situated on the Wasatch Front, the strip of land separating the Wasatch Mountains from the Great Salt Lake, Salt Lake City was designed in 1847 by its Mormon founders. Noted for its broad, spacious blocks designed around the Temple Square, Salt Lake is now a thriving city in a thriving metropolitan area. This success has led to problems such as pollution and an outdated infrastructure, but it remains that Salt Lake City is the cultural center of the state. Cultural Bike & Brew opportunities? You bet!

Salt Lake City is loaded with brewpubs and dozens of biking opportunities right out of town. Cut into the rock outcrops above the city is a shoreline terrace, which was left behind by the ancient Lake Bonneville that once covered the entire Salt Lake Valley. This old shoreline is now home to the Bonneville Shoreline Trail that when completed, will stretch all the way from Provo to Ogden. And with hundreds of miles of other mountain-bike trails, most within an hour of the city, and four brewpubs and two microbreweries cranking out the suds, Salt Lake City is a premier Rocky Mountain Bike & Brew scene.

Literally right around the corner from each other are two fantastic pubs—both very similar, but one gets the nod for dining and the other for a biker-friendly atmosphere. The beer? It's like splitting hairs. First, to the trails.

Mueller Park Trail

THE SCOOP: Perfect singletrack, better-than-perfect views.

RIDE LENGTH AND TYPE: An out-and-back totaling 12 miles of singletrack, it can also be made into a 13-mile loop with the finish on pavement.

THE BIKE: Looking for perfect singletrack? Then how does this sound? A switchback-filled ascent, which never leaves you kissing your handlebars, through lush forest that only breaks for occasional views of the Salt Lake Valley. If this is what you crave, the small town of Bountiful (how perfect a name is that?) just north of Salt Lake City has the solution in the form of Mueller Park and the **Mueller Park Trail.**

The first 3 miles of perfectly smooth singletrack, with barely a root or a rock in the way, get you to The Rock where a branch in the trail offers a bench and incredible views of the Great Salt Lake and Antelope Island. If the trail was all you could handle up to this point, turn around and enjoy the ride back down. Got more in you? Then continue past The Rock for another 3 miles to the summit. Things get a little tougher on this section of the trail with erosion-preventing waterbars, loose-rock sections, small bridges to navigate, and a steeper incline. But the view! The whole valley now stretches before you, making the extra work all worthwhile.

Once you've reached the summit, you have a few options. One, go back down the way you came for one of the smoothest singletrack descents the Wasatch Front has to offer. Two, explore some of the off-shooting trails along the summit before returning down the way you came. Three, head down the other side of the hill. This last option puts you out on **Canyon Creek Road,** which

"It's like saying you can go mountain biking but you can't go down-hill."

—SQUATTER'S BREWMASTER AND EX-PRO MOUNTAIN-BIKE RACER, JENNIFER YOHE, WHEN DESCRIBING BREWING WITHIN UTAH'S 3.2% ALCOHOL BY WEIGHT LAWS.

empties into **Bountiful Boulevard**. Take a right, pass the golf course, and turn right on **Mueller Park Road** to complete the loop.

Then it's back to 2600 South and Nielsen's Frozen Custard, which *Men's Journal* listed as one of the 100 Best Things to Eat in America, to hold you over for the trip back to Salt Lake City and some of the best brews Utah has to offer.

DIFFICULTY: Beginner to intermediate. The first 3 miles is about as novice as biking up a mountain can be. Which is to say, not that easy considering you're starting at an elevation of 5000 feet. After The Rock, things get a little sticky, and intermediate is the best way to describe it.

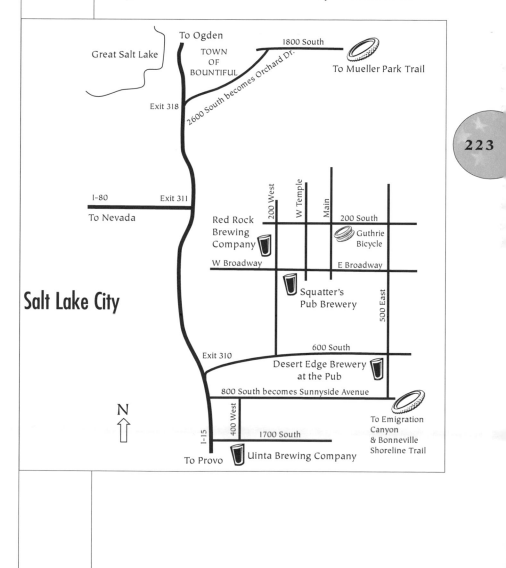

AEROBIC DIFFICULTY (1–5)

Up to The Rock 2 and 3 thereafter

TECHNICAL DIFFICULTY (1–5)

Up to The Rock 2 and 3 thereafter

WARNINGS: Mueller Park Trail is a very popular trail in the area. Not only will you encounter other bikers, but hikers are even more common, especially up to The Rock's scenic overlook.

OTHER TRAILS IN THE AREA: The **Bonneville Shoreline Trail** is a mountain-bike trail system that, when completed, will stretch all the way from Provo to Ogden. Much of the Salt Lake City part has been completed and offers singletrack options leaving right from downtown. So if the drive to Bountiful is too much for you, stop by Guthrie Bicycle downtown for a map and directions to the nearest trailhead. Ask about the **Bobsled** section for a particularly tasty slice of track.

The most popular high-elevation ride in the area is the **Wasatch Crest Trail.** This is an advanced ride along the top of the Wasatch Front that offers up to 20 miles of trails. Please be aware that bikes are only allowed on the **Millcreek Canyon** sections of the trail on even-numbered calendar days.

CONTACTS: Bountiful Department of Parks & Recreation, 150 West 600 North, Bountiful, UT 84010; (801) 298-6220. Bicycle Utah Vacation Guides, *Great Salt Lake Country Hiking and Biking Guide,* P.O. Box 738, Park City, Utah 84060; (435) 649-5806. Salt Lake City Chamber of Commerce, 3330 South 700 East, Suite H, Salt Lake City, UT 84101; (801) 467-0844.

MAPS: The *Great Salt Lake Country Hiking and Biking Guide* lists almost 20 rides in the Salt Lake City area. It is available free of charge at Guthrie Bicycle.

BIKE SHOP: Guthrie Bicycle (downtown shop), 156 East Second South, Salt Lake City, Utah 84111; (801) 363-3727. This shop is located right around the corner from the breweries and right down the street from the Bonneville Shoreline Trail. Stop in for information and a free copy of *Great Salt Lake Country Hiking and Biking Guide,* which lists the rides outlined here and many, many more.

Red Rock Brewing Company

254 South 200 West
Salt Lake City, Utah 84101
(801) 521-7446
www.redrockbrewing.com

ATMOSPHERE: Great open feel with skylights, large windows in back, glass french doors in front, and exposed wooden beams up top. The huge U-shaped bar has the brew kettles behind and multiple beer awards hanging above.

THE BREW: The Red Rock Brewing Company opened up in 1994 with just three styles of beer. The brewpub now has over 35 recipes to wheel out over the course of the year, thanks, in part, to an aggressive guest-brewer program. Of the three regulars, the **Red Rock Amber** is the best seller, but the **Nut Brown Ale,** a silver medal winner in the 1999 Great American Beer Festival, is the one you can really dig into. Red Rocks has the fine dining appeal and the food to back it up. This is without question the place for a beer and a meal. However, if you're still in your shorts and looking for a little brotherly love, Squatter's Pub is the place for you.

PRICE OF A PINT: Pints are $3.75 all day long except for the Beer of the Day, which will ring up at $2.50.

Squatter's Pub Brewery

**147 West Broadway
Salt Lake City, Utah 84101
(801) 363-2739
www.squatters.com**

ATMOSPHERE: Another old brick building, Squatter's offers a down-to-earth atmosphere with a four-seat bike, said to be capable of reaching speeds of 70 mph, hanging above the mantel of the huge fireplace. Here you can even have a beer by the name of Full Suspension Pale. Also, to make the outdoors person inside you feel more at home, Squatter's has an outdoor patio in back.

THE BREW: Not quite as many beers as at Red Rocks, Squatter's offers six regulars, plus various blends and serving techniques. There's even a **Shandy** right on the menu (about one-fifth Slice, four-fifths **Street Provo Girl Pilsner**). As far as hardware goes, **Squatter's Vienna Lager** took home a gold medal at the World Beer Cup, so check out this tasty Euro-style brew. The **Emigration Amber** and the **Full Suspension Pale** both have a very nice balance of malt and hops, and the pale gets even better when served via the nitrogen tap.

Tired of hops? I know, who would ever get tired of hops? Well, long before hops were used in beer an herb called yarrow was used to preserve and flavor beer. Yarrow is also an ingredient in gruit, along with sweet gale and wild rosemary. Yarrow is highly intoxicating and also an aphrodisiac. You can now try a yarrow beer here in the form of **Earth Hop Ale.**

Regardless of whether the aphrodisiac works or not, don't leave without at least one pint of Squatter's hand-pumped **Millcreek Cream Stout**—a tasty little beer perfect to finish up, or begin, for that matter, the night. **PRICE OF A PINT:** $3.49 a pint and no happy hour in sight.

OTHER BREWS IN THE AREA: Interested in sampling Utah's most decorated beer? Check out **Uintah Brewing Company's King Uintah Porter** fresh off the tap at Uintah's brewery and taproom located at 389 West 1700 South. As Utah's largest microbrewery, it offers tours and tasting six days a week. Plus Will Hamill, the owner of Uintah, is a mountain biker, so you can't go wrong buying local here.

And where do the brewpub employees go for a beer when they're not drinking their own? Check out **Desert Edge Brewery at the Pub** in Trolley Square.

CHAPTER FIVE

WYOMING

Wyoming's terrain is very similar to the western slopes of Colorado with the combination of alpine forests and high-desert plains. Although not quite as organized on the mountain-bike advocacy front as Colorado, Idaho, or Utah, Wyoming nevertheless offers nearly unlimited riding.

The problem is, although Wyoming is the ninth largest state, it has the smallest population of any state in the country. This fact means that there are just not enough mountain bikers out there to mark, map, and maintain all the trails! Regardless of this unusual predicament, Jackson and Laramie have emerged with plenty of charted trails. And Green River and Pinedale are working on it.

Wherever there's good mountain biking there is also good beer. Wyoming brewers are not inhibited by any 3.2 law, and they're not afraid of showing off that fact. They've got big beers where there's enough people, and beer education, to support these products. Unfortunately, that's just not that many places.

Jackson Hole

Jackson Hole: mountain-bike destination meets tourist town. Jackson will greet you with beautiful mountain vistas, a happening western town feel, gateways to both Grand Teton and Yellowstone National Parks, and all the traffic and tourism that goes with such a location. Fortunately, Jackson Hole also delivers as promised in the Bike & Brew realm, making all the hassle more than worth it. There is no question that Jackson Hole is a classic Bike & Brew destination. Epic trails are everywhere, and the exceptional brews at the Jackson Hole Pub & Brewery are what every beer drinker dreams about.

Wyoming

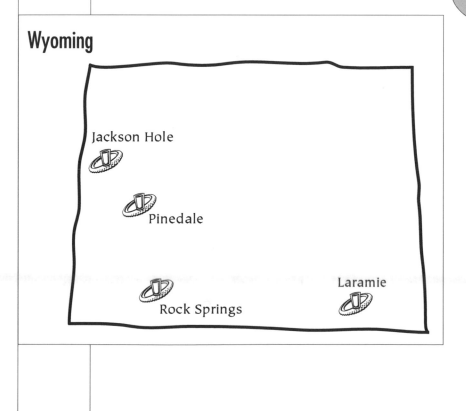

Cache Creek to Game Creek

THE SCOOP: Buff mountain singletrack straight from the brewery and back.

RIDE LENGTH AND TYPE: 19-mile loop or 23-mile out-and-back.

THE BIKE: The most accessible B&B ride, and the local's favorite before and/or after work, is the Cache Creek to Game Creek Trail. **Cache Creek** begins as a dirt road heading east out of town at a slight but steady incline. Once underway, you'll notice multiple singletrack trails running off to the left and right of the road. Some of this tangle parallels the road and will get you where you're going, and some of it does not. First timers should stick to the road and ensure themselves an eventual arrival at the **Game Creek** singletrack turnoff.

The loop is an intermediate trail with only one difficult climb, after which you have almost 5 miles of incredible mountain meadow and valley downhill singletrack riding before you pop out onto U.S. Highway 89. Here you have a decision to make. Not quite ready to give up the single-track? Then turn around and those 5 miles of graceful downhill become 5 miles of manageable climbing. Had enough? Right across the highway, a paved bike path takes you the 7 scenic miles back into town and to the award-winning microbrews at the Jackson Hole Pub & Brewery. One last option, reserved for those with masochistic tendencies, is also available. Turn off the trail onto the single-track coming down over the backside of Snow King Mountain, and a monster climb will bring you back over the top of the ski resort and into town the hard and fast way.

DIFFICULTY: Intermediate to advanced. Turning west onto the Snow King singletrack makes this ride heroic. By sticking to Game Creek, chances are you'll still be smiling, if not darn right pleased with yourself, when you get to the brewery.

AEROBIC DIFFICULTY (1–5)

Loop 3

Out-and-back 4

Over Snow King 5

TECHNICAL DIFFICULTY (1–5)

Loop 3

Out-and-back 3

Over Snow King 4

WARNINGS: Keep in mind that Jackson Hole weighs in right around 6000 feet and things just go up from there. Even though most of your climbing will be done on a dirt road, it can still make for a long day if you're not ready for the elevation.

OTHER TRAILS IN THE AREA: There's a reason why you see so many mountain bikers riding around town: there's a lot of riding here. A move 5 miles west to the slower-paced town of Wilson is where you'll find the **Black Canyon Loop**, a 13-mile town-to-town ride providing you with some great downhill opportunities. From Wilson, if your travels take you over Teton Pass and into Idaho, you'll go by Otto Brothers' microbrewery (and sometimes brewpub) and end up in the fun little town of Driggs, Idaho, for a choice selection of real estate known as the **Aspen Trail**. This ride can either be done as an out-and-back from town (18 miles) or from the trailhead (9 miles). Either way, you're in for a treat of climbing, incredible views of Teton Valley, multiple stream crossings, and, you guessed it, plenty of aspen trees.

CONTACTS: U.S. Forest Service, Bridger-Teton National Forest Office, 340 North Cache Drive, Jackson, WY 83001; (307) 739-5500. Also, a couple of doors down North Cache Drive is the Wyoming State Information Center, which is also another excellent source for maps and information. Jackson Chamber of Commerce, 990 West Broadway, Jackson, WY 83001; (307) 733-3316.

MAPS: Hoback Sports carries free copies of the rides mentioned here as well as the *Jackson Hole Ride Guide*, the local turn-by-turn guide to all the rides in the Jackson and Wilson area, for about $4.00.

BIKE SHOP: Hoback Sports, 40 South Millward, Jackson, WY 83001; (307) 733-5335. This shop is two blocks from the brewery and has free maps to the Jackson and Wilson rides mentioned here.

If you make it over to Driggs, check out Big Hole Mountain Sports, 99 South Main Street, Driggs, ID 83422; (208) 354-2209; www.bikesnboards.com. This shop is definitely Bike & Brew's kind of place. During its annual spring snowboard blowout sale (when boards go two for one), the shop gives a free **Pabst Blue Ribbon** beer to anyone over 21 who makes a purchase. Any purchase. Sure it's only Pabst, but hey, it's the thought that counts. The Aspen Trail town-to-town loop leaves right from the shop, and—if you mention you heard about Big Hole Mountain Sports in this book—the employees will even ride and drink with you. That is, if they're not too busy fixing up your bike.

Jackson Hole

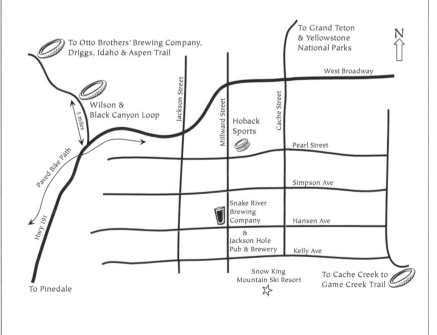

Snake River Brewing Company & Jackson Hole Pub and Brewery

265 South Millward Street
Jackson, Wyoming 83001
(307) 739-2337
www.snakeriverbrewery.com

ATMOSPHERE: Huge operation just off the main drag filled with the sunburned noses of various outdoor types: bikers, hikers, climbers, kayakers, and rafters. Very casual and noisy, perfect after a day on the trails.

THE BREW: Don't let the noisy crowd and the size of the place scare you away. This is the place to go for a little relaxation après mountain biking when in Jackson Hole. The size fits the demand, and the noise just means it's good; a quick glance at the menu shows the long list of awards Snake River has won throughout its history.

In addition to restaurant beer sales, Snake River does a healthy business as a microbrewery. This accounts for the size of the brewhouse and number of fermentation vessels you see surrounding the mock industrial warehouse interior. Fortunately, it's not all business here with excellent food, wood-fired pizza, and a daunting list of award-winning beers to choose from on any given afternoon.

Staples include the gold-medal–winning **Snake River Lager** and **Zonker Stout,** as well as the exceptional **Snake River Pale.** The brewers also do at least three other seasonal brews along with a cask-conditioned beer to round out the selection at seven or eight handles. All come highly recommended except their lightest, which seems to be focused toward a more mainstream beer-drinking crowd. That's fine as long as they don't start messing with their bigger beers.

233

"Michael Jordan rocks!"—
"Yeah, he was a great ball player."
—GROUP OF 20-SOMETHINGS DRINKING BEER AT 1:00 ON A SUNDAY AFTERNOON IN DRIGGS, IDAHO, MAKING A PLAY ON WORDS WHEN DISCUSSING THE NEW BREWER AT OTTO BROTHERS' BREWING. HIS NAME? MIKE JORDAN.

If there is any knock on this place, it's the fact that it's in Jackson Hole. If you're not sitting in that chair, someone else will be, so don't expect any kind of special treatment. Comes with the territory of being a popular restaurant in a popular destination town. So stake out your territory, be it on the patio, at the bar, or upstairs playing pool, and join in the fun.

PRICE OF A PINT: Jackson Hole has happy hour from 4:00 to 6:00 P.M. every day (even on the weekends!) where pints drop from $3.00 to $2.00. Now that's a nice happy hour.

OTHER BREWS IN THE AREA: If you're headed over Teton Pass and into Idaho, be sure to stop in and check if **Otto Brothers' Brewing Company's** brewpub is open. Although known for outstanding pizzas and calzones, not to mention fresh Otto Brothers' beer, as of this writing the pub part of the brewery was, how do you say, between restaurant managers (and employees). Although the pub has some problems staying open in the summer because everyone's out riding bikes (no kidding), the brewery itself is open year-round and can set you up with a tour if you catch them during a lull in the action. Call ahead at (208) 787-9000 if you're worried about missing them.

Downstairs dining in the Jackson Hole Pub & Brewery, from the dizzying second floor "catwalk." (COURTESY SNAKE RIVER BREWING CO.)

Laramie

Incorporated in 1874 and named after the French fur trapper Jacques La Ramie, Laramie sits directly north of Colorado's Front Range and is the first and last bastion of good beer and riding for all of eastern Wyoming. As such, Laramie has been blessed with two great—yet very different—breweries. The Library is located across from the University of Wyoming, and the Altitude Chophouse & Brewery is in historic downtown Laramie and around the corner from the Pedal House bike shop. Both have great atmospheres and great beer, so it comes down to what you feel like today. How about both?

Miles of well-marked trails in the Pole Mountain area puts Laramie up there with Jackson as one of the top riding destinations in Wyoming. Situated right off Interstate 80, with great beer and fresh singletrack, Laramie makes an excellent Bike & Brew destination.

Laramie

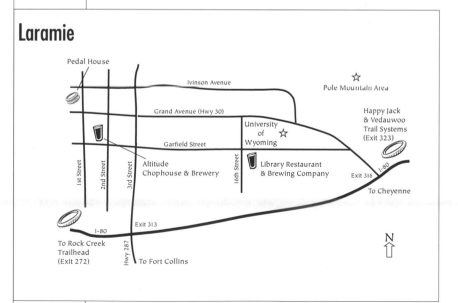

Pedal House
Ivinson Avenue
Pole Mountain Area
Grand Avenue (Hwy 30)
Happy Jack & Vedauwoo Trail Systems (Exit 323)
University of Wyoming
Garfield Street
1st Street
2nd Street
3rd Street
Altitude Chophouse & Brewery
16th Street
Library Restaurant & Brewing Company
Exit 316
I-80
To Cheyenne
I-80
Exit 313
To Rock Creek Trailhead (Exit 272)
Hwy 287
To Fort Collins
N

Happy Jack Trail System

THE SCOOP: Smooth and fast with many miles of trails through pine forests to explore.

RIDE LENGTH AND TYPE: Variable—"Happy Jack" proper consists of about 6 miles of trails, but a network of trails surrounding the area can connect with the nearby Vedauwoo Recreation Area for epic-ride potential.

THE BIKE: The Pole Mountain area, which includes the Happy Jack and Vedauwoo Recreation Areas, consists of 55,000 acres of public land and hundreds of miles of singletrack, doubletrack, and dirt roads. The meat of Happy Jack is actually a well-marked cross-country ski loop and just the tip of the mountain—literally and figuratively—as far as mountain biking is concerned in this little bike sanctuary of southeastern Wyoming.

Despite the abundance of trails, Happy Jack is still the place to begin your exploration of the area. If you like starting your ride with a downhill glide, park at the Interstate 80 rest area and use the **Headquarters Trailhead (no. 791)** directly across Blair Wallis Road to access the beautifully constructed x-c ski loops. However, if you're like most and prefer to start by climbing and finish with a nice little downer, follow State Highway 210 east (although, strangely you will actually be traveling west) to the **Happy Jack Trailhead,** an old ski area where some of the old runs are still visible.

Now at your fingertips is a pine-shrouded maze of singletrack that includes the **Upper and Lower UW Loops, Ridge Loop, Meadow Loop,** and **Blackjack Loop** for a total of 6 miles of well-marked singletrack fun. These loops are just the beginning of riding in this area with connector trails and roads all over the place. The riding all depends on how hard or easy you want it. If you want it hard, you can pedal all the way to the huge granite mounds of the Vedauwoo Recreation Area. Primarily a climbing paradise, the multiple access trails, cow paths, and doubletrack make this area an excellent way to see the incredible rock formations dominating that region. If you want it easy, stick to the well-trodden Happy Jack trails and happy you will be.

DIFFICULTY: Beginner to advanced. Stick close to the Happy Jack trails, and this area makes a great beginner ride. Strike off into the unknown, and you can make it whatever you desire. The local bike guide does an excellent job of labeling each trail with difficulty ratings even if it is a bit obscure with actual mileage.

AEROBIC DIFFICULTY (1–5)
2–4
TECHNICAL DIFFICULTY (1–5)
2–4

WARNINGS: Laramie is over 7000 feet and the Pole Mountain Area is even higher, so be prepared for a lack of oxygen and all the dizziness, shortness of breath, and cursing that goes with it. Like all mountain riding, be prepared for sudden shifts in weather—bring that jacket! Also, be sure to have a map if you plan on leaving the safe confines of the Happy Jack trails. Although all the forest service roads are well marked, you still need a map for the signs to do you any good.

OTHER TRAILS IN THE AREA: Aside from the excellent riding in these two areas, a great advanced ride is the out-and-back ride known as **Rock Creek Trail.** About 40 miles west of Laramie, take Interstate 80's Arlington exit (no. 272), and you're at the trailhead. This is a great ride—16 miles each way—for those tired of the Pole Mountain area.

CONTACTS: U.S. Forest Service, Laramie Ranger District, Medicine Bow–Routt National Forest, 2468 Jackson Street, Laramie, WY 82070; (307) 745-2300. Laramie Chamber of Commerce, 800 South Third Street, Laramie, CO 82070; (307) 745-7339.

MAPS: Pedal House in downtown Laramie publishes the *Happy Jack/Vedauwoo Mountain Bike Guide: Bicycle Rides in* *the Pole Mountain Area of Southeastern Wyoming.* This is an excellent guide of the area including trail descriptions and ratings. It only costs $3.50. Well worth the price of admission.

BIKE SHOP: Pedal House, 207 South First Street, Laramie, CO 82070; (307) 742-5533. The large painting of Thomas Stephens riding his Ordinary bicycle around the world points you in the right direction. Located in Laramie's historic downtown, two blocks from the Altitude Chophouse & Brewery, stop by and pick up a copy of the trail map from the guy who created it.

Library Restaurant & Brewing Company

1622 Grand Avenue
Laramie, Wyoming 82070
(307) 742-0500

ATMOSPHERE: Sitting across from the University of Wyoming, the décor of "the dome" reminds one of endless hours of cramming for finals. Looks like kids these days are studying the same subject they always did—only these days, the beer's better.

THE BREW: The sign in front of a nondescript stucco building directly across from the UWyo (pronounced U-Y-O) dorms announces the Library Restaurant and Brewing Company. Walk in the entrance of the restaurant, and you just might believe it. A large and airy circular room greets patrons with stacks of library books lining the walls as well as antique writing tables and wooden chairs under a lofty domed ceiling. Light streaming through the large circular skylight lends credence to the fact you have entered an institute of higher learning. The presence of a brewhouse behind a low brick wall covered in books proves it.

A wooden footbridge leads from the textbooks, encyclopedias, and reference books to the smoky bar area you'd expect to find across from a major university. Filled with TVs, video games, and pool tables, the bar at the Library makes for a great hangout and primer-bar before heading downtown for a big night out.

The brews at the Library are worthy of beer intellectuals such as ourselves. The lightest brew aimed at the domestic customer is the **Thomas Stephens Ordinary Extra Pale Ale.** Named after the famous high wheeler who rode his bike around the world in the late nineteenth and early

239

"Don't lie to your mom. Tell her you're at the Library."
—THE LIBRARY'S MOTTO, ONE TO LIVE BY.

twentieth centuries, Thomas Stephens may have been the original mountain biker. Wonder if he drank beer too?

On to bigger and better is **Bantom Pale Ale.** A nice India pale ale, it's named after the India port where the English would dock to unload this precious liquid for the troops. The Bantom is brewed with oak chips in the boil to impart a slight cask flavor as if fermented in a wooden cask. The **Red Eye Ale** is a full-bodied, medium-alcohol ale, making it a great session beer. Either study session or one of seemingly more enlightened content. The **Dubliner's Stout** has a nice reputation from the time the quality controllers from Guinness, who were visiting from Ireland and looking for a decent beer, came through town and wound up spending the day drinking it. Not a bad endorsement.

PRICE OF A PINT: No happy hour at the Library, but pints are always a reasonable $2.25. If it's a happy hour you're after, then get to the Altitude Chophouse & Brewery in downtown Laramie between 4:00 and 6:00 P.M., when pints are a buck and Cuervo margaritas and brewery snacks (which are actually full-blown appetizers) are only two bucks if you hang out in the bar area.

OTHER BREWS IN THE AREA: If the college scene is not for you, then head to the more traditional downtown location of the **Altitude Chophouse & Brewery.** More what you've come to expect in a brewpub, Altitude started brewing in 2000 and gives you a great alternative to the Library with wooden floors, open interior, and brewhouse behind the bar. Next to the bar and dining area is a separate pool room with music and TVs. Beerwise, Altitude brews up some unique varieties of your old favorites with the **Expedition Porter** and **High Plains Pale** anchoring the lineup. Definitely put this place on your list, and take advantage of its outstanding happy hour when riding in the Laramie area.

Pinedale

Surrounded by the Bridger-Teton National Forest, Pinedale is a great little western town complete with log-faced buildings, one main street through town, a combination hardware and bike shop, and a brewery. Now what could be more western than that?

Because this place is located a mere 70 miles from Jackson Hole, it may not get the mountain-biker attention it would anywhere else. So, although there is incredible riding here in the Pinedale area, the lack of charted and mapped trails means you'll need an adventurous and determined spirit to find it. However, you'll realize it was worth the effort as you sit on LaVoie's patio, sipping on a pint of LaVoie's finest ales, and watch the sun dip below the Continental Divide.

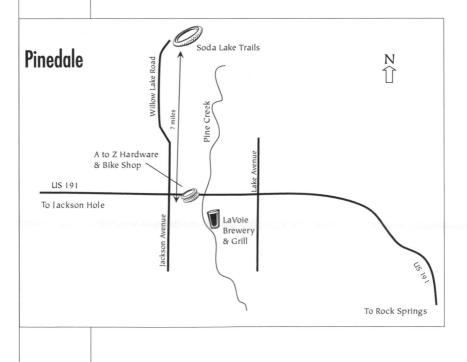

Pinedale

Soda Lake Trails

Willow Lake Road

7 miles

Pine Creek

N

A to Z Hardware
& Bike Shop

Lake Avenue

US 191

To Jackson Hole

Jackson Avenue

LaVoie
Brewery
& Grill

US 191

To Rock Springs

Soda Lake Trails

THE SCOOP: Incredible views, remote riding right outside of town.

RIDE LENGTH AND TYPE: 18 miles out-and-back with a mix of doubletrack and singletrack.

THE BIKE: The closest trails can be found at Soda Lake and in the **Spring Creek Park Trail System** located just 7 miles due north of the local bike shop. Starting at Soda Lake, you basically bike into a sagebrush-, cedar-, and conifer-filled bowl, which is hemmed in by Lake Fremont on the east, Bridger Wilderness to the north, and Willow Lake on the west. And, although the exact trail is some-times hard to follow, it's very difficult to get really lost here—you just head back down the hill, and you'll eventu-ally return to Soda Lake and your car or truck.

As for the ride, expect rough doubletrack, wide single-track, and finally, 2½ glorious miles of pristine winding singletrack as you near the Bridger Wilderness boundary and the ride's turnaround point. By the time you hit the wilderness, where bikes are not allowed, you are over-looking some of the most incredible scenery imaginable with the 600-foot-deep Fremont Lake (seventh-deepest natural lake in the lower 48 states) and the incredible granite expanses of the Wind River Range straight ahead. As tempting as the trail beyond the wilderness boundary looks, unless you want to park your bike and take a hike, it's time to turn around with the consolation of knowing it's all downhill on your way back to Soda Lake.

DIFFICULTY: Intermediate. Nothing is easy above 7000 feet, and adding climbing, singletrack, and some unmarked intersections doesn't make it any better.

AEROBIC DIFFICULTY (1–5)

3

TECHNICAL DIFFICULTY (1–5)

3

WARNINGS: Although it is very hard to really get lost, it is not very hard to lose the trail. Be sure to get a map from Dale Hill at A to Z Hardware. Also, no matter how tempting that little piece of trail looks winding off into the distance, there is absolutely no riding in the wilderness area.

OTHER TRAILS IN THE AREA: A little over 32 miles southeast of Pinedale is some great riding in **Irish Canyon.** Irish Canyon offers logging roads for novice riders and destination rides to Lamreaux Meadows, Twin Lakes, and Boulder Lake for the more advanced riders. One last place of note, about 34 miles northwest of Pinedale, is the **North Horse Creek** area. A bit of a drive but, according to Dale, there is "more riding than one can do in a week" up there. Both the **North Horse Creek Trail** and the **South Fork Trail** are excellent places to start your week of explorations.

CONTACTS: U.S. Forest Service, Pinedale Ranger District, 29 East Fremont Lake Road, P.O. Box 220, Pinedale, WY 82941; (307) 367-4326. Pinedale Chamber of Commerce, 32 Pine Street East, Pinedale, WY 82941; (307) 367-2242; www.pinedaleonline.com/mtnbiking.htm.

MAPS: The rides mentioned here are remote and mostly unmarked, so a stop at A to Z Hardware for free maps and information is an absolute must. The owner, Dale Hill, has been riding these trails for over 13 years and has even started a guidebook on the area (now if he'd only finish it!). In the meantime, he can personally supply you with all the necessary info to get you on the trail of your choice.

BIKE SHOP: A to Z Hardware (and bike shop), 777 West Pine Street, Pinedale, WY 82941; (307) 367-2116. Don't be fooled by the nontraditional mix of merchandise this bike store carries—the store has what you need, be it maps for biking in the area or that bathroom remodel you keep putting off in lieu of riding.

LaVoie Brewery & Grill

492 Pine Street
Pinedale, Wyoming 82941
(307) 367-1337

ATMOSPHERE: Situated a little back from the street to accommodate a very casual picnic and cable-spool table gravel patio, LaVoie's is a small cinder block building that looks almost tiny on the outside but has exactly what you're looking for on the inside.

THE BREW: Since 1996 Susan and Mickey LaVoie have been brewing up beer and serving food from their place here in downtown Pinedale. Opening with happy hour at 4:00 P.M. each day, you're likely to find Susan behind the bar pouring beer and Mickey not far away brewing or drinking his wares.

Although the interior of the building is concrete floor and cinder-block walls, don't let the simple construction fool you. The brewhouse is behind the wooden bar, pool table, and real cork dartboard. A casual seating area offers easy chairs, board games, books, and magazines, which all combined give the place a comfortable, cozy English tavern feel. It's definitely a place where you can come and relax while sipping on a pint or two and reliving the day's ride.

Mickey specializes in English-style ales, all of which are filtered and very smooth, without a lot of bitterness because he uses hops with an extremely low bitterness value. The **LaVoie English Bitter** is a very smooth example of an English-style ale that will have you staying for more than one, and the **LaVoie Porter** is the beer of choice among the regulars—dark, creamy, and again very, very smooth. Adding to the English feel of the place is **Bass** and **Guinness** on tap alongside **Fat Tire Amber.** Fat Tire is not very English, but it is a nice addition all the same. Be sure to try the house specialty before leaving—grilled pizzas and calzones. That's right, grilled. You'll have to see it to believe it.

PRICE OF A PINT: LaVoie's doesn't open until 4:00 P.M., but it does so with the bang of a happy hour until 6:00 P.M. Happy hour pints are $2.00—down from $2.75—so be sure to come early and enjoy a little LaVoie hospitality.

OTHER BREWS IN THE AREA: Remember this is Pinedale, Wyoming, and you should be happy just to have a brewpub here in the first place. The LaVoies sell by the six-pack, growler, and Party Pig, so you can always get some to go. Also, you're getting closer to Jackson so you'll start seeing Snake River Beer in the stores and bars.

Rock Springs–Green River

Situated at more than 6200 feet above sea level, Rock Springs is an important mining community with a rich and colorful past that includes a brief stay by Butch Cassidy, who, as legend has it, received the name "Butch" while working as a butcher's assistant here before turning to banditry.

Rock Springs

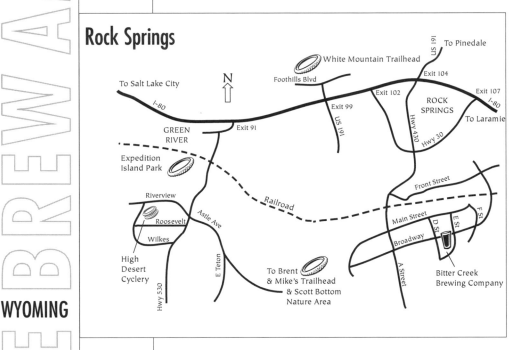

To Pinedale

US 191

White Mountain Trailhead

Foothills Blvd

Exit 104

To Salt Lake City

Exit 102

Exit 107

I-80

ROCK SPRINGS

I-80

Exit 99

To Laramie

US 191

Exit 91

Hwy 430

Hwy 30

GREEN RIVER

Expedition Island Park

Front Street

Railroad

Riverview

Main Street

Roosevelt

Astle Ave

D St

E St

F St

Wilkes

Broadway

High Desert Cyclery

E Teton

A Street

Bitter Creek Brewing Company

Hwy 530

To Brent & Mike's Trailhead & Scott Bottom Nature Area

The area in and around Rock Springs is loaded with singletrack, doubletrack, rough dirt roads, smooth dirt roads, hills, mountains, and breathtaking vistas all just waiting to be explored, much like Fruita, Colorado, was in the early 1990s. Enter present-day Rock Springs, which has been going through a trail-access struggle for the past 5 years, but without the political clout and numbers of the migrating Colorado Front Rangers.

Here's where you come in. The Rock Springs and Green River folks are busy finding, building, and mapping the trails. In fact, these trails are just waiting to be ridden. And as more cyclists ride them, the trails will become better, and mountain biking will have a larger voice in the community. Isn't this a great place? The locals actually want more riders on their trails!

Now calculate in the fact that Rock Springs has the first Interstate 80 brewery east of Utah, and at this brewery, larger than 3.2% beers are brewing. That's right, a mere 176 miles east of Salt Lake City is real riding and real beer. Now all you alcohol-starved Utahan riders can start making the journey east to some prime biking terrain and even finer beers. The biking is in Green River; the drinking is in Rock Springs. Got that? The 14.1 miles separating the two is a small price to pay for some of the best Wyoming has to offer of each. The terrain is here, the shop is here, the trails are here, and even the beer is here. Now all this little undiscovered region of southwestern Wyoming needs is some riders.

Brent & Mike's Trail

THE SCOOP: Classic high-desert Fruitistic-type riding (that's a new mountain-biking "technical" term referring to the quality of mountain biking available in Fruita, Colorado).

RIDE LENGTH AND TYPE: 10 miles out-and-back with more under construction.

THE BIKE: One great ride filled with singletrack, desert hills, and incredible views of the Flaming Gorge National Recreation Area follows the newly constructed and completely legal **Brent & Mike's Trail.** Currently about 5 miles in length, this out-and-back is a great intermediate ride with tight winding singletrack and plenty of moderate climbing. Expect to encounter antelope, dwarf-growth trees, and high-desert vegetation whose stark beauty will entrance even the most veteran rider.

Construction is underway (and with luck will be complete by the time you read this) to continue the trail another 5 miles or so, terminating at the 7644-foot Wilkins Peak radio tower. In the meantime, a way to add more miles to the ride—and keep your vehicle parked in town—is by leaving from the Expedition Island National Historic Site in downtown Green River. Expedition Island gets its name from being the launching point from which a one-armed Civil War hero named John Wesley Powell began his famous geological exploration of Colorado and Utah in 1869. The island is now a city park with the **Greenbelt Bike Trail System** running through it. Follow this mixed pavement and dirt path east about 4 miles until you reach the Scott Bottom Nature Area and the start of Brent & Mike's Trail. Add Brent & Mike's 10 miles, and you're in for a good 18-mile round trip.

DIFFICULTY: Novice to intermediate. This ride is perfect for a strong novice rider, but will keep any level of rider interested with its tight turns and elevation gain. Once the trail is complete, the additional miles and elevation will make this a solid intermediate ride.

AEROBIC DIFFICULTY (1–5)

2

TECHNICAL DIFFICULTY (1–5)

3

WARNINGS: There are many, many trails around this area, but not all are mapped or marked very well. Be sure you know where you are going and how to get back before you strike out on your big adventure. Even though this is high-desert riding, it's still the desert, and it still gets hot in the summer. Be sure to bring lots of water on any excursion, even the shortest.

OTHER TRAILS IN THE AREA: Across Interstate 80 from Green River and right between Green River and Rock Springs is **White Mountain.** Starting at the Cruel Jack Truck Stop at exit 99, you can traverse along the edge of the mountain all the way to Rock Springs and beyond (up to a 12-mile out-and-back total)—a technical affair with narrow off-camber trails, short dips, sharp climbs, and plenty of exposure. Although you may lose the trail at points (locals say always go up when there is a split in the trail), it's impossible to lose yourself. Interstate 80, Rock Springs, and the brewery are always to the south and the top of the mountain is always to the north. There are many trail networks on White Mountain, and it's possible to get so far back that you may even see the local herd of wild horses.

Scott Bottom Nature Area, the launching point for Brent & Mike's Trail, is also the home to a few miles of novice dirt trails. A great afternoon starts at Expedition Island by riding the Greenbelt to Scott Bottom, continuing around Scott Bottom, and then heading back to the island (or on up to Brent & Mike's). A mere 15-minute drive takes you to downtown Rock Springs and the Bitter Creek Brewing Company.

CONTACTS: Bureau of Land Management, 280 U.S.

"You can ride dirt for 100 miles in any direction from here."
—LOCAL RIDER JOHN JAMES DESCRIBES THE AREA WHILE TAKING A BREATHER ON BRENT & MIKE'S TRAIL.

Highway 191, Rock Springs, WY 82901; (307) 352-0256. Rock Springs Chamber of Commerce, 1897 Dewar Drive, Rock Springs, WY 82901; (307) 362-3771.

MAPS: High Desert Cyclery has free topographic maps of Brent & Mike's Trail as well as maps and directions to many other trails in the area.

BIKE SHOP: High Desert Cyclery, 520 Wilkes Drive, Suite 2, Green River, WY 82935; (307) 875-5569. Even though the pub is in Rock Springs, Bike & Brew America is sending you to Green River for all your biking needs, because the folks at the High Desert are mountain bikers. They know the trails, ride the trails, map the trails, and even make the trails. They have shop rides Tuesday and Thursday evenings where all are welcome, so stop in and find out what the Rock Springs–Green River area has to offer the Bike & Brew community.

Bitter Creek Brewing Company

604 Broadway
Rock Springs, Wyoming 82901
(307) 362-4782

ATMOSPHERE: A perfect historic spot in a downtown that is still recovering from a slowdown in coal mining and oil exploration. Located in a newly remodeled brick building one street south of Main and right behind where Butch Cassidy used to hang out at a bar called the Fountain Club. Why that building has not been reclaimed as a national monument, or at least a local tourist trap, is as much a mystery as Cassidy's death.

THE BREW: Maybe it's the fact that this is the first brewery across the Utah border or maybe it's the fact it brews darn good beer, but this place is like spotting a gas station after the low-fuel light has been on for 20 miles. From the moment you walk in, you know this place means brewing business. The light-wood interior is broken only by sky-lights and a long row of labeled fermentation tanks dividing the bar from the rest of the restaurant. This is the closest you will ever sit to your favorite beverage while it is being birthed—so order up a pint, settle in, and enjoy the miracle called beer!

From start to finish, Bitter Creek has what you're looking for in beer. Even its lightest beer—the **Boar's Tusk**—is an incredible example of how you don't have to lose flavor to make a light beer. And it just gets better from there. Both the **Red Desert Ale** and **Mustang Pale Ale** are unfiltered blessings in a glass. Bitter Creek's most famous beer—and the local favorite—is a big stout known as **A Beer Named BOB**, which took the bronze medal at the 1999 Great American Beer Festival.

And, just to keep things interesting, there's always the Test X Batch, which is what Bitter Creek calls the "Brewer Playing Mad Scientist" game, so you never know what else may be brewing. To get some of this incredible beverage home—but not across the state line, of course, because that might be illegal—growlers are available to go, and even little insulated beer huggies for the half-gallon glass jugs are for sale. How's that for solving one of the world's problems?

PRICE OF A PINT: There's no happy hour and there's no games, just great beer. But remember, Big Bad BOB's parking is always reserved at the Bitter Creek Brewing Company.

OTHER BREWS IN THE AREA: An oasis in the desert comes with a catch: it is usually called an oasis because it is all by itself. That's true here in Rock Springs as Bitter Creek is the only brewery operating in the area. However, because you'll be in Green River anyway, there are a couple of places along Main Street that deserve note. The first thing to check out is the castle-like structure on the western end of the strip—the old **Green River Brewery,** circa 1900. Admire this building for what it was back then, an incredible architectural achievement, and for what it is in the present, a bar just begging to be turned into a brewpub. After gawking and dreaming about what may someday be, head over to the **Embassy Bar** where the local bike crowd goes for micro taps, pool, and the best CD collection in Wyoming . . . well, in Green River anyway.

GLOSSARY

ALE – Beer made with ale yeast; the most common type of beer found in brewpubs. The short fermentation period and minimum aging requirements of ale make this type of beer more practical for small breweries as it spends less time in the fermentation vessel and more time in the serving tank ready to drink. See also **Lager.**

B&B HOTMILE – Simply put, a B&B Hotmile describes the sweetest section of an already sweet trail. A slice of mountain-bike nirvana. The part of the ride that leaves you grinning like a fool and drooling for more. The true Bike & Brew America goods.

BALLOON-ON-A-STRING – A combination of a loop (the balloon) and an out-and-back (the string). Basically, travel to a point where the trail diverges onto a loop. Take the loop all the way around. Then return to the trailhead on the out-and-back trail.

BEER – There are two basic types of beer: ales and lagers. The difference is all in the yeast. See **Ale** and **Lager.**

BEER ENGINE – See **Hand pumped.**

BREWHOUSE – This is where the magic of brewing actually takes place. Some brewhouses are fancy state-of-the-art presentation breweries, and others consist of dairy equipment hidden away in the basement. Regardless of what they look like, all serve the same purpose: to make you fresh, unique beer.

BREWPUB – Accept no imitations. A brewpub is a restaurant or bar that brews its own beer, of which 50% must be for on-premises consumption. Although the various states have different laws further defining a brewpub, this characterization forms the essence.

CARBON DIOXIDE (CO$_2$) – Most of the beers served on tap use carbon dioxide gas to carbonate the beer and propel it from the serving tank (or keg) through the tap lines to your pint glass. These beers are typically served cold, somewhere around 38 degrees Fahrenheit.

253

CASK CONDITIONED (also called **Real Ale**) – A beer is considered cask conditioned when a secondary fermentation is induced inside the keg (or bottle) from which the beer will eventually be served. This secondary fermentation is the beer's only source of carbonation. A cask-conditioned beer is usually served at cellar temperatures (around 52 degrees Fahrenheit) via a **Hand Pump**.

CRYPTOBIOTIC CRUST – A thin, dark, mineral-looking crust, usually found in the southwest region of the United States, cryptobiotic crust is a critical part of the desert soil-building process. It takes many years for the slow desert lifecycle to accumulate enough algae, mosses, bacteria, fungi, and lichens to retain water, reduce erosion, and support larger forms of plant life. A single footprint, bike track, even old thrown-away food that will attract scavengers could set an area back decades in this process. If you're new to the area, ask someone to point it out to you so you don't accidentally cause unintentional damage to a sensitive area.

DIRT ROAD – When all else fails, a nicely maintained dirt road ride is available almost anywhere in the country. Not usually destination rides, dirt roads are still the preferred route for great town-to-town rides and very useful when connecting multiple singletrack trails to create epic rides.

DOUBLETRACK – Also called "two-track," many trails begin as old logging roads, mining roads, fire breaks, railroads, or four-wheel-drive (4x4) roads. These are rediscovered for the use of hikers, bikers, and horseback riders. And, although some may complain that they're not singletrack, sometimes these crazy old roads are little more than glorified goat trails with only one rideable way up, or down, and make the best epic rides in the business.

ENDO – An Endo occurs when you unintentionally go over your handlebar headfirst. This stunt happens most frequently when you are riding downhill and your weight is shifted too far forward. Your front wheel comes to a stop either because you applied the front brakes or because your front wheel lodged against an immovable object such as a log or large rock. This situation generally leads to a **Face Plant**, the sudden meeting of your face with the ground. Just the hazards of having too much fun.

FACE PLANT – For whatever reason, the inelegant, rapid pressing of a bicyclist's face into the ground. See also **Endo**.

FERMENTATION – The process of turning wort (the boiled-down, sugary liquid extracted from barley) into beer. Basically (and this is very basic, so take a tour of the brewery the next time you're in a brewpub), the wort is mixed with water, and either lager or ale yeast cells are added to the concoction. A yeast is a tiny (microscopic) single-celled organism that eats the sugar in the solution and whose metabolic byproduct is alcohol and carbon dioxide gas—the building blocks of beer.

GROWLER – The original and traditional method of taking your beer home before there were six-packs. Usually a growler is a half-gallon (64-ounce) reusable glass jug sold at the brewpub for a nominal cost. Once purchased, the growler can be filled with a house-brewed beer, taken off-premises, and consumed at your leisure. Unopened in a chilled, dark place, growler beer can stay fresh up to five days. Once the seal is broken, the beer's best when consumed in one sitting, so make sure you have a couple of friends around.

HAND PUMPED (or **Hand Pulled**) – A traditional serving method designed for cask-conditioned ales, although any beer can be served via this method. A hand pump (also called a beer engine) uses vacuum pressure to "pull" beer from the keg to the tap. This serving method creates a less carbonated brew, typically served at a warmer temperature (around 52 degrees Fahrenheit) than a typical American beer. Usually the warmer temperature and reduced carbonation result in a smoother beer with enhanced flavors and exceptional characteristics.

HAPPY HOUR – Usually sometime between 3:00 and 7:00 P.M., during these few magical hours, the beer is discounted, the sun is still shining, and all is right in the world.

HELMET – A light-weight and rather hip-looking device that will help keep your brain properly suspended in your skull. As cool as you think you may be foregoing its use, not wearing a helmet whenever you get on a bike is just plain dumb. Please see **Endo** and **Face Plant.**

HIKE-A-BIKE – A section of terrain impossible or illegal for anyone to ride. Over this section, which is not usually considered a single obstacle where a dismount and remount are required, you must carry or "hike" with your bike. Common hike-a-bikes are large river crossings, unreasonably steep trails (for example, Jacob's Ladder, Moab, Utah), an impassable technical section of trail, or any part of a trail that is illegal for riding your mountain bike.

LAGER – The vast majority of beer produced in the United

States consists of American Pilsners, which are made with lager yeast by the likes of Anheuser-Busch, Coors, and Miller Brewing Companies. Occasionally, you'll find a microbrewery or brewpub making a beer or two with lager yeast, although most use ale yeast owing to the longer aging periods required by lager yeast.

LOOP – Just as singletrack is the desired riding medium, a singletrack loop is the desired ride type. On loop rides, you travel in a fashion that brings you back to your original starting position without riding the same terrain twice. Usually some sort of circular situation, the singletrack loop is the Holy Grail of mountain-bike rides worldwide.

MACROBREWERY – Also called a large brewery, companies in this category produce over 2,000,000 barrels of beer per year. Examples in the United States include Anheuser-Busch, Coors, and Miller Brewing Company.

MICROBREWERY – A brewery that produces less than 15,000 barrels of beer per year for off-premises consumption, although many have tap or tasting rooms.

NITROGEN – A growing trend is to use nitrogen to "carbonate" and serve beer. The higher pressure of nitrogen gas means a tight and creamy head and an overall smoother character. A true delight!

OUT-AND-BACK – An out-and-back ride returns you to your original starting position by your riding the same trail back as you rode out. Although not as exciting as a loop ride, the out-and-back is still worthy. Remember, a trail will ride differently in the reverse direction.

PAVEMENT – Not a favorite of most, but still an option. Like dirt roads, paved roads are often used to ride to a trail or to connect different dirt routes together.

PHAT – As in hip, cool, "I wish that were mine," awesome! You may have a phat ride, a phat bike, or a phat time, but you won't have a phat chance for any of that if you don't get out there and ride!

PINT – The almighty pint, a beer drinker's equivalent to single-track. The most common method for ordering and serving a microbrew in America. Pint glasses range in size from 14 ounces, to the standard 16-ounce glass, all the way to the rare and much desired 20-ounce English pint.

POINT-TO-POINT (Shuttle Ride) – Though always fun, a point-to-point ride is the least accessible, because it requires coordination of multiple cars or trucks and drivers. Also called shuttle rides, you leave a vehicle (or arrange pickup) at your destination location (say, the bottom of the mountain) and then travel in another vehicle to your starting destination (say, the top of the mountain) to begin the trail ride back to the arranged destination location. Of all the rides, you can cover the most distance on some of the best terrain (as in "all downhill") on a point-to-point ride. Unfortunately, the need for multiple vehicles, the reliance on others, and arranging the pickup time is often time consuming and prone to error. And retrieving the second vehicle from the trailhead at the top of the mountain delays visiting the brewpub.

REGIONAL BREWERY – One that produces between 15,000 and 2,000,000 barrels of beer per year.

SHUTTLE RIDE – See Point-to-Point.

SINGLETRACK – This is it, what you're all after, the reason you left the road behind and dove headlong into the trees! Simply stated, singletrack is a dirt path too narrow for cars and trucks. But, oh, it's so much more! Singletrack comes in many forms, from smooth and flat to steep and rocky with everything in between. For every variety of singletrack there is someone out there looking for it, and it's all good!

SLICKROCK – Made famous in Moab, Utah, by the classic Slickrock Trail, the term slickrock is now often used to refer to any section of trail that is made of rock. Usually this rock offers unparalleled traction (at least when dry) and a unique riding surface that is much sought out and treasured.

SWITCHBACK – A switchback is a sharp turn up or down an incline. Building switchbacks is a trail-creation method that reduces erosion and helps human-powered machines (including hikers) up a mountain. When properly built, a biker has enough room to complete the switchback without dismounting. This usually requires about 6 to 8 feet of turning radius.

TOWN-TO-TOWN – Often spoken of in only the most hushed of tones, the fabled town-to-town ride is a glorious thing indeed. Typically epic in distance and time, this ride allows the mountain biker to start from town (the brewpub is always nice), travel by bike to the trail, and then return some time later. When planned correctly, the return time usually coincides with **Happy Hour**.

TWO-TRACK – See Doubletrack.

WATERBAR – Waterbars come in all shapes and sizes, but they invariable serve the same purpose: to divert the flow of rainwater from the trail and reduce erosion. Usually, nothing more than a

half buried log, trench, or pile of dirt running almost perpendicular to the trail, these seemingly annoying fixtures are the reason you have pristine singletrack instead of a rocked out, eroded, and crumbly mess to ride on. Volunteer to work on a trail maintenance crew to learn more about waterbars and other trail-building techniques.

WIDETRACK—At some point in its life, singletrack can no longer be called thin, or tight, or even narrow. Whether it is from excessive use or by design, there comes a time when a trail is no longer singletrack and not yet a road, even though it is a single dirt path making its way through the woods. Though some of the thrill may be lost, it's still dirt, still mountain biking, and still fun. Enjoy!

GLOSSARY

INDEX

259

INDEX

261

INDEX

263

INDEX

INDEX

TODD MERCER

Todd Mercer is a former collegiate swimmer who realized there was more to sport than the structured confines of the pool. After much time spent scuba diving, rock climbing, and competing in triathlons, he found his true calling in mountain biking. Perhaps a factor in this revelation was how well a pint of fresh beer in the company of good friends tasted after a day on the trails.

Mercer began writing about his outdoor adventures in various club newsletters. Soon his articles were appearing in regional and national magazines. Finally, so there would be no regrets, he abandoned the cubicle world of a nine-to-five computer desk jockey to pursue his dream of traveling and writing. He and his wife, Amanda, a successful prosecuting attorney, sold their nineteenth-century home in Indiana, and along with their dog, Nikki, left behind the secure and predictable for a life on the open road.

They currently live without a fixed address. The red Bike & Brew America truck could be anywhere.